Lucy

Mishagas, misfits...
I'll bet Jarvis had
hats in different area codes...
Merry Christmas!
Love Joanne
xxx

FREAK OUT THE SQUARES

FREAK OUT THE SQUARES

LIFE IN A BAND CALLED PULP

RUSSELL SENIOR

Aurum Press

First published in Great Britain
2015 by Aurum Press Ltd
74–77 White Lion Street
Islington
London N1 9PF
www.aurumpress.co.uk

A catalogue record for this book is available from the British Library.

ISBN 978 1 78131 438 8

eBook ISBN 978 1 78131 471 5

2015 2017 2019 2018 2016

1 3 5 7 9 10 8 6 4 2

Typeset in Spectrum MT by Saxon Graphics Ltd, Derby
Printed and bound by CPI Group (UK) Ltd, Croydon, CR0 4YY

Contents

Picture credits

Plate 1, top: photo R.S; Plate 1, bottom left: design R.S.; Plate 1, bottom right: Neville Elder/Redferns; Plate 2, top: design R.S.; Plate 2, bottom left: Collection R.S., designer unknown; Plate 2, bottom right: Collection R.S., designer unknown; Plate 3, top: design R.S.; Plate 3, centre: design R.S. – central image Jo Blascos; Plate 3, bottom: design R.S.; Plate 4, top: © Des Willie/Redferns; Plate 4, bottom: Collection R. S., photograph sent in by Cesare Guerguess; Plate 5, top: Collection R. S., photographer unknown; Plate 5, bottom: Collection R. S., photographer unknown; Plate 6, top left: photo R.S; Plate 6, top right: © Topfoto/UPP; Plate 6, bottom left: © Rex; Plate 7, top: © Stefan Rousseau/PA Archive/PA Images; Plate 7, bottom left: photo R.S.; Plate 7, bottom right: photo R.S.; Plate 8, top: © Gary Wolstenholme/Redferns; Plate 8, centre: Photo – Ralph Parmar; Plate 8, bottom: © Gary Wolstenholme/Redferns

2011
SHEFFIELD

1
Tsunamis Permitting

On the bus with Gareth and Ralph. The bus is a camper van. It has a wobbly little table with four seats, a sink and a fridge, which we do use, and a toilet – which we don't. In the back are two long padded seats that face each other, which you *could* lie down on – but aren't supposed to in transit. It is nominally a six berth, but that would be very snug. It does however have a button that makes a pair of stairs mysteriously emerge from the side: very James Bond.

Gareth is the driver, I have only met him once before. He was down at the rehearsal rooms when I was 'styling' them, helping to put up the giant neon P.U.L.P. signs. He did this in a curious way using complicated knots and fastenings.

Me: 'You a climber, mate?'

Gareth: 'No, caver.'

Me: 'Got lots of anecdotes about caving?'

Gareth: 'Yeah, quite a few.'

Me: 'Know much about minerals?'

Gareth: 'Yeah, a fair bit.'

Me: 'Do you drive?'

Gareth: 'Yes.'

Me: 'Do you want to drive me on tour?'

I *had* presumed Gareth was one of the many roadies who periodically turned up at the rehearsal rooms in preparation for the tour. As I found out later, he was just someone's mate hanging about and had never encountered the crazy world of rock and roll before. You wouldn't have known it to look at him. With his Mott the Hoople straggle cut, Maglite, extra-length shorts, reckless climbing skills and dissolute air he had all the hallmarks of pondlife. 'Pondlife' is road-crew slang for lighting engineer: presumably because, however depraved road crews may be in general, lighting engineers always take it that much further into the swamp.

On the road you spend a lot of time in close proximity with those you are working with, and a ready supply of anecdotes can enliven an otherwise dull journey, as well as diffusing the inevitable cabin fever that will set in. Gareth seemed like a good egg, but could just as easily have been a maniac.

Now here he was skulking about in front of my house in Sheffield, about to drive us thousands of miles in a rickety little charabanc, enjoying a crafty toke of special relaxing herbal tobacco. Not the ideal start, but in the grand scheme of things not a biggie. What was I going to do? Pull out of the tour?

Ralph is my manager/stylist/carer for this tour. When the prospect of the Pulp tour came up we were writing an ill-advised musical about the miners' strike and he took on the managerial role by default.

I had first seen Ralph many years before, swanning around town in a purple suit, trilby hat and lightning-strike sideburns. Typical student, I thought: all outrageous now, when outrageousness is conformity, give it a couple of years and he'll be kowtowing to The Man as if it had all never happened.

A couple of years later, he was running the much-loved club Razor Stiletto, from which he picked up the moniker 'Ralph Razor'. I ran into him next at a Saxon concert he was promoting. Saxon were the model for the fictional band Spinal Tap and it was for this reason, rather than any deep-seated love of heavy metal, that Ralph was putting them on. He was wearing pink winkle-pickers. He invited me to his thirtieth birthday party, which I had expected to be populated by mwa-mwa hairdresser types – it wasn't. It was in an old casino and Ralph was sat on a throne wearing a full Marie Antoinette dress and pompadour wig with a model galleon on top, surrounded by Russian girls who called him 'Meester Ralph'. The cat had style.

What I do is play guitar and violin in the band Pulp. I am on the way to my first concert engagement in fifteen years. This is a long time of absence. I'm not a fan of reunions in general – but somehow this one feels okay – at least in principle.

How did it happen?

Well, a couple of years previously, Pulp's singer Jarvis had rung me up out of the blue and said: 'Do you want to play Glastonbury?'

Me: 'Ooh, I don't know about that, I'm not really keen on reunions.'

Jarvis: 'Just the one show.'

Me: 'Well, we can talk about it.'

Jarvis: 'Okay, I'll ask the others, see what they think.'

Glastonbury was the scene of our perceived greatest triumph and stands outside the general world of touring, having an exalted semi-mystical status. People will put aside their differences for Glastonbury and play football in no-man's-land before going back into their trenches. It was tempting and, as I had left Pulp in circumstances that I still resented, it seemed like a way to attain some kind of 'closure' on the whole unfinished business.

Well, the months passed and no return call came (not atypical this). It was well past the moment we would have needed to prepare for a show, so I booked my holidays elsewhere for the time of Glastonbury, to make it impossible to be tempted to cobble something shoddy together at the last minute – we owed it to 'The Kids'.

The phone rang.

Jarvis: 'Are you still up for playing Glastonbury?'

I'd mentally rehearsed my response ('Fuck off', followed by phone slam). But I couldn't resist the jibe …

Me: 'You've left it a bit late, mate, Glastonbury was weeks ago!'

Jarvis: 'No, no, next year: I've talked to the others and they're up for it.'

Me: 'Oh, *next* year. Oh, right: well, I suppose we could talk about it.'

We arranged to meet at Nick the drummer's house in Sheffield for the summit. Everyone was nervous, but on best behaviour. Jarvis and I kept popping out for cigarettes to postpone the inevitable encounter.

I had left the band acrimoniously fourteen years earlier, at the peak of its fame. They had continued for another seven years, recording another two albums and touring, before it all petered out. In the intervening time, posterity's assessment of Pulp had been kind and there was, it seemed, a demand for us to play concerts. I had my reservations: there was something glamorous about quitting at the height of success and to go back now might seem a sell-out. My life had moved on and I hadn't picked up a guitar for years.

I was proud of my time in Pulp and quit before I could become one of those crozzled-up old rock stars doing the circuit, not knowing when to stop. I got out well before hitting forty – at which age, in my opinion, pop stars who don't know when to quit should be pushed off a cliff in the Brigantian fashion, for the greater good of the tribe.

By now I was fifty, carrying a pound or two too many, and had a bad back: you'd think there was an obvious answer to the question of a reunion. But there was something nagging. The end had seemed premature; we'd struggled for years to get to a high point. I'd done all the transit van load-your-own-gear hard work and had barely stayed around to enjoy the success.

The original proposal had now expanded from one concert to ten and my doubts increased, where would all this end? I had no intention of getting back onto the treadmill permanently and the nostalgia circuit was complete anathema to me.

As it turned out, what was being proposed was not some 'Relive the glory days of Britpop and sing along to your old favourites,' but rather a summer tour of European festivals, which is about the most fun you can legally have on the road. And 'The Kids' go to festivals, not just middle-aged ladies in feather boas who ought to know better; and apparently The Kids dug us. I had kids – they were little when I was last doing this, now they were grown-up – they didn't listen to Pulp.

When my son was little, he once said, 'You used to be cool, Dad!'

Thinking he was being ironic, I said, 'Oh yeah, when was that then?'

Flatly he replied, as if explaining the obvious to someone with that forgetful thing you get when you're old, 'When you were in Pulp.'

To me this was all the more reason not to revisit that other country. Coolness is my one great vanity and to cash in even retrospective coolness for a handful of silver was something I didn't want to do.

How many handfuls of silver? Oh, well, that bears serious consideration then. And a ten-date tour of Europe you say? Travelling in style, staying in the best hotels – something that had hardly begun when I left. A kind of long summer holiday with a concert once a week, a chance to do it properly and enjoy it in a way we never had before. A victory lap, a testimonial match: basking in the affection of our justly won status as national treasures; to give those songs which, whatever our differences, we all more or less loved, one last outing. Tempting.

But then there was the actual reality of, 'Could we hack it?' Yes the music deserved another outing, but were *we* up to it? I looked in the mirror and at my fellow bandmates: not so sure. Perhaps we owed it to 'The Kids' *not* to inflict this on them. Jarvis shared my misgivings as to whether the people we now were could inhabit those songs any more, and whether a middle-aged man with a beard should be singing about hiding in wardrobes looking at schoolgirls' underpants. There was only one way to find out – have a rehearsal. So we arranged one in December in a Victorian redbrick building of the 'Little Mester' type.

Little Mesters were small-scale steelworkers who occupied cramped Dickensian workshops which, as the steel industry declined, became the spiritual home of Sheffield music. It was a marriage of convenience because the remaining Little Mesters made too much noise to complain about the horrible racket the bands made. Without it being articulated there was, I think, a common assumption that if we were to resurrect this monster we had best do it in an authentic and auspicious environment.

It was cold and damp; we huddled in fingerless gloves round a one-bar electric fire once more with the snow outside, looking like the tattered survivors of the Siege of Stalingrad – and not sounding much better. I'd insisted that we should book three days of rehearsal (in the event that, as was more often than not the case with this fickle butterfly, we had an off-day) and was glad we did because on day two … we sounded ace! Songs that I couldn't remember the name of, my fingers knew how to play: they sounded fresh, sparky and exciting. And it was emotional. You see there was a lot, and I mean a *lot*, of heart and soul put into those songs and, all of sudden, we were transported back to the start of the racing season – with all the raw emotion of the first time. There was something contemporary about the songs, we had actually got better! We played as a team, so much more than the sum of the parts. It was meant to be.

So that was it, we didn't need another day to make our minds up. We had no choice but to give it a go: if we made fools of ourselves, well that's just the chance you take for living a day as a lion rather than a year as a lamb. It was on.

The first thing was to get out of that fucking freezing practice room. We hired studios in the centre of town and I put a lot of work into making it 'Pulpy'. The Pulp style isn't exactly my style – only one or two of the items came from home. Actually it's sort of my style, but in Jarvis's colours (shades of mustard, snot-green and brown banned under the

Geneva Convention). Then there's keyboardist Candida's rinky-dink magic Celtic toyshop thing. Anyway, I know what Pulpy is and I got together the HQ of a seventies villain/pimp with some aplomb with the help of local film-set suppliers. Nick supplied a fridge for beer and I think someone in the band even thanked me for it rather than moaning, which was novel – things might be different this time.

They weren't actually; during rehearsals, nerves got jangled, emotional silt got stirred up and if I'd known what a ball-ache it would have been I would never have gotten into it. But, by the time I'd realised it would be business as usual, I'd bought too much gear and got into debt. I had to see this thing through, whether I liked it or not. The tour had been advertised, tickets had been sold and we owed it to The Kids … oh, and the music got better and better, there's that small thing.

Well, somehow we got through the rehearsals and now here I am rather looking forward to the tour, in a terrified sort of way. There is eager anticipation amongst not only friends and family but also, judging by ticket sales, the wider public. Any concerns that it might be a damp squib have gone, to be replaced by trepidation about how well we will perform and be received. You can never, should never, be able to predict how these things will turn out – that should be in the lap of the gods. That's part of the buzz, part of the terror, part of the challenge, part of what keeps you awake at night, part of what drives you to drink and drugs and novelty and distraction, and the feeling that by doing this you are apart from other men and somehow special. But for the muse to flutter into your lap, there has to be humility somewhere, a willingness to let go and let the wind blow you where it will.

This kind of existentialism takes an awful lot of planning. Let's be right, it's not the kind of thing you do every day, and you should try and make the most of it. Ralph and I have put much effort into the arrangements – we hope to make every leg of the tour have a different flavour by inviting different guests, but always to conduct things with a certain aplomb. The look I have opted for – 'Englishman abroad in linen suit and panama hat' – works well and Ralph has made the great sacrifice of *not* wearing the same outfit – I'd look rather too much like his sugar daddy if he did.

Ralph is sat in front with Gareth and I am in the back. Perhaps Ralph is taking his role as a tour manager very seriously … or just avoiding the minerals quiz.

Me: 'What is the orange-coloured microcrystalline form of quartz?'

Gareth: (Shouting over the rattle of the van) 'YER WHAT?'

Me: 'What is the OR-ANGE coloured MIC-RO-CRYS-TALINE form of QUAAARRRTZ!'

Gareth: 'CARNELIAN! ... Ooh, ar've gorra good-un for thee; what is the yellow and blue banded form of fluorite?'

Me: 'Blue John! Too easy ... What value is calcite on Mohs scale of hardness?'

Ralph isn't getting many of these; he smiles benignly, feigning interest, and tries to suggest other, racier, quiz topics, but Gareth and I are having too much fun. Ralph is content to let us exhaust this topic now so that we can move on to something hipper when we have company. In short, Ralph fears that minerals, like beards, are not a fanny-magnet. But it can't be absinthe and Russian girls *all* the time.

We pull in for a last fag break before customs and Gareth's face is obscured by the fug coming from his evil-smelling joint.

'You can't take that dope through customs you know? If you get busted I'll miss the show.'

'It's not dope though is it.'

'Well what is it then?'

'Coltsfoot, mugwort, raspberry leaf, catnip and valerian.'

'All fuckin' soporifics aren't they!'

'No Coltsfoot in't' that's for your throat.' I give up.

It's a mighty long way to Barcelona by road – but each mile travelled is a mile further from home and closer to Barcelona, and what a splendid final destination. I'm not staying in the same hotel as the rest of the band for the Primavera festival, due to it being too close to sea level. I have always had a morbid fear of tidal waves. Tsunamis permitting, the tour should be a good laugh, though of course a little scary.

I can see the sea! One of the quintessential joys of living far inland. I pity those who live within familiar distance of the sea. They can't experience the frisson an inlander gets on an annual basis. And, of course, there are the tidal waves.

Customs, then the vacuum hush of the tunnel, then France.

1980
FRANCE

2
1980, The First Fifteen Minutes

I'd never been abroad before and Europe Endless lay before me. I'd got spiky hair, an InterRail ticket and all I needed on my back for a glorious escape from the stultifying meat-and-two-veg, suet-pudding pastiness of England and grey grimy gritty Sheffield. Away from blank-eyed teenagers, 'keep off the grass' signs, Sunday afternoons with acrid privet hedges and annual holidays with lovely couples from Rhyl – to a world of excitement and possibility.

I didn't talk to anyone on the train, people are strange when you're a stranger, but I'm not naturally chatty or approachable and perhaps a little scary looking – the swivel-eyed hitcher you don't want to pick up.

The Parisian station was so damn French; they all spoke French, looked French and were fabulously unreal and exotic in a familiar way. I breathed Marcel Duchamp's air. Paris looms large in the imagination, from countless films and books: *Down and Out in Paris and London*, *The Rebel*, *Irma la Douce*, Utrillo cafés, the bar at the Folies Bergère, tarts with hearts and artists' garrets.

The improbable art-nouveau metro entrances led to a seamy underworld where pouty young Parisians sat smoking Gitanes. It was better than England, it was different, it was foreign, and foreign was good.

I loved everything about it. The hiss of the coffee machines, the way the waiter nonchalantly stroked the foam off the beer, the wizened old men saying '*merde!*' into their espressos. I dipped my croissant into the coffee because we were taught in school that Parisians did this: 'Er, miss, they don't, do they? That's just weird!' Well I was just weird too. They had better lives, better food, better art, better buildings, more beautiful women and more intense conversations: I wanted in.

Two Frenchmen had a heated argument about politics in a café, shook their fists, then shook hands and parted like old friends – clearly they were better at life. Somewhere a distant accordion played – bliss.

But, with rudimentary baguette-French, one is still a stranger. And the Parisians don't exactly clap their hands in joy at meeting an Englishman. Still, they were right and we were wrong and I didn't blame them for being snotty about the English; I was snotty about the English. Hopefully they would realise this and take me into their stripy-shirted conversations – but they didn't, so I went home.

On the journey back, an earnest German punk – no doubt encouraged by my spiky hair – asked if he could borrow some hair gel. I didn't have any, nor had I heard of Bad Brains, whom he was very struck on. He seemed disappointed by my lack of punk credentials. However, when I told him I was from Sheffield, he got very animated and reeled off a list of bands from there, which I'd heard about but not seen – so Sheffield was cool, apparently!

What know they of Sheffield who only Sheffield know?

I'd tried to escape but the tractor-beam had drawn me back, yet this time the familiar smokestacks looked exciting and filled with possibility. In the post-punk period, Sheffield's unique take on electronic experimentation produced a buzzing swarm of intense new bands. The splendidly titled Neutron Records EP – *1980: The First Fifteen Minutes* – captured the urgency of the times. The Sheffield I returned to in 1980 was briefly the most dynamic place on earth and I wrote about it in my fanzine.

Jarvis was working as a crab-scrubber on a fishmonger's stall when I met him. He was a striking figure and had a neat line in jokey patter with the old ladies. I went to see his band Pulp and wasn't terribly impressed. They were eighth on the bill out of nine bands – too high in my estimation. My review described all their songs as 'dirges' but did concede that 'the appearance of the front man is entertaining'. They were shambolic, which was fine, but they played it for laughs, which wasn't to my taste. They murdered 'Wild Thing' by The Troggs and 'Steppin' Stone' by The Monkees – which Jarvis claimed to have written. They stumbled through two of their own ridiculous songs, were hideously out of tune and the bassist fell off the stage.

A member of The Naked Pygmy Voles ripped my fanzine up in front of me in protest at the less than glowing review I had written. So I thought I'd interview Jarvis before he had a chance to read what I thought about Pulp in their first-ever review. He was sparky, bright, engaged, unpredictable, funny, risqué and everything else you could want. Pulp weren't as good as Cabaret Voltaire, Clock DVA, New Model Soldier, Artery, I'm So Hollow, Vice Versa, Vendino Pact, De Tian, The Scarborough Antelopes, or even The Naked Pygmy Voles but Jarvis was by far and away the best interviewee.

I went to every available local concert, including everything local band haunt The Hallamshire pub had to offer. Somewhat to my dismay I saw that Pulp were on the bill. Most of their fans came from City School, which was near Ashleigh, the school I had attended. Ashleigh would be considered rough by most standards, it was in the bottom 10 per cent and Barry Hines (who wrote *Kes*) set a play there. However we regarded ourselves as Eton to City School's Grange Hill and avoided them if we could. Jarvis soothed these savage beasts and clowned around to their half-mocking, half-admiring urgings. There will always be bands that can make a good night out for their mates and get rapturous encores. The real test is if you can get someone you don't know to come and see you again. To my mind Pulp were best suited to their staple fare of school discoes, friends' houses and 'battle of the bands' competitions.

Jarvis and I were friends now, so, rather to my embarrassment, I was one of his mates clapping along too: there was a likeable brio to the band, Pulp were fun.

But I wasn't that interested in fun; I was interested in serious music and politics.

My father had on occasion taken me through the industrial district at night to see the glow coming from the factories as hot metal was poured to the clang of the drop-forges – a powerful sight. He lost his job in the steelworks which were rapidly demolished and we went through the same area, and saw the flattened apocalyptic landscape where the factories had recently stood – it was heartbreakingly sad.

There was a big march against unemployment and the lead marchers wore chartist-green Harrington jackets, like skinheads did – radical chic. My father and I joined this march, along with the brass bands and union banners. We went past some factories and in one doorway a man shouted out my father's name. My father shouted back to him to, 'Get your lads out!' (it's all getting disturbingly homo-erotic this!) and the man beckoned the workers out, black-faced to join the march. It was the kind of stuff you get in films, it seldom happens like that – but this time it did.

Fortunately there was no shortage of angst in Sheffield music to slake my thirst. Cabaret Voltaire, the great pioneers of the scene, put on darkly hypnotic multi-media, strobe-lit shows. They claimed to be 'practising Dadaists' and sparked my interest in the movement. At The Limit club one could dance to 'The Passenger' and 'Lust for Life' by Iggy Pop but also 'Nag Nag Nag' by Cabaret Voltaire, 'Being Boiled' by The Human League, and '4 hours' by Clock DVA – many of our heroes were local.

Sheffield had embraced modernism in the sixties and all schoolchildren were shown a film called *Sheffield: City on the Move*, which depicted our Star Trek-like future. The city had much in the way of prize-winning Brutalist buildings that the architects wouldn't want to live in themselves, or walk through at night.

One such a landmark was 'The Hole in the Road', a series of pedestrian subways converging under a traffic island; with a concrete oculus, open to the sky, round which the traffic revolved. A large glass panel behind which tropical fish once swam in a giant aquarium was now vandalised and abandoned – a place to avoid at night.

By early 1981 the hard-edged abstraction of the early electro scene was falling apart and many from that scene crashed and burned. They became casualties and sometimes fatalities – junkies, tramps and thieves; who died of overdoses and motorbike accidents. A wino tried to ponce ten pence off me in The Hole in the Road and I recognised him as someone I had been cheering onstage only a year before. Being in a band seemed the most important thing you could do, but it was death or glory.

But some reinvented themselves, survived and made a defining and credible contribution to the futurist scene of the early eighties. Bliss was it in that dawn to be alive, but to be young was very Heaven 17, Human League and ABC.

The indefinable Artery played a memorable concert at The Marples pub one winter's night. The lead singer walked out of a second-storey window as the band kept playing. He was waiting for a bus to pass underneath so he could leap onto the roof and make a dramatic escape, but none came. He reappeared several minutes later, having somehow worked his way along a narrow snowy ledge to come in at the other side of the building still singing. Half the audience were in bands. Although we didn't know each other yet, the people who would later form the new Pulp were adding their voice to this crowd, as outside unemployment rose and the city decayed.

By charm, persistence and luck Jarvis had managed to get a Peel session and it wasn't that bad. They did the best of their set: the anarchic 'Please Don't Worry'; 'Turkey Mambo Momma': 'Wishful Thinking'; and the genuinely moving 'Refuse to Be Blind'. (Jarvis had been told at a young age that he was going to go blind and determined that, by force of will, he would refuse to do so). Pulp, while still not in my top-ten Sheffield bands, were no longer an embarrassment.

In 1982 I organised a concert featuring Sheffield bands with Bath University's Dadaist Society. Headlining the bill were the dark and drummerless New Model Soldier, with their songs about suicide, serial killers and Lovecraftian trans-dimensional horror. Second, by dint of them having a Peel session, were Pulp. Pulp went down well – they were crowd-pleasers.

Headliners New Model Soldier weren't: by the end of their set, the 300 people that had been enjoying Pulp dwindled to fifty – impressive, I would book them again. I wanted to be in New Model Soldier. The night was a laugh though; there'd been a teeny bit of trouble, which can give an edge to things. About fifty hard-to-impress cider punks from town had jeered and sneered through the event. There was a tiny fracas and a security guard (called Mr Ball) got his hat knocked off. This made the front page of the local rag, accompanied by a picture of me looking particularly thuggish, with my shaven head, army boots and a black-and-white stripy jumper. The article was vague and you could be forgiven for thinking it was I who had assaulted the hapless Mr Ball – who made a right old palaver for someone supposed to be a security guard. I remember his name because there was much puerile merriment that had he been called Mr Hat then the outcome might have been much more grave.

I caught Pulp again at The Limit Club in Sheffield and they weren't much better. They suspended different-coloured cut-out fish from the ceiling to create an impressive aquarium effect – they sounded crap but looked good. The irreverence of their approach made a welcome break from the ubiquitous greyness of the more serious Sheffield bands, they were free. Sadly the line-up that produced such gems as 'I Scrubbed the Crabs that Killed Sheffield' folded.

In 1983 a new and more po-faced line up of Pulp produced the slicker and more polished album *It* and premiered songs at The Leadmill – I hated it. Jarvis had dropped the comedy routine and replaced it with saccharine whimsy. The album failed to make waves and that incarnation folded too. Pulp were defunct.

I recruited Jarvis for a Dadaist play I had written along with a largely silent but enigmatic character called Magnus Doyle. The play was performed in the Crucible Studio Theatre, where it fell absolutely flat. We had more success in pubs, clubs and abandoned warehouses, where its edginess was more appreciated. There was one scene with the stage instruction; 'Woman walks to front of stage, leaving hoover running in front of microphone until first audience member walks out.' Usually it was more than one and was pleased with this. It's not that I didn't want anyone to like it; I just wanted them to be committed and prepared to suffer. Cabaret Voltaire were unprepared to suffer. Despite describing themselves as 'practising Dadaists' they stayed drinking downstairs in The Hallamshire pub rather than come upstairs and see perhaps the first Dadaist play ever performed in Sheffield.

There were 'sound poems' in the play too, accompanied by rhythmic banging, so there was music of a sort, though nothing you'd call pop music.

3
Island of Bohemia

When the play had run its course, Jarvis and I were talking about music and I gave him a frank appraisal of his output. I loathed the twee and introspective album *It*, considered it a sell-out, and told Jarvis so in no uncertain terms.

He said, 'Do you think you can do any better?'

I said, 'Yes.'

He lived on the edge of the roughest area of the city, called 'The Manor' (a district which will only be familiar to you from programmes about social breakdown; *Police, Camera, Action!* Chases; fly-tipping; and RSPCA rescue missions to dirty houses where old women have ninety-three neglected cats). Jarvis, however, lived in a delightful walled estate, an island of Bohemia in the hood with no woodchip on the wall. With that physique and that name and his mother's insistence on him wearing lederhosen to school, his outsider status had been guaranteed.

So we rehearsed in his mother's garage and he turned my crude psychobilly tunes into poetry. My version of the song 'Maureen' went:

> Maureen, Maureen, Maureen, Maureen, you knocked me down you knocked me over, you were wearing your red dress at the red car races.

When Jarvis had finished with it, it went:

> Maureen's divine incision slits through my sense of reason
> Mind jerks back to the first time, start of the racing season.

I spiked up his poncey ballads with acidic guitar lines and something new started to happen.

The Sheffield scene that contained many of our personal musical heroes had fallen apart but in that garage we kept its flame alive, drawing upon a melange of musical influences that excluded very little. Jarvis might have borrowed his stage moves from Alvin Stardust and Les Grey of Mud but was more than willing to be freaked out by my Throbbing Gristle albums.

We had a discussion on what to call the new band, Jarvis didn't like the name of my previous psychobilly band The Nightmares, and I quite liked the name Pulp but didn't particularly want to be associated with it. We tried sticking a pin in a dictionary but all the names were rubbish and he persuaded me that keeping the name Pulp would bring a few people in, so it stuck.

We got Magnus Doyle from the play in on drums. Magnus was a man of few words but many remarkable actions. He liked to demolish his drum kit at the most inappropriate times. You could understand it in some rocking-out encore, but Magnus seemed to cause the most destruction during the quiet songs.

I used to put on 'performance nights' in out-of-the-way locations. These had five-minute open mic slots for anything anybody wanted to do; preferably *not* music. At one of these, in an abandoned warehouse on The Wicker, a run-down inner-city street in Sheffield, it had attracted a large hippy crowd – lured in by the chance for self-expression. Magnus's 'performance' consisted of putting a metal bucket on his head and charging off in all directions. He hit walls and got up, knocked a ladder over onto his head and got up. In the end the room was clear, with just Magnus crashing into walls.

At the next performance night at the Hallamshire pub he was introduced as a 'famous rapper' and proceeded to put records on a Dansette and scratch them while wrapping up gifts. It had the disquieting air of a David Lynch film.

Then he put another record on and lined up a pint of beer, a pint of baked beans and a pint of tinned tomatoes and drank them one after another, as if conducting a magic show. In the dreary light amidst flock wallpaper, with the Dansette scratching away, he induced himself to vomit back into a pint glass. The audience gasped in disgust, but Magnus wasn't finished, he drank the pint of his own vomit as well. It had an odd edge to it.

Magnus then got out a selection of soft fruits with a manic gleam in his eye. Fearing the worst, I scarpered out of the room, only to see

Magnus's parents coming up the stairs – I desperately tried to engage them in conversation until the groans from the room subsided and Magnus came out with a grin on his face.

We were always trying to find interesting locations to play concerts and Magnus and I went to enquire at a Victorian theatre. There was an audition on for Peter Shaffer's *Black Comedy* and Magnus and I were taken for auditionees. We just played along with it for a laugh. We had to act out a duologue in which one of the characters is blindfolded. Well, this was easy. Magnus did his berserk thing and I did my mad staring-eyed thing and we got the parts – but never showed up for the play.

We needed a bass player and Magnus knew someone called 'Manners'. His real name was Peter Mansell – which would make a good name for a serial killer, if not a bassist. He had a yobbish, young offender air and looked like he should have been in Sham 69.

But he was a good bass player, by which I mean he hit it hard and didn't play anything too complicated. We were trying to learn a song and Manners was playing something completely out of tune.

'What you playin' at, Manners? Do you even know what key it's in?'

'No, no, that'll be it, I've got the wrong key: what key is it?'

'It's in "C" …'

'Oh, right. "C." Yeah, yeah, I've got it now.'

So we started again and Manners just played a 'C' note all the way through. This makes it sound like he was crap, but he wasn't, he was a very punky but sensitive player.

He never took himself or anyone else seriously, was hilariously funny and I tried to book him as a comedian for my performance nights, but he was too shy.

My most abiding memory of Manners was seeing him from the upper deck of the last bus home at 1.30 a.m. on a Saturday night. Town was lively and lairy as people headed drunkenly out of clubs with their takeaways, pissing in doorways and puking up. I saw Manners coming down High Street on his own with his bouncy, almost Mancunian stroll, with his hands in the air clapping, cheering and extolling the virtues of Sheffield United, 'Come on ye blay-eds waaay, arrrghh, waaaayyy'. He had a good-natured smile on his face and would hit no one. On the other hand he would almost certainly get hit. He was always getting hit.

3a
Extreme Hair Topiary

Our friend Tim Allcard was the caretaker of a complex of abandoned factories that acted as a drop-in centre for Pulp and various waifs and strays with names like Crazy John and Rabid. It was a madhouse but it had rules: no meat, no booze, no waste. Tim didn't believe in throwing things away and kept toenails, earwax, belly-button fluff and hair combings in separate jars. Whether this was an extension of his austere creed or Situationist humour I couldn't say, and you wouldn't get a straight answer out of Tim.

Tim sported a variety of what I hesitate to call haircuts – extreme hair topiary would be more accurate. Elements of Farrah Fawcett-Majors, Hasidic Jew, Wolverine and Anglo-Saxon warrior competed with pigtails, tonsure and braids to give him a distinctly Neolithic air. For clothes he wore a variety of tabards, smocks, pantaloons and tunics – held together with belts and rope.

There was no television or radio, just a wind-up gramophone and a virtual museum of fossils, scrap metal, ancient motorbikes – all painted yellow. A yellow 1950s school bus with the destination set at 'Riddley-Diddley'; jars full of marbles; horseshoes, which Tim could date; a dolphin's skull; salvaged errata from demolished factories; a half-scale gypsy caravan-cum-market barrow of Tim's construction lit by a tilly lamp; several hundred yellow-painted bas-relief heads made out of concrete, which Tim called 'gobbo bonces'; life-size straw men, which he called 'familiars' etc. etc. etc.

Tim's empire was pretty spooky at night, with the noise of mice scurrying away and the building shaking from the pounding of the drop-forges. Occasionally one would come upon a Nosferatu-like character who lived there. He was a skinhead, wore a black trench coat, had a 'borstal glove' and kept a pet rat on his shoulder. He set up a black-magic shrine and brought in skeletons from Cemetery Road graveyard to decorate it, which possibly contravened the rules and certainly exceeded even Tim's tolerance.

Tim got a new lodger in the form of Jarvis and knocked out the partition walls that housed the factory's service ducts to make a room for him. It was pyramidal in form and had pipes, three foot in diameter, running in from each corner at two foot above the ground that you either had to limbo under, do an ungainly clamber over, or a potentially painful splits across. Not a place to entertain the ladies.

Down several dusty corridors in Tim's complex was a recording studio called Vibrasound where Jarvis, Magnus, Manners and myself recorded our first four songs together.

'Maureen' was the song we saw as a single at this time, but the recording didn't do it justice, hence the Demo's name: 'Bad Maureen'.

This new Pulp had a darker and more experimental edge but also catchier bits than before. The paucity of our equipment meant that in order to be able to hear one's own part it had to be particularly textually striking. So, whilst others pumped up the bass, I tweaked up the treble. The ragbag of instruments we came across accidentally gave us some distinctiveness.

The drumming and bass on all of these tracks is frenetic and urgent but I can't really hear them so much as feel them. My hearing range is flawed from childhood deafness. I *can* hear bats though, but have yet to find a practical application for this skill.

Pulp never approached the studio as a way in which to get down the live sound. We were always playing around with things we couldn't do live. This left us with the problem of how to play the new and improved songs in concert. I could just about – albeit with some difficulty – switch between plectrum and violin bow when playing the guitar but Jarvis couldn't play the guitar and the keyboard at the same time, so we got Tim in to do his parts. To say Tim 'joined' Pulp feels almost insulting to him in the same way that if a raven was to take residence in your loft you wouldn't regard it as a family member. Tim was effective guru and talisman to the band and helped us by playing occasional keyboard and doing sound poems in between the songs.

We were keen to distinguish ourselves from run-of-the-mill demo-tape presentation and did hand-drawn pictures of aquarium fish on the inset sleeves. I sent these tapes off to venues with the objective of playing shows as far away as possible – perhaps even outside the city boundaries.

5
Brown Light

A friend of Jarvis's at Brunel University offered us a show. It was in Uxbridge, about twenty miles out of London; which is *technically* London if you ignore the fact that it isn't London. As slightly the eldest and definitively the least flaky member of the band, most of the organisational work fell to me and I became de facto tour manager, which was a little like trying to get indecisive octopi into a very small jar.

I got the van booked but a call was passed on informing us that the concert was cancelled. There'd been a double booking and the rugby club had got the venue for the evening. I decided to pretend we hadn't got the message and set off hoping to blag our first show.

It looked as if we weren't going to be allowed to play, but the rugby club band cancelled and they were left with us. The audience had been expecting a bawdy band but instead got the early Pulp at its most raw, amateurish and confrontational.

Manners was a joker but at show time he got terribly nervous; he shook, he panicked and was wide-eyed with terror. Manners' nerves calmed everyone else's, because we could laugh at his conniptions and forget our own. This added to the intensity of this early incarnation of Pulp. There was no danger of us being taken for a bunch of art-school trendies with him in the band, we were for real.

Taking an idea from the Dadaist play, we started the set with a blast from a factory siren Tim had salvaged. Unfortunately the bloody thing wouldn't turn off and we took to the stage with this ear-splitting racket and Tim desperately trying to get it to stop.

It was a hostile audience from the start and they heckled us. We didn't play well: during the song 'Back in L.A.', Manners played completely the wrong thing and Jarvis chanted along to the tune of the song, 'What you doin' I wish you were dead!' The audience threw coins. Manners gave them the rods and did the 'offer out' sign for a fight. Some blokes turned their backs and took their trousers down. Jarvis kicked one up the backside and chairs started to fly. There was a hostile stage invasion, the drum kit went over and we bolted to the dressing room – barricading ourselves in and waiting until the venue was cleared before we dared venture out and load our battered equipment into the van for the long journey home. Strangely we weren't that downhearted, we'd certainly got a reaction and presumably it could only get better from here. A perceptive reviewer described us as 'the escape party from *One Flew Over the Cuckoo's Nest*'.

In the absence of somebody proper to do the job I became de facto booking agent. I decided to avoid mates of mates fiascos and looked around for a striking venue to do our own show. Eschewing the habitual pub venues, Jarvis and I went to look round The Library Theatre. It was a cool arty place with a whiff of the vaudeville, which suited our oeuvre perfectly. It held 200 people and put on independent films.

Jarvis and I scoped out the venue in preparation for the show. There was a conflict about the lighting. Jarvis was adamant that he wanted 'brown' light and I was convinced that no such thing existed, arguing that brown was black and orange, and black was the absence of light – so brown light was merely dim orange light. However, after much debate, brown lighting gels were actually found and Jarvis got his 'brown' light – or dim orange if you are a rational being.

I printed tickets and we sold them to our mates and in a couple of record shops. We sold around seventy, which wasn't bad. I gained night-time access to a photocopier and wearing nothing but a trench coat, photocopied distorted images of my entire body which, when stretched out like a skinned tiger, made an image six foot wide by twenty foot long. I stuck this onto a roll of corrugated paper and hung it from the back of the stage, where it would be illuminated by red uplighting.

With Tim's poetry, my spoken-word stuff and the dramatic lighting it was more of an art happening than a concert and perhaps not quite where we wanted to be. I felt self-conscious jumping about to the faster songs in front of a seated audience and rued the day that we had chosen to keep the name 'Pulp'. We played no songs from the album *It* and some of the audience shouted out for them. But it was by far and away our best show thus far and nothing got thrown. We got applause from an odd mix of friends, other bands checking us out, puzzled habitués of independent films and a few skinheads that Manners had sold tickets to.

6
The River Porter Expedition

We were all fascinated by urban exploration in our decaying industrial city – particularly its hidden underbelly.

A culvert near Sheffield station lead to an intriguing-looking tunnel out of which issued the river Porter and I mounted a Pulp expedition to 'Trace the source of the Porter'. This odyssey into the secret world of the metropolis was to be a formative experience for us all.

So, with torches, we stooped to conquer the Porter and followed the redbrick tunnel, which led away in winding arches deep into the dark. We ventured fearful, and, after nervous crouching in the grime, Manners wanted to go back. But no one would go with him so he stayed, afeared to return in the dark on his own with no torch. The tunnel seemed never-ending and we hugged the edges, shining a dim light down the side tunnels that disappeared into the gloom. Everyone was at the point of turning back when a shimmer of uncertain light was seen in the tunnel ahead – but was it just the distant reflection of our own torches? We turned them off and in the darkness visible was a thin sliver of light, gleaming off a curving arch like a sickle moon. We pressed on towards the light and eventually were able to stand up in the daylight with a delirious sense of relief. We tried pushing people up the high barbed-wire-topped walls, but there was no way out. There was junk, smell, flotsam and jetsam and everywhere the vile black silt of endless industry. A further tunnel led off but that had visible light at the end, so we pressed on. The water was an unnatural translucent yellow with red oily blobs and it deepened as we clung to the sides. We made lightfall and gazed up black-bricked sides to a window ten feet up. A woman leaned out with a pint in her hand. It was a pub in the old industrial part of the city and they gamely passed drinks down to us, intrigued by these maniacs stuck down in a storm drain. Refreshed and emboldened by our ability to conquer these tunnels – and perhaps not wishing to appear cowardly to the curious boozers leaning out of the window, warning us that the river often flooded – we went with no courage but much braggadocio into the next tunnel.

Great oval ironclad culverts discharged industrial effluent of various noxious hues into the river; rust red, purple. But neither fish, nor fowl, nor vegetation had made this sewer its home. A rumbling noise as a rusted iron cover plate rib-reinforced cranked sideways, dolloping its goop of acrid effluvia into the river behind us. The nameless fears that had beset us were now added to by the more tangible dread of some more colossal voiding of the bowels of the city that might wash us away in anonymous filth, unfound by parents or police. Side culverts now became the source of a less spectral trepidation and we dived past them, relieved to be upstream of their trickles, which could at any time become a fatal flood. But the river was deepening as it became sluggish and we clung to the crumbling sides, leaping from one disappearing bank to another through the structures from the Victorian and earlier eras; which dwarf the ambitions of the present with their scope, scale and ornamentation. Ours were the only human footprints, but there were others; the myriad marks leading this way and that of a rat, and behind us in the dark, eyes gleamed. So we rushed on mindless, clinging with fragile fingers to the sloping sides. The bank had become but inches wide and fell away as we passed – there was no way back. In this moment of babbling, a ray of hope befell us. It was the Spirit of Dark and Dirty Water which, we convinced ourselves, held no power over sensible children but over such a folly cast a protecting eye. This familiar figure from public safety announcements thus became our guide. And to this day I don't pass a river without reaching into my pocket and casting in the first coin I find in supplication to this spirit.

7

Candy-Coloured Keyboard

I had seen Candida around in The Beehive pub; looking very cool, sophisticated and unapproachable in a Scandinavian way (which wasn't far off the mark with her coming from the Shetland Islands). Candida was Magnus's sister and, joy of joys, a keyboardist: rather a good one. She had a unique jerky style that evoked music boxes, abandoned funfairs and sinister clowns – bittersweet yet strangely disquieting. Candida joined us in 1984 and did Jarvis's keyboard parts, adding flourishes and ornaments. We referred to her style as 'rinky dink'. Her personal appearance was somewhere between sixties waif, fairy-tale princess and seventies teenager.

This five-piece felt like a solid line-up: there was something cool about having a girl in the band and while the bawdy banter continued, at least someone was rolling their eyes at it. She must have liked bad lads though, as she started going out with Manners.

The more intellectual and self-conscious side that Jarvis and myself exhibited was enlivened by Magnus, Candida and Manners' more chaotic and anarchic Celtic spirit. There wouldn't have been a Pulp worth the name without them. It would have been some clever art-school nonsense that withered for lack of soul, they were the missing ingredient in the pot. Pulp was a clash of oddballs but what we made was greater than the sum of the parts.

The first concert we played with Candida was at a pub in King's Cross called The Pindar of Wakefield, which was actually genuinely in London. Candida was terrified because Manners had been telling her about having to dodge bottles at our previous excursions. We half expected some of the ruffians from our first show to turn up looking for trouble but she relaxed when the headline act, Pride of the Cross, turned out not to be the feared goths the name implied. They were a bunch of local London Irish who took their name from the area and included members of The Pogues, whom she adored. Her organ had a candy-coloured keyboard that we angled towards the audience so they could see the flying fingers of the nearest thing Pulp had to a decent musician.

Bands and their camp followers often comprise the majority of the audience in small venues and if you get on and clap each other then everyone feels better. Concerts in London like this which the press or record companies may attend are more important to your career than much bigger ones elsewhere. They are not entirely real though, it's about buzz: who is checking you out, who sees who checking you out, who is on the guest list and how cool your fans are.

The show was so-so but nonetheless we had a strong sense that we were bringing something earthy and real down from the north.

A guy from a small record company was supposed to see the concert but he missed the show, having gone out for a pizza – a fantastic pizza by all accounts. He kept raving about it and was in such a good mood that he agreed to sign us.

8
Bag of Spanners

The light of illumination can destroy the shadows that are the essential nature of the matter under scrutiny. But I'd like to think that art is robust enough to bear a little understanding. A song is like a motorbike, you can lay all the parts out on the floor, but it is only when you fire it up that it has any real purpose.

There was a lot of rationality in my approach, I had read Stanislavski and applied 'The Method' to our music. This might seem contrived and disappointing at first glance. The musician is supposed to be an organic idiot-savant speaking in tongues they barely comprehend – that's appealing, but in our case it wasn't the truth. I tried out techniques from drama workshops and psychology. This manifested itself in turning the lights down low and, let's say, trying to conjure up the sea. So the keyboard would be the waves, the drums the rocks and the guitar a boat. Then we'd swap instruments and take it in turns to play a note so as not to be hidebound by anything so quotidian as actually being able to play. After long, gruelling hours of this kind of guff we would, for light relief, knock out something catchy … so, in a way, the deconstruction worked, however perversely.

A lot of this boils down to monkey-at-typewriter stuff: if you chuck enough tunes around, some will end up being pleasing. But it's a good way to get yourself off the route you normally go from A to B, and hopefully end up somewhere original. Of the twelve notes in the scale, there are only so many permutations and inevitably anything good will have a few echoes elsewhere. If something sounds totally original, it will be because it wasn't pleasing to the ear and, though thousands of others will have come across it, they will have had the sense to discard it and leave it for King Crimson and Frank Zappa.

I adhere to the concept of 'the muse'. That the art is out there, trapped in the stone and you just have to be sensitive enough to allow it to flow through you. I would sit at night in front of the coal fire at home awaiting the muse and sometimes had a very tangible sense of its presence. Taking that into a cold garage on a Sunday afternoon is another matter and I can imagine my fellow band members guffawing at this pretentiousness – because I'm not talking about bringing in a chord pattern, but an attitude of mind.

It doesn't always translate that well, though. The most powerful occasion on which I've ever experienced this was when Jarvis, Magnus and I were experimenting. I played one of those decorative copper hunting horns that used to adorn peoples' walls in the seventies, Magnus played some portentous chords on an organ and Jarvis tore his soul apart singing. The song was called 'Silence' and when we first played it, it was frightening in its intensity.

We looked at each other: 'Did you feel that?'

'Yeah! It's like it's coming down through the roof at us!'

We had called down some primal force, something ancient and eternal, the God of the Wild Woods had walked amongst us and we were humbled in reverential awe at its majesty.

But when we played the tape back it sounded like a bag of spanners.

The Miners' Strike was getting into gear: I went to the NUM headquarters and volunteered for active duty. The NUM was almost as casual as Pulp and put me on a bus to a large demonstration in Mansfield, sat behind the leader Arthur Scargill. He had a rubbish sense of humour – like something from a sitcom.

But when we marched into Mansfield the huge crowd parted and fell silent as he spoke. It was like the return of the once and future king – this ordinary bloke was transformed into a charismatic leader by the will of the crowd. Crowds have their own dynamic; they can stir from seeming quiescence into a roaring beast, like a thunderstorm on a sunny day. An idol doesn't have to be a special person to do special things, they just have to be in the right place at the right time and let the power of the crowd flow though them.

I went into our next recording session straight from that demonstration. There's a lot of angst in the early Pulp songs and that was where it was coming from at my end.

9
Crisps *Are* a Free Meal

The following Sunday we played a pub in Sheffield. Sunday is not the best night to pull a crowd but it was packed. It was enough time after The Library Theatre show for word to have got around Britain's largest village that Pulp were doing something different.

We opened to hushed anticipation, people danced to our songs for the first time and there was enthusiastic applause. There were enough ballads to please older fans and enough avant-garde stuff to please those raised on a traditional local diet of experimentation. It felt like we were a serious proposition and a fanzine glowingly praised our new direction. Sheffield dug Pulp.

The landlord was very gruff and always had a cigar in his mouth, but I think he must have liked us because he mumbled something through his cigar about wanting to give us a kettle. Well, kettles are always useful and we said yes and he set about unlocking several padlocks on a sliding grilled door. He disappeared up some dark steps for a while and came puffing down the stairs with a kettledrum. The scrap value of the copper on this battered old thing was tempting but we opted to fix it up and use it as an instrument.

With it we wrote 'Mark of the Devil', which marked a turning point for the band. Up until then, songs came from ideas that either Jarvis or myself had been kicking around previously. If the band had split, the division of songs would have been obvious.

'Mark of the Devil' had its origin in swapping instruments – with Jarvis on drums and me picking up a violin I'd found buried in the detritus of the garage. Unable to figure out how to play the thing, I just droned the open strings and created squalling harmonics by sliding my fingers up and down and putting it through effects (a technique I still use). It's totally original, even though – like most of our music from that period – neither the performance nor the recording does it justice. So in my eyes it's the first fully Pulp song. After 'Mark of the Devil', they all felt more or less like Pulp songs and I find it hard to disentangle the origin and the process from the welter of collaborative ideas flying around.

Orgreave, 18 June, 1984

I heard on the radio that there was a mass picket at Orgreave coking plant. So I got my boots on and walked the six miles from my house. The police were well prepared – it was brutal. But I thought we'd won, that when the news showed what was going on the government would fall. However the news didn't show what was going on at all.

A day or two after Orgreave, we played Psalter Lane Art College. I'd seen Cabaret Voltaire there, so the fact that lowly Pulp were walking in such hallowed halls was desperately exciting.

I used to 'sing' in Pulp and I'm not quite sure why this came about, because I can't sing for toffee and have never been under any illusions about it. I'd done vocals in previous bands and was always keen to get a singer in, no matter how bad, so I didn't have to do it myself. I really wasn't comfortable with singing in Pulp but Jarvis was keen on it, he said it gave him a break. On mature reflection, I think a part of it might have been that he was assured of huge relief amongst the audience when I stopped bellowing.

Nonetheless, I had a certain presence. We uplit the black-and-white backdrop with red searchlights and, with expressionist shadows cast onto it, it really looked quite something. If you were thinking that this has a touch of the 1930s, you'd be right. The 'stewards' armbands with a Brutalist typeface given out to members of the audience gave it the feel of a political rally. It really never occurred to me that, with my guitar plastered with 'coal not dole' stickers, we might be taken for some kind of crypto-fascist sect. You'd think you could safely muck about with constructivist imagery at an art college, wouldn't you?

There were more skinheads in the crowd, some of whom Manners brought backstage after the show because they wanted to meet me. They muttered a few things then just hung around, the younger ones with gluebags and the older ones who 'had been inside for ABH, but didn't mean nuffin' by it', I didn't have the little moustache but did look a bit like Hitler in other regards, with mad staring eyes, khaki clothes and the trendy floppy fringe of the time.

No discussion of Manners can be deemed complete without an exploration of Nietzsche. In a nutshell Nietzsche says, 'God is dead ... Behold, I give you the superman', who must enforce his tragic destiny with *The Will to Power* – something I broadly adhered to. Nietzsche, being a smart cookie, knew what was coming, but I didn't.

Our song 'Will to Power' had a line in it where I screamed, 'where are the broken bottles? where's the fanaticism!!!!?' So you can maybe figure out what I hadn't at the time: that this might have appealed to these lads. So there was some kind of power to it – but it was a dark one and best left buried under the patio and my vocal contributions dwindled, which was a relief to all. So in a roundabout way you can thank Manners for that.

Psalter Lane, unaware of events in the bunker, booked us for fresher's week and we got offered three more concerts in Sheffield, including two on the same day – something that we figured would save money on van hire.

The first, at Pitsmoor Vestry Hall, was in the East End and thankfully few of our fans elected to go. It would have been uncomfortable for the arty ones and incendiary if the skinheads turned up. It was a tense atmosphere at the time of the Brixton riots and some of the Afro-Caribbean crowd didn't take to us. Outside, nine-year-old kids with mini-pops bottles tapped them on the wall and threated to cut us up. As the van departed, it came under a hail of bottles and sticks and we piled across to the West End to set up for the next concert.

The second venue, Rockwells, had Norman Rockwell prints on the wall and pretensions to be an American-style cocktail bar/speakeasy. In an attempt to bring yet more sophistication to the proceedings, we had put pictures of cocktail glasses on our flyers and offered a free meal – but it wasn't exactly Tony Bennett at Vegas. The skinheads turned up and the landlord asked us to 'do a few cover versions', which we didn't have in our repertoire.

Now, the 'do a few covers' thing was a bit worrying. I'd been to working men's clubs and knew people in local bands who made good money playing them. Bands were expected to do cover versions of popular songs and could slip in a couple of their own tunes. It was a slippery slope that potentially awaited any local band of the time. You started out punk and ended up in a frilly shirt with a droopy tache and aviator shades playing 'Wichita Lineman' to pensioners. The version of working-class life where you wear out a groove on the same seat where your father and his father before him sat, playing cribbage for all eternity in a working men's club, was an all-too-possible alternate reality. I was baffled by Jarvis's taste in clothes which put him uncomfortably close to that particular nightmare.

Fortunately, the only song we all knew was 'Hurry Up, Harry' by Sham 69 and Manners was dragooned into singing this, to my secret satisfaction – he could deal with his own skinhead following. But the skinheads didn't much like Manners' matesy take on it and wandered off muttering about the free meal we'd advertised – or 'crisps' as they are referred to down south.

10
The Secret Shop

A stone's throw from Rockwells was a doorway to a shop which seemed to be in different places at different times. Sometimes it was open and a few chipped enamel pans were put out for sale. Inside, the shop went on for ever – ending up in a dusty garret with a mouldering Morris Minor and pigeons cooing through holes in the rafters. What we referred to as 'The Secret Shop' was the inspiration for a leaflet I produced for our upcoming Christmas show at Sheffield's prestigious 800-capacity Leadmill club.

It began: 'This piece of paper is magic. It can take you out of this room, into the street, past the hole in the road … the door is never in the same place twice for the same person … the door is always at the same place for everyone at the top of the stairs … at first all is silent … you shut your eyes for a second and it all grows … ' This leaflet had a Christmas theme, but others were specific to other venues.

This was a chance to try out some new material and we wrote a special winter song called 'Snow' for the occasion. To the best of my knowledge, Pulp have never played the same set twice. It was quite usual for more than half the songs to change between one show and the next – each show was a unique event.

Stage sets have always been a massive deal to Pulp. My initial take on things was that we were artists who also played instruments. In the early days, the playing instruments side of things wasn't what got the most attention. It seemed perfectly conceivable that the direction we would take would be performance art or experimental films. The band part eventually became the dominant element, but this was not always the case and the look and style of presentation always remained something that huge care was taken with.

My Dadaist play had fruit marked-up as pool balls suspended from the ceiling – hanging three feet above the ground, as if lying on an invisible pool table – to be pierced by players with snooker cues. So stuff hanging from the ceiling was something we liked and used to great effect in many shows. This was all on a dole-money budget. But five pounds' worth of toilet rolls of different colours draped around a stage like streamers can be remarkably effective. Bags of water, each with a different food colouring inside, interspersed with upside-down umbrellas was another one. And silver foil was something I was always keen to have industrial quantities of: it can transform an otherwise impersonal venue into your own space. You can wrap ugly items of equipment in it, you can line a wall with it, you can crinkle it, you can make giant icicles, you can drape it from string and make a maze and you can even have yourself wrapped in it like a mummy. This isn't comfortable, but it does retain cooking juices, which slosh about in your shoes.

Candida looked resplendent in an all-white outfit, with snowball pom-poms and baubles for earrings, and she had a mini Christmas tree lit up on her keyboard.

We opened with a Hawkwind/Test Dept/Einstürzende Neubauten-style sound piece called 'Hydroelectric Dam', to alert people in the bar that we were on, then went straight into live favourite 'Mark of the Devil'.

The sound was terrible and, to the bemusement of the crowd, Jarvis began a furious argument with the engineer while the rest of us jammed, waiting for the endless dispute to finish. The budget set collapsed around our ears and maddeningly the audience thought this was deliberate. So, where I saw a Dadaist agitprop statement, others saw a bunch of wacky zany funsters. But there were around 500 people and we entertained them, even if for all the wrong reasons. We got paid a band record of £50, which I later discovered was a support band's fee, not a headline one – but we weren't complaining. It was the last act of 1984, a year that started with chairs being thrown and ended with an enthusiastic encore in Sheffield's leading live venue.

11
What to Wear?

Negotiations with the small record company were proving intractable and we sent more demos off to other labels with an air of desperation. But we had no takers and decided to do the dark deed and go down to meet our only suitors. What to wear?

Jarvis's arty mum had forced him to be different when he was younger so he'd never had all the seventies gear, whereas I'd had Brummie bags, Oxford bags, high-waisters and a shamefully 'in-the-knit' brown star jumper ... I loathed this stuff and couldn't figure out what Jarvis saw in it. I liked sixties gear and thought Jarvis's dress sense was absurd. I appreciated its originality though, and that's how it was: we were all very different and hated each others' style but knew that the whole gained from the sum of the parts.

There was nothing contrived about this, I genuinely pitied Jarvis for his lack of fashion sense. At the meeting with the record company I wore a smart and sombre suit and Jarvis angled for praise for his own outfit, which was all purple. But they were all completely different and clashing purples, a browny purple, a fuchsia, an imperial purple, a reddy purple – hideous, simply hideous. Flares, frills, kipper ties and 'fuck-off' lapels, he looked like a bad working-men's-club comedian. To my eyes, and I firmly believe in the eyes of the God of Aesthetics, he looked a fright, but he thought he looked great. And, insanely, the rest of the world ended up agreeing with him.

If you want to know why we signed with a label more interested in pizza than music – it was the only offer on the table. It seemed they would sign anyone for £500 and many, including Pulp, rued the day they did. But we'd got a record deal and that was a big step up.

At night the thinning ranks of striking miners tried to throw off the police by calling surprise pickets at wavering pits . . . only to find that their phones were being tapped and the police arrived before they did. Away from the cameras, things got ugly. In the dying days of the strike, I joined a minibus evading border checks between Yorkshire and Nottinghamshire. Cold floodlights illuminated the constructivist majesty of the pit headgear, which now turned as the miners returned to work.

Two men in a red Ford Escort, both with moustaches and blue shirts, followed me home to my squat. I ducked behind the concrete wall, pushed the door open and crawled to bed in the dark so they couldn't see where I lived. The defeated miners marched back to work with banners waving and a brass band playing. It seemed like something from another era.

After the strike, there was a sense that idealism would get you nowhere, let the devil take the hindmost. Being in a band seemed an unbearably light and inconsequential thing.

At a scrapyard near Orgreave I produced a low-budget film – using an affordable new media called 'video' – for our song 'Maureen', which we hoped the record company would release as a single. This video was added to the package I sent off to get shows, hoping that the recipients would be early adopters. I sent it off to the TV companies but there were no shows playing videos.

We played a set at The Hallamshire, bookended by a spoken-word piece by one of our friends. The landlord noted with approval that we were using the kettledrum and gave us another one. There was more debate as to whether we should cash these in for the not-inconsiderable scrap value of the copper.

We thought that the record company would be champing at the bit to have us go into a studio and record something, but they seemed to be prevaricating rather than urging. They resisted releasing 'Maureen' and gave us enough money to record the ballad 'Little Girl' as a single. The clock was ticking but we managed to get down five tracks.

By September kids were going back to school and we'd managed to play five concerts, only one outside Sheffield. I was sending tapes and information off but we weren't getting any takers. Promoters of small venues in other cities would rather pay a local band with a few mates £30 than take a chance on an unknown.

After talking with some similarly hungry and frustrated local bands we decided to combine forces and offer a 'Sheffield taster menu', where we could share costs and present a more appealing package to venues. Venues would ask to talk to 'the grown up' – in Pulp that was me. But these other acts all had at least one 'grown up', people that gave a damn and had ambition, so it was good to have a bit of backup. The other 'grown ups' supplied tapes, images and press cuttings, which allowed me to hype up the profile of the package higher than it was in reality.

I printed off individual information sheets for the acts on an A4 sheet of thin pastel-coloured tracing paper – then stuck them together and rolled them up to make a scroll, which looked pretty good. The venues didn't just get a band with no profile, they got a complete night with a Sheffield theme at a time when Sheffield's star was riding high. We offered a compère (Henry Normal) and supplied the venues with posters and leaflets. I knew, because I'd promoted shows before, that this package would stand out from the crowd. Most bands handed in a cassette tape with the songs written in biro and, if you were very lucky, an A4 sheet of black-and-white information saying how brilliant they were. Our offering was low budget but distinctive and we got nine concert offers – in effect a national tour.

12
Five Go Touring

At The Leadmill, Pulp drew the short straw and went on first out of the three bands: the place was virtually empty. Many of the audience would have paid to see us, but they arrived after we'd played. As booking agent and promoter I had somehow contrived to demote us from headliner to third on the bill and reduce the audience by a factor of ten. I didn't care though, the bands were taking it in turn to open the show, which meant we would headline at the more exotic out-of-town shows where none of the bands had any profile to speak of.

The next show was in Bristol and we went to the camera obscura and Clifton Suspension Bridge, which was a fun day out and a bit like a school trip. People kept wandering off and doing naughty things. When members of the public showed concern, I tapped my head, gave them a knowing raised eyebrow and herded the offending parties off. Not for the last time, I pretended to be the carer for a group of delinquents and used this to get us out of trouble.

On our way to the venue we found an unusually shaped metal container in the street and opened it. Inside we found a judge's wig and a telephone number: we rang the number and the judge came driving round to collect his wig as he was due in court. He could have given us a fiver for our trouble though, we had a concert to play and took time out to make sure he got his wig, but who are we to judge?

(There's a saying about this kind of occurrence, the surrealism that seems to cleave unto bands on the road, 'When on tour you *will* find a porcupine in a bucket.' And this is very true, apart from the fact that we've not found a porcupine in a bucket ... yet.)

The concert was on Vivian Stanshall's boat *Thekla*. This was quite a coup: he'd been in the Bonzo Dog Doo-Dah Band, with Neil Innes from Monty Python, and had starred in a film called *Sir Henry at Rawlinson End*, which Rover, our driver-cum-roadie, liked to read extracts from at soundchecks.

Vivian Stanshall's world was through the looking glass. He would bark out things in German and ask me join his band, with the stipulation that I would have to play an instrument made out of rubber – a bona fide English eccentric. There was a very beautiful middle-aged woman from some sixties Scandinavian dream involved in putting the shows on who probably used to be in Can or the Baader-Meinhof Gang. Rover, ever the romantic, said wistfully: 'I'd use her shit for toothpaste.'

On the way back we went for something to eat in a high-end antique centre in the Vale of Evesham. We took our seats at the cottage-style benches amongst jams with chequered mop caps. But alarm bells must have been going off in the minds of people around us, they weren't used to our sort round there. A teddy boy had once stopped there in the fifties but had been seen off with a stern talking-to and a flea in his ear before he'd had a chance to pull a flick knife, jive or gob on the floor.

There was an air of tension: a look, a raised eyebrow, a tone of voice. The staff and clientele were elderly, middle-aged and female – apart from the guy serving, who took it upon himself to be a hero and stand up to this barbarian invasion by having a very truculent attitude. You should always stand up to bullies, even if they haven't actually started bullying you yet, and he got his retaliation in first by being extremely curt. Middle-aged ladies clutching smelling salts were all a-swoon at his bravery. He was Robert Kilroy-Silk, Nigel Havers and Richard Madeley rolled into one and would get his end away that night if he kept this up. The prices were extortionate. It was £1.40 for a bacon butty, which would have bought you a small house in Sheffield at the time. But the cavalier Rover, who was getting paid unlike the rest of us, went ahead and ordered one. When he opened the butty, there was one tiny streaky rasher inside and – in spite of my pleas not to make a scene – he went to the counter, smiled ever-so-politely, and said, 'Excuse me, but when I pay £1.40 for a bacon butty, I expect to get more than one rasher of bacon.' (Rover had a very polite manner for someone with such long hair.)

You could hear a teaspoon drop. 'Certainly, sir,' said the man through gritted teeth and put an extra rasher on. When the bill came, there was 40p extra for the additional rasher of bacon. They were taking the piss and I was concerned that things might kick off, but Rover just threw his head back and laughed uncontrollably, tears streaming down his face – like Errol Flynn as Robin Hood confronting Guy of Gisbourne. It made everyone feel uncomfortable but I'm glad he did it.

Magnus liked to spin round and bounce up and down on his drum stool. At our concert at the Darlington Art Centre the padded seat finally gave way and he sat down on the sprocket to quite eye-watering effect. He screamed and leapt back up – demolishing his drum kit, thus ending the concert.

Magnus could take an awful lot of legal highs – banana skins, lobelia, *Amanita muscaria*, a pipe of hops, pickled broom buds – but he was surprisingly reticent to have booze. On the night we played Adam and Eve's Nitespot in Chesterfield, Magnus had a pint, but it made him go bonkers. He wrecked his drum kit during the opening song, 'Little Girl', which is a very soft ballad indeed. And he wasn't angry when he did this, just one of those legendary crazy drummers.

We met up at compère Henry Normal's mad house in Chesterfield, which he shared with members of a punk band called The Bland. Strangely, they all seemed to be prog rock fans and had the most infantile sense of humour, of the student *Bottom* variety.

Manners snarled, 'Let's smack 'em!'

In Middlesborough we did some local radio and it became apparent that the interviewer was just reading off a crib sheet. 'So, how would you describe your music?' 'A mixture of funk and jazz,' I said, deadpan.

The support band was a crusty white-rasta-with-dreads outfit. As behooves hippies, they hadn't brought their snare drum and asked if they could borrow ours. Magnus, a fellow traveller, let them and they broke it, so we weren't best pleased. We played at one end of a bar with no stage and an uninterested crowd wandered about chatting in front of us – as if we were workmen in the corner fixing something. So we pretended we were playing to a stadium rock audience and went completely over the top, throwing shapes and making grandiose gestures, largely for our own amusement.

Our concert at Sheffield University was advertised as a 'Workers Against Racism' benefit. Very few 'workers' in the bands, even fewer in the audience and all white, of course.

At any concert we played, Manners would go into town for a takeaway and there was a fifty-fifty chance he would come back with a bloody nose. 'What happened, Manners?' 'Oh, some kids smacked me.' It was just the norm, but it only happened to him. So he always had a black eye or his arm in a sling. The rest of us seemed to be able to acquire a late night kebab without this.

This was our first taste of life on the road and I loved it. A new day, a new place. Pop music is fun: this is why you do it. I had learnt that hippies rip you off and patronise you, and that gangsters are much better people to deal with. If the promoter has a sheepskin coat, a ruddy face, a cigar, and owns greyhounds and a chain of nightclubs from Batley to Cleethorpes, then the treatment will be OK, and he'll probably send a crate of beer back for you. If they've got a nose piercing and have just come back from backpacking in Machu Picchu, then you are in trouble. When a venue ripped us off, we weren't averse to sending in a light-fingered hanger-on to 'liberate' goods and redress the balance. And we'd drive off in apple-scromp delight with the crate of beer he'd extracted as a fee. We never stole anything from a place that had been fair to us though.

12a
The Man Who Fell to Earth

The single 'Little Girl' was released after the tour that was supposed to be promoting it. All the cylinders were firing at different times and little staggers forward weren't followed up. It was very frustrating. I knew what needed to be done to advance the band, and therefore sell records. You put up posters, you get press, you give out leaflets, you release records, you tour, you get round radio stations – it ain't rocket science. And it was costing us money we could ill afford. A small band loses a bit of money doing their hobby. A small band who tours nationally loses a lot of money.

For the sleeve we had specified gold lettering, aiming for a Klimt-like opulence, but the tightwad record company fobbed us off with mustard. It sold a few hundred copies, mainly in Sheffield. 'Little Girl' got slated in one review by a feminist and described as 'filth'. This was pretty ironic because it was, if anything, a feminist statement, though obviously a subtle one. Radio One banned it: literally whipping it off the decks halfway through – though unfortunately not in such a high-profile way that we got any publicity. Getting banned usually ups record sales, but not in our case.

Perhaps I should be thankful that Pulp didn't get a breakthrough at this time, we weren't quite the finished article. Had we had a minor hit with a less than brilliant song before slipping back into obscurity I would have thought, 'Okay, we've had our shot.' But, as it was, I felt I had to keep pushing.

Still, all things considered, things were looking up, we got mixed reviews but with enough decent ones to swell the press pack. We were offered more shows, what could possibly go wrong?

I was living in a flat above a sex shop with a girl who had a bit of a Béatrice Dalle thing going on and was the object of much pining amongst local musicians, including Jarvis. In a bid to impress her, he climbed Artery-style out of the window and made his way along the ledge, only to fall twenty feet onto the pavement in front of the sex shop – his broken glasses and splayed limbs serving as a dire warning on the dangers of pornography to several adolescent boys who had been plucking up the courage to go in.

It seemed touch and go for a bit, he'd broken his hip and was in hospital for a while, then moved out into residential care. But he slowly improved and was able to come out in a wheelchair. We had to cancel a couple of shows but he gamely did the rest in his wheelchair.

I shamelessly milked the mishap for all it was worth and took Jarvis down to London to do press, which included a surreal photo shoot pushing him round a skateboard park in the chair.

For the next show at The Clarendon, London, we brought a coach party down from Sheffield. The trip down to London was always filled with expectation. On the way into the metropolis, the excitement mounted: there were famous people just walking down the street, bold as brass. Rover always seemed to spot Oliver Reed just disappearing into a pub and demand that the van stop, but no one else ever saw him. It was probably just wishful thinking on Rover's part, like the time when he went past Felicity Kendall in the street and she 'gave him the eye'. Can't remember the concert, it got some reviews.

Never one to avoid advancing the greater glory of Pulp by resorting to bad taste, I cut out a picture from a *Romania Today, 1968* magazine of a forlorn man wired up with electrodes – onto which I drew broken glasses to make it look like Jarvis.

There was a gale blowing and I pushed Jarvis in the wheelchair down the middle of West Street wearing crash helmets to avoid the flying slates.

Sheffield's legendary Limit Club was full, with a crowd drawn at least in part by ghoulish curiosity. Jarvis resisted my urgings to have himself wheeled out on a hospital trolley, with electrodes attached like the poster, but went on in his wheelchair; head lolling to one side cradling the microphone claw-like in his hand. He kept this up all the way through the set – then rather ruined the effect when he ran back on for the encore and danced: but such was his dancing that, if you weren't an aficionado, it may well have compounded the impression of loss of faculty. The show was slated by the *NME*.

At Chesterfield Arts Centre we were interviewed by a local youth called 'Zig' who wrote a fanzine called *Cosmic Pig*. Pulp were genuinely weird, no two ways about it, but I'm not sure we've ever been weirder than that night. Magnus was off his head on something, possibly fly agaric mushrooms; I was barking at Manners' dodgy mates, who were trying to nick things, with the thousand-yard stare of a miners' strike veteran; and the seemingly sound-limbed singer kept sitting down in a wheelchair. It freaked poor old Zig out, but in a good way because he came to all the concerts after that.

14
Get a Flat Above a Shop

Jarvis and I got a flat above a shop, which was always a tip – he was not a man who did the dishes. He did once hoover though, afterwards setting the vacuum cleaner up like a Viet Cong punji trap, to hit me in the kidneys and let me know he'd done it.

I bought a VW camper van. The thrill of ownership was exquisite, it had a tiny sink and cooker, and curtains you can draw – saucy! My mates were impressed, it had a sliding side-door and we cruised round the town with water bombs at the ready, looking for a particularly miserable-looking goth to pelt before making our getaway.

I attempted to teach Jarvis to drive in this vehicle, which, with its ridiculously underpowered lawnmower engine, was very challenging on the steep hills of Sheffield. He had a curious technique, which must have come from owning a pedal car as a child whereby he pumped the accelerator to make the vehicle go. So the van lurched along in fits and starts, stalling in alarming places.

Jarvis, like myself, was an inveterate jumble-saler – but with no filter button and his room soon filled up with innumerable jigsaws and tatty board games: all with missing pieces. Things became critical after a trip to the auction across the road, where they had job lots of house clearances after the good stuff had been taken out. So you might get ten odd-chairs, a bed, a table, an elephant's foot umbrella stand, a mangle and a stack of *Good Housekeeping* magazines. I left Jarvis to bid, with the instruction not to pay more than ten pounds. What I didn't impress on him strongly enough was that I only wanted *one* of these lots. So he bought them all, and we ended up with seven tables, fifty-three chairs, a Regency commode, a cement mixer, five beds etc. etc. etc… . which had to be piled up so high that getting in the flat was like coming through a tunnel.

It was okay living with Jarvis but you couldn't watch the telly without him shouting at it and giving a running commentary: doing a little sketch then looking round for approval. It was wearing thin and I had outbursts along the lines of, 'Aren't you *ever* offstage?'

We needed to make some room. Jarvis wouldn't be parted from his seven full-length mirrors but he did reluctantly part with some clothes. A second-hand dealer gave him £10 for a transit van full of them, not trendy stuff at the time you see, all that seventies clobber.

There *was* woodchip on the wall and Jarvis *did* date a girl for a year without bringing her home. Thinking he was making her up I said; 'So when are we finally going to meet this "legendary girlfriend" of yours, then?' But she did exist and he brought her round and cooked her boiled potatoes and lettuce, served in very dim candlelight so she wouldn't notice there was no chicken in the chicken dinner advertised. She was rather special and found her way into several songs: things between them were stable for a bit, but there was a lyrical lull. A guy from the record company said, 'I hope she breaks his fucking heart soon because we need a new album,' and that did kind of happen.

Jarvis treated the world as a giant jumble sale, to pick through for ideas; and our rather ordinary lives found their way into songs and, eventually, the zeitgeist.

The way in which Pulp differed from many of our contemporaries on the 'indie' scene was that we admitted we wanted to be successful. Not for us the succour of: 'You can't really reject us because we aren't really trying.' Selling a couple of hundred records was a mark of failure rather than a badge of honour. Indie was a label we never sought or liked, and I surreptitiously switched our records from the 'indie' section to 'pop' in record shops. We were trying to make pop music, albeit unsuccessfully. I wrote a manifesto saying we wanted to make 'the fairground music of the future'. The greatest accolade a piece of music could have was not to be praised in avant-garde circles or win a prestigious prize but to be played on the waltzer.

We played Hull Adelphi quite a few times during this period. I've heard that venue slagged off as the archetype of the kind of dive you don't want to play, however our experience was different. Paul, who ran it, was always friendly, the place had atmosphere and you could crash there if you needed to. We made detours to Flamborough Head, the Humber Bridge, Spurn Point and the magnificent Flixborough chemical plant – which is a sight to see at night. It was a bit like a geography field trip. But the favourite and repeated detour was to Withernsea – a forgotten seaside town that was a budget alternative to Bridlington or Cleethorpes in the fifties. We loved this *Scooby-Doo*, end-of-the-pier-falling-into-the-sea place and wandered around with candy floss and chips, and played games on the beach, while lesser bands sat backstage, staring at the dressing room wall. There was a game (there is always a game) and this one was called 'groynes'.

Groynes are wooden walls that project into the sea to make sure storms don't wash away all the sand. In our game, one person placed a pebble on the groyne, then the next person walked along and moved the pebble further along, so it got further into the sea. After a point you had to wait for a wave to pass, then rush to push the pebble further on before dashing back. On one occasion, the sea was choppy and Jarvis spindled his way uncertainly along the wall. He waited well shy of the pebble for the increasingly vigorous waves to die down, dashing back to save his Chelsea boots as big waves washed over. Urged on by jeers, he finally made a dash for it, then slowly toppled over the side of the groyne into the sea. He wasn't going to get his Chelsea boots wet so dived in head first, leaving his feet sticking out, and somehow scrambled back onto the wall, to much laughter. Miraculously his Chelsea boots were dry, but they were the only things. He had to play the concert with seaweed-strewn clothes, standing in a puddle of water.

Quizzes, almost always at my instigation, and almost always accompanied by groaning, were a staple of Pulp tours. One that particularly sticks in my mind was 'name a sexual perversion', which we played on the way back to Sheffield from a concert in Manchester. Most people had dropped out before we'd even left the city but Jarvis and I were still contesting it as we left a rainy Glossop, wound through the treacherous Snake Pass, descended down into Sheffield and unloaded – which might explain some of the lyrics.

At another show at London's Rock Garden the publicity was non-existent so we busked in Covent Garden using the timpani and gave out fliers to puzzled tourists, with Candida vainly hammering away at an unplugged stylophone. (We had various goes at busking and garnered a total of less than £10 across our entire career.) Our new songs, which were both more avant-garde and more poppy, baffled reviewers. The journalist Jon Wilde wrote; 'Pulp have to choose between the charts and the asylum soon.' He was right.

15
Freaks

We recorded *Freaks* in 1986, at Sheffield's Input studios. This was exciting, we were recording an album like proper grown-up bands; here was our chance to shine. But the budget was £600, time was limited and the circumstances were not ideal. The noise of a mystery drill kept appearing on recordings. Rover encouraged Jarvis, much against his better judgment, to do fairground calls such as; 'Roll up, roll up'. Jarvis immediately regretted this and we tried to erase it, but to no avail, it's there for all eternity.

The opening track, 'Fairground', is a true story.

> As the signs outside proclaimed, nature sometimes makes mistakes. Was it the mother or the father to blame, inside the damp grass and tilted tent?

It came from a childhood visit to a decrepit freak show, which must have been a survival from an earlier era. There were exhibits such as 'The cat with two heads and the dog with eight legs.'

'I sought shelter from the storm in a small inn by the coast.' This was The Ox at Lebbeston, which had Victorian freakshow exhibits in the children's room. I was about thirteen and had been left there by my parents, along with a family who never spoke.

> In the children's room three identical sisters sat,
> Except for the one who was hideously deformed;

> her grotesque features seemed to parody her sisters' beauty,
> ridiculing and mocking everything I held dear.

There were three identically-dressed girls, two of whom were meltingly gorgeous and one of whom was disabled. Their parents were sat in the room too and must have been as uncomfortable as I was.

> Won't you come with me to the fairground?
> Your head
> will be spinning,
> I said your head
> is your feet.

I could write an essay about sexual awakening and all sorts of stuff, but there you go. I'd say 'Fairground' is a song and *Freaks* is an album I'm embarrassed by but not ashamed of – if that makes any sense.

We were not laughing at freaks, we were saying: 'We are freaks and maybe you are a bit of a freak, too?' The ever-present voyeurism that runs through Pulp is always empathetic to the subject. The theme of mistakes, misshapes and misfit outsiders remained.

For some reason, our roadie Rover played drums on a song called 'Tunnel', which didn't make it onto the album. Rover's style was completely different to other drummers; it was what I would call 'stodgy'. It sounded like he was playing with two suet dumplings on the end of sticks, which suited 'Tunnel' perfectly. 'Tunnel' was about what it was like to be in the band at the time: a long dark tunnel that you had to keep going down because there might be light at the end.

When a journalist asked me what it was like to be in Pulp I said, 'Imagine a boot stamping on a human head for all eternity.' It was paraphrased from George Orwell but got repeated as if it was my own. Another quote that *was* my own was in answer to the question, 'What is your greatest nightmare?' My answer was: 'That I'm stuck in a crap retro novelty band with no hope of escape or prospect of success.' They were hard times.

Songs the audience like are, in my opinion, an almost infallible guide to what makes a good single. (There may be exceptions, due to local factors: let's say a song that lists all your mate's names and says they are great, then perhaps that is the exception.) So I never trusted the record company and always trusted 'The Kids'. The twelve-inch single 'Dogs Are Everywhere' was released in June 1986, with the lead track one of the weakest. We consoled ourselves that, as it had five tracks, including live favourite 'Mark of the Devil', people could make their own minds up.

Melody Maker made it 'Single of the Week', highlighting 'Mark of the Devil' as the standout track. But radio stations were getting the lacklustre 'Dogs Are Everywhere' as the A-side. It didn't get played much and it didn't chart anywhere. I'd not minded 'Little Girl' being a single, even though it wasn't the direction I would have chosen, because it was still a good track. But 'Dogs' wasn't in our top-ten songs, people weren't calling out for it. I can remember doing a few interviews and having to be chipper and big-up the track, but it felt false. We were in the uncomfortable position of doing what we rightly or wrongly believed to be groundbreaking material and the record company was choosing to put out the most compromised part of our output. I sent the record off but the only out-of-town show we got was the Inner City Blues Club at The Bristol Tropic, which put some good acts on but was a teeny bit seedy.

We got yet another show supporting someone we had never heard of at The Leadmill but no tour and no fun. 'Desperation, Death, Doom, Dogs' was our in-band saying.

The live shows were sometimes fantastic but it didn't seem to be getting us anywhere. We weren't selling many records and were in serious danger of going down the pan.

If I could choose to be in the audience of a Pulp concert I'd definitely choose the line-up that produced *Freaks*, it just felt so powerful. But there were problems with that line-up, the main one being that they didn't turn up for rehearsals. To put none too fine a point on it, everyone else in Pulp was lazy. While Jarvis was still living with his mum, rehearsals had often started with me throwing stones up at his window to wake him up and then waiting for the others, who didn't always turn up.

Jarvis and myself were pretty committed and put quite a bit of our own time and money into doing the band. I'd quit the various odd jobs I was doing to give it my full attention, so there were tensions when the others weren't taking it as seriously. This came to a head when we were filming the video for 'They Suffocate at Night' in one of Tim's abandoned warehouses. We had been at it all day, it was two in the morning, and I'd been running, around picking up equipment and organising things.

Jarvis had been decking out a vehicle inspection pit as a living room so that it could be filmed from above and get some interesting angles. Magnus, Manners and Candida were getting increasingly bored, cold, hungry and fed up. They refused to continue, climbed into the rafters and sat there, dangling their legs like three big sulky pigeons. I gave Jarvis an ultimatum, 'They go or I go', and that was the end of that line-up, sacked whilst twenty foot in the air in a cold warehouse.

Pulp were now a two-piece.

16

The Curious Case of Captain Sleep

Then began a Dark Age for Pulp, a long struggle to find a stable line-up and keep the band together. A full two years would elapse before the boundaries of the new kingdom were finally settled and the seminal line-up that produced all the songs you hear on the radio was set in aspic. We'd got an album (*Freaks*) about to come out and several shows booked – including a support slot at The Leadmill in a fortnight's time – so there was no time to mourn the passing of the old order. The hunt was on for new members. Pulp had a profile locally and various bods came through the garage doors, some of whom assured their rejection by being suspiciously competent at playing and making us look like fools by asking questions about keys and scales. I was keen to preserve our musical naivety.

We got a keyboardist called 'Captain Sleep' on account of how he kept falling asleep when playing. I never got to know his real name or much else about him, so have no idea whether he had narcolepsy or just a lot of heavy nights.

We played The 100 Club in London and my first impression was that I'd come to the wrong place: for a legendary venue it looked awfully like a down-at-heel northern club. But it was a lively show and we got the best reviews we'd ever had, even though Captain Sleep kept dropping off during the concert and had to be prodded awake.

Captain Sleep went missing for a while and, not knowing his real name, we had no means of contacting him. I chanced upon him sat on a bench outside Birmingham St Martin's market, where I had a stall selling antique glassware at the 'Big Brum' antique fair. I went over with the intention of dragging him back into the bosom of Pulp, then noticed he was asleep and decided to give it a miss.

The record company released another dolorous ballad, called 'They Suffocate at Night', which had the distinction of out of tune vocals and justifiably failed to make an impact. The most favourable review said, 'there's a lot worse around'.

We had another concert booked at The Leadmill, which was impossible minus a keyboardist. So I got in two performance artists and it turned into a surreal event that involved them dropping balloons full of water while we swapped instruments. This puzzled the rest of the band and must certainly have puzzled the audience. I could spout some kind of nonsense about what it all meant, but then I'd have to know what that was – I'd been watching a lot of Luis Buñuel films. Jarvis read out a self-penned horror story that was the lyrical precursor to a number of songs. It was a short set and something of a twenty-minute jazz odyssey, but this was not a willing return to our avant-garde performance-art roots, but rather a cobbled-together attempt to produce a show in the absence of a full line-up. Fun though, and possibly quite good, in its own way.

We tried auditioning other people but it just didn't feel right, there was something magic about the old line-up. We missed them, so we asked them back – on best behaviour mind, and no running in the corridors this time – but only Candida came. Manners says it was for the best, that we'd never have made it with them mucking about all the time – which is very big of him in the circumstances. And at least we'd got Candida back, so the Celtic fringe remained intact, if a little thinner.

We already knew drummer Nick Banks from around town. He had a good style, little round specs and Nehru collars. He worked in a very trendy new-wave clothes shop where I'd bought the punky T-shirt that encouraged earnest German punks to approach me on trains.

I met Nick at a place called Manor Top, where we were followed by a heavily pregnant white bulldog to Jarvis's house. Jarvis's dog, a burly male Staffordshire bull terrier called 'Bonzo', went mental. We had an audition of sorts as Bonzo hurled himself at the door, yowling. Then Nick and I went off, still followed by the panting bulldog, which was about to give birth. We took it to the police station, which was shut and, in desperation, ended up hoisting it into someone's front garden before running off – the perfect audition.

When Nick joined the band, Manners said he was glad to see we'd 'still got the yob element'. Nick did *The Times* crossword and worked as a supply teacher, but did a very good yob impression. He was from Rotherham but – like many arty people in South Yorkshire and beyond – had naturally migrated to Sheffield, where the action was.

Like Jarvis and myself, Nick was a musical magpie and the stylistic options open to Pulp expanded. In rehearsals, a new and beatier direction emerged. Nick was particularly good at disco; so we had a bit of a jokey go at it and it turned out well. But he had only one volume setting: LOUD. Which resulted in much bad feeling as he twatted cymbals inches from our ears – this garage wasn't big enough for Nick.

At The Limit Club in March 1986 I got together a sci-fi grotto with silver foil, bubbles, orange globes and projections and gave an oft-repeated pep talk before we went onstage – that we had to walk the tightrope of absurdity and risk making complete fools of ourselves. We'd not played Sheffield for a while and Jarvis made an announcement along the lines of: 'This is the new Pulp – tonight will be an experimental evening.' We introduced the more up-tempo 'disco' songs to our already eclectic set, to the puzzlement of reviewers and the admiration of the audience. The album *Freaks* wasn't released but we'd grown tired of it; of the eleven songs we played only a couple were from that album. Mercifully relieved of singing duties, I now played half the songs on violin. There had always been a slightly dark underbelly to Jarvis's lyrics but now it was the main course. Pulp were no longer a performance-art event, a freak show to observe, we were a band: one you could dance to.

Freaks was released into the community on 11 May 1987. We'd almost given up on this album ever coming out and it was made available with little fanfare. All of the songs had been written and recorded in a different era, with a different line-up. There was minimal to zero publicity and no tour. *Freaks* was not critically well received and sold a few hundred copies, but it picked us up more fans locally and, unbeknown to us, was sending its tentacles of influence into the bedrooms of a number of people we were to later encounter.

We never sold more than a few hundred records and kept playing a series of straggling concerts in 1987: some local and some out of town, including Derby's 20th Century club, which set an attendance low of six people. It cost us money to play but we were getting better live and, in the fierce crucible of winning round initially hostile audiences, we honed the songs and performance.

Whilst our complete volte-faces of style between songs baffled critics, we picked up a few fanatical local fans – people whose favourite band was Pulp. We still got hecklers but hecklers are usually knobheads and most people aren't knobheads. The squares were slagging us off and the freaks were cheering us on. The Limit Club was the perfect venue for this clash. During the week they had free nights for the freaks, then at the weekend the townies arrived to poke fun at the freaks and there were almost always fights. So we'd play a concert at the weekend with quite a bit of booing going on at the back and after the show a few people would come up and say 'That concert changed my life.' We were setting down a defiant marker, risking ridicule, but sometimes pulling it off. If you take a strong stand you invite hatred or devotion, and we got both. I went for a pee and saw graffiti slagging us off in the toilets, which on one level was hurtful, but on another was something of a landmark. I walked taller when I came out. We were receiving the kind of reviews, record sales, and setbacks that would make most people pack it in, but when a small but growing coterie of people absolutely adore what you are doing it is hard to feel that you are on the wrong track.

17
The Day That Never Happened

1988 was the leanest year so far, we recorded nothing, we released nothing and played only five concerts. One concert was advertised as: 'Pulp return from the dead!' Our bass player went from hard partying to hard religion and back again, with very little discernable difference, and had to be persuaded not to take his clothes off at shows – not always successfully.

The Leadmill had given us the odd support slot, but the fees stayed low – which was particularly galling as most of the audience was coming to see us. They were also extremely rigorous in enforcing fire regulations and we were often debarred from putting our sets up. This from a venue happy to put on fire-eaters – but, hey, they're hippies, so it's cool, man.

After much haggling, I managed to get The Leadmill to give us a headline slot. This felt like a critical show: the band was in danger of splitting up and I determined to make it special, if only as a swansong. To add to my tension, it was scheduled for a week before I was about to become a father and my girlfriend obligingly went into labour three days before the show. The show was conceptualised as 'The day that never happened' and I produced charts delineating curtain closes, intro music (the theme from *La Dolce Vita*), dry ice, lighting, films, visuals, costume changes, positions of band, neon lights, falling snow and smells – for which I'd made incense, which was to be volatilised by a wind machine during the appropriate song.

There were only two members of Pulp who had the remotest interest in this kind of thing. Jarvis, who had the kind of interest that mainly manifested itself in talking about it in the pub at ten in the evening and myself, who had the kind of interest that manifested itself in actually turning up and doing it. Nonetheless, things got done with the help of various local artists; weird-beards and fey flappy-armed youths who were more enthusiastic than practical. The entrance to the club was transformed into a tunnel that the audience emerged through to be handed a leaf made iridescent with formaldehyde, and a small Alice in Wonderland 'drink me' bottle. Then they worked their way round a fortune teller and a tombola, then through a maze of silver foil where a giant and malevolent Santa's head with gleaming red eyes raised its mouth and said 'Ho ho ho,' before disgorging a present; if it didn't bite your hand off.

Things did not go according to plan.

The Leadmill fire officer took exception to almost everything, even the dry ice: I enjoyed pointing out to him that dry ice was what fire extinguishers contained. Testing our projection screen for flammability, he set fire to it. Visuals that were supposed to be projected onto an entire wall were instead transmitted on a telly on a chair in the middle of the stage (wrapped in silver foil of course). During the set, the confetti that was supposed to be blown through the wind machine clogged it up and spattered the audience with gobbets of damp smelly paper. Four clockwork manikins – one with a gumball machine for a head – jerked about onstage, articulated by cogs, chains, pulleys and other robotic conveyances. There was dry ice too and, say what you like about dry ice, dry it is not. It's very slippy underfoot and so, unrehearsed due to putting this menagerie together, I slipped and skidded my way through the set as this pandemonium collapsed around us. The audience laughed.

I had my head in my hands in the dressing room. It was horrible to be in the band but possibly good to watch because of that. Desperate people playing Russian Roulette with ill-advised stage sets who want to make it big but think they are about to have their dreams shattered in public are quite compelling viewing.

The bassist announced that if we didn't all move to London he would leave. It was his fifth concert and I had a two-day-old daughter. I didn't take kindly to his ultimatum and told him to bugger off.

Jarvis took me to one side and said that he was packing it in: he'd got a place at Saint Martins college and this caper was going nowhere, he was moving to London.

And I gave a speech that went something like this: 'What is so special about those 500 people out there, the ones that were clapping for an encore, even after that terrible show? What is so peculiar about them that we can't be as popular as that in every city in this country and every city in this world?'

It seems a stretch of the imagination to draw too many parallels between the radicalism of the eighties and the story of Pulp, but I did just that. The sheer bloody-minded defiance of the miners' strike had been inspiring and, when all around seemed dark as night, I was always hopeful that it might suddenly change. The strike's most tangible effect on Pulp was my unshakable conviction that something can arise from nothing. So we didn't split up, despite escape bids by all parties.

I vowed that if we ever got another show I would tone it down and concentrate on just playing my instruments and staring intently – that was enough. I'd been snapping at the good people who'd come to help us, was knackered and didn't know the songs.

But of course I did get involved again – I couldn't help myself. I want everything to be special all the time and get frustrated when it isn't. At every cool party there's someone frantically sellotaping fairy lights to the ceiling while everyone else sips their cocktails. Magic doesn't happen by magic, people make it.

18
The Wilderness Years

We got a new bass player in the form of Steve Mackey and the line-up felt a little bit more relaxed. We had the odd rehearsal, but there were no more concerts for almost two years. We recorded an album called *Separations*, but again the record company seemed in no hurry to release it and things pretty much ground to a halt. The patient lay unconscious with the odd flicker of an eyelid to indicate life as the eighties turned into the nineties and we got on with our lives.

1990 was an even leaner year than the previous two. Pulp made no recordings and released no records. We were offered the support slot at The Leadmill on 29 December, a full two winters since our last show. We thought that everyone would have forgotten us and feared that the attendance would be derisory.

To add to the ignominy we were supporting a band we believed had drawn influence from us. They were the current darlings of the music press and were on the covers of magazines doing what appeared to be a watered-down wacky version of Pulp. We were none too happy to be supporting people who had commercialised a style and attitude we felt we were the originators of. This bitterness says very little about them and everything about us. We were approaching our thirties and getting a bit long in the tooth for this. To watch the boat depart with them aboard was a bitter pill to swallow. They tried to be friendly but we wandered off muttering 'Twats!' and they gave us a wide berth. There was nothing personal in this. It was just two teams going up against each other: we wanted to beat them.

We kept peeking through the curtain to see if the venue was filling up but it wasn't – there were maybe fifty people half an hour before show time. We moaned bitterly that it would fill up with students checking out the flavour of the month when we'd gone off. It seemed that our journey was at an end and, steeling ourselves for the shame of playing to an empty room, we headed to the stage.

The curtains opened and the place was full, people had remembered us and turned out in force. We hit them with the old favourites and some sexy new material and came offstage ecstatic. We'd have packed it in if things had been otherwise.

1991 proved to be a busy year for Pulp, though you would hardly notice. That a glacier starts moving at two feet per year rather than two inches doesn't register at the time. We were tired of being paid £50 to bring in punters as local support for bands with lots of column inches but no fans. Instead we concentrated on playing out of town, particularly London. We were bottom of the bill and playing to a few dozen people but at least we got reviewed and the reviews weren't always bad.

The Barry White-inspired single 'My Legendary Girlfriend' was eventually released, two years after we had recorded it. It got 'Single of the Week' in one of the music papers but it didn't seem to be pushing us up the billing. 'My Legendary Girlfriend' takes as long to get to the chorus as most pop songs take to finish, so it didn't get much airplay, but unbeknown to us at the time it sold an astonishing 1,500 copies! Mostly in Sheffield of course, but also nationwide; particularly in Manchester where they were doing their own variant of disco (with a wacka wacka guitar) called 'Baggy'. We got our first TV slot on the *New Sessions* – a regional Manchester programme that went out in the wee hours, so we didn't see it.

Being unemployed is depressing and being poor is depressing. We'd had a tiny bit of success, but if that was all there was to it then you could keep it. It didn't change your life and it didn't pay the bills. It was looking like a lost cause, but I still yearned for the open road so I applied for a job as an ice-cream man.

But there's nothing quite like clearing out your drawers and throwing away that odd sock to make the right one turn up. When the last person who believed we could make it (i.e. me) gave up, something remarkable happened: we got a booking in France.

19

By Rights, This Part of France Belongs to Us

Paris was the first place outside England that Pulp played. This was exciting: not only was it international but, rather than the usual dreary round of local bands, we were supporting bands that got onto the front covers of magazines.

We somehow ended up with an ungainly fellow bumming a ride in our van.

'By rights, all of this part of France belongs to England,' he said. Well, I suppose we did win at Agincourt, but he wasn't our kind of guy. He had somehow claimed kin with support band Huggy Bear, but they'd wearied of him and palmed him off on us.

'I'm gonna stage dive for you lot, I know the Frenchies won't catch me, but I don't care.'

He did, they didn't: his vast bulk furrowed into the floor face-first, like a crash test dummy. He stood up confused and bloody – it was an ugly moment.

Huggy Bear were the leading lights of a movement called 'riot grrrl', which was a neo-feminist assault on the senses by Young Ladies Who Could Not Play Guitars Very Well. Or, indeed, at all. But they made a glorious shrieky racket, very like Pussy Riot. And, like Pussy Riot, they had the added allure of at least one very pretty one, called Jo, who went out with Graham Coxon, the guitarist of Blur: so they got some press as well as being good. There was an 'anything might happen' atmosphere and we were buzzing with anticipation for the Paris show. After years of slogging round pubs it felt as if we had arrived.

The venue was La Cigale and we were third on the bill – supporting Blur, who were supporting Lush. The venue was magnificent, a proscenium-arched theatre with a high stage and thirty feet of headroom. Venues usually reacted with hostility to our attempts to put up stage sets but here they seemed to know who we were and treated us with a respect we weren't accustomed too. We arranged giant mobiles on the stage, which comprised a pair of footballs sprayed silver hanging either end of a flexible rod from fishing line, with another such assembly hanging beneath so that seven pairs of balls slowly rotated either side of the stage.

It was an impressive spectacle on such a small budget and somehow very French, in a late-sixties Kinetic kind of way. Whilst many of our attempts at grandeur on a budget had been notable more for the comedy of their collapse than the effect intended, this one held.

The audience loved us and, much to our surprise and delight, knew songs that an English one wouldn't have. I can only describe the reaction as reverent. And we rose to the occasion: we played our disco songs 'She's a Lady' (the recorded version never did it justice), 'Death Comes to Town' and 'Countdown' to a rapturous response. Flushed with the adulation, we watched Blur and Lush in the charged atmosphere of that night. It was a strong bill, vital and spunky, and all the bands went down well.

Afterwards we were mobbed by journalists, who were better informed, more attractive and hygienic than their English counterparts; and asked interesting questions such as: 'What is your favourite planet?' 'What literature influences you?' and questions that might have started with a long quote from Rimbaud or Baudelaire. We were seen as kindred spirits: they were fascinated by the ragbag assortment of budget instruments we used and took us very seriously indeed – unlike the British press, who lazily seemed to regard us as some kind of comedy band.

We had a keyboard with a unique feature. It did a pitch shift when you slid your finger above a magnetic strip – you didn't need to touch it. One of these earnest journalist/fans was being shown this puzzling feature by Mark Webber (Pulp's new rhythm guitarist). The guy didn't really get it and touched the strip. Mark, by way of explanation said; '*Non, ne touche pas!*' To which the guy leapt back, mortified and apologetic; thinking he had transgressed some great taboo by presuming to touch the sacred instrument of the maestros.

This was a new feeling: we were recognised in the street, asked to sign autographs and sold twenty T-shirts. This might not sound like a lot, unless you are in a band that has played a lot of pubs. The Hull Adelphi held the previous record, of seven – often we sold none. Quietly, and without our being aware of it, hip French radio stations had been playing our songs and we had a profile there we didn't have at home. We felt like stars.

We'd been invited to join Blur in their dressing room for a drink. Nothing like this had ever happened before. We had usually seen other bands as rival cats on our patch. We thought we were better than them and they thought, with some truth, that we were a bunch of weirdoes who were best avoided. We often hated the bands that we played with, with their £300 guitars that cost more than all our equipment put together. We'd never been to a backstage party worthy of the name. This was about to change ... As we entered Blur's dressing room, a frenzied Graham Coxon was demolishing the mirrors. Singer Damon Albarn was casually pouring the contents of a bottle of champagne out of the window and bassist Alex James was flicking caviar round the room while drummer Dave Rowntree grinned nervously, as if he'd accidentally fallen in with the rough lads on a school trip. I think Justine Frischmann and Donna Mattheus from Elastica may have been there. (This really is a blur and separate events may have merged into one here). Lush were there, of course: the lovable drummer Chris Acland and singers Miki Bereny; and Emma Anderson, who were already the objects of much lust amongst earnest young men; and now they were our mates!

We crunched off over the broken mirror-glass to lug our gear into the van and Damon sat on an amp smoking a fag watching us. He couldn't believe that a band whose records he'd bought didn't have people to do it for them. Blur didn't lug their gear, probably never had. I think we learned a lot from Blur and the first lesson was: if you want to be a pop star, act like a pop star.

Back at the party, champagne flowed and people spilled out onto the Parisian cobbles, jumping into fountains. We went back to the hotel to dry off and someone shagged someone else's partner over a balcony. Alas, the balconies overlooked a central square and this was seen by many others, including said partner, who lobbed the contents of the offending party's suitcase out of an upper window – much to the amusement of the gathering crowd. This eventually alerted the heedless shaggers to the fact that they had an audience.

This was not how concerts normally ended and, although Blur were probably more hedonistic than us, I think something about the edgy clash of styles and accents drove us all to try and outdo each other in excess. It was a collision that could have ended in a fight but actually ended in a party.

If I look back on it now, I think there's as good a case as any for saying that this night in Paris is when Britpop was born – although the term didn't then exist. Blur and Lush were regarded as 'shoegazers', in the same category as Catherine Wheel, Slowdive and Curve. The shoegazing bands used a lot of ethereal washes of effects and gazed at the floor where their effects pedals were. In some ways, shoegazing was a bit like prog rock, in that you were supposed to take it very seriously and not jump about too much. It was introspective music for angst-ridden student bedrooms. It wasn't Britpop.

But something was in the air; we had all tasted it and wanted another bite. Pulp weren't regarded as 'shoegazers'. We were more flamboyant and showy, had a greater sense of dash and flourish and looked the audience straight in the eye. For a number of years it had seemed anachronistic to have a sense of showbiz and razzamatazz amongst the prevailing grungy ethos. But these once-unfashionable characteristics spread through Britpop in the coming years. The foppish loucheness of shoegazing was out and Pulp's star-spangled glamour was in.

The collision of styles musically and personally was combustible and liberating. Whilst the music of the shoegazer scene was often gloomy, it was also known as 'The scene that celebrates itself' because the bands were a right laugh and knew how to party. The constraining orthodoxy in the music press praised their sometimes po-faced and worthy music – but they were bored and straining at the leash. In a mirror image, Pulp were derided for our over-the-top attempts at glamour, yet also expected to play up to the dour northern stereotype offstage. That night we each found some kindred spirits to party with and the mirror cracked.

The great criticism of Blur is that they are musical chameleons: constantly borrowing others' clothes and therefore lacking in soul. I don't think that's true. I've watched them live perhaps twenty times and they have a rare ability to connect with an audience that transcends the sum of the, sometimes derivative, parts. One of their many influences was Pulp. We were a little older, had been knocking around for years and had sold very few records – the few we had sold were almost exclusively bought by people in other bands. We didn't own any Blur records, but they did own ours. The first words Graham Coxon ever said to me were: 'We like your band, we're going to copy you.'

I was amused/piqued when I next saw Blur and Graham had copied an arm gesture of mine – a cross between a Pete Townsend windmill and a gay Nazi salute.

A few years later, when I first saw Blur perform 'Boys and Girls', I didn't really make the connection but their producer, the always charming and well-suited-up Stephen Street, said: 'I know we've kind of stolen your clothes with this one.' And to some extent they had, it was very Pulpy. The queasy disco beat on the octaves was very reminiscent of our disco period from La Cigale. But then we'd nicked it from Blondie and New Order, who nicked it from Divine, who'd probably nicked it from the Venerable Bede. Pulp had even more influences than Blur but ours melded into something that passed for originality. I was jealous to death that Blur had had the balls to be that cheesy and still stay cool. To walk the tightrope of absurdity and get away with it we needed more courage and better producers. No more hiding behind being meaningful, clever and indie: go for the raw pop nerve and have a hit – yes, we learned a lot from Blur.

The satellite launched that night turned its gaze back to the planet we had left, which was by then a single pixel in a distant solar system.

Down to earth the next morning with a bump like a fat stage-diver, we dragged our sulphuric bones into the foyer, nursing our hangovers, where Blur were conducting interviews. They were on the ball, sharply incisive and had a hint of appealing dishevelment, implying junkie chic. They allowed the journalists to feel like they were 'hanging out with the band' and, when the journalists had gone, returned to their real selves.

But our drummer Nick had a question for Graham Coxon:

'Is tha owl or is tha blade?'

Graham couldn't answer this and I think he was slightly intimidated. Nick just kept repeating the question (which is basically asking which of the two Sheffield football teams Graham supported). Graham referred to this encounter later, he seemed to think Nick was a master of surrealism. Like many Yorkshiremen, your humble narrator included,

Nick was playing the time-honoured game of turning up the Yorkshire to freak out the southerners.

So that was the next lesson: work hard, and feed the press what they want to hear. Play up, play up and play the game.

FRANCE
2011

20
Minerals *Are* a Fanny-magnet

Back on the bus we are playing the game.

Me: 'The regular pulses of which mineral are used to make accurate timepieces?'

Gareth: 'Quartz!'

Me: 'What naturally occurring black silicaceous form of glass did ancient man use to make scrying mirrors?'

Gareth: It's ob-something, isn't it?

Me: 'It *is* ob-something.'

Gareth: 'Ob-what?'

Me: 'Not telling you.'

The countryside is open and the distant sea glows a milky opalescent yellow. The particular light is familiar from a Ruskin acolyte's watercolour, which captured a frozen moment like this; of wispy mare's tails hanging over other jaunty-angled Gothic steeples destroyed in the Great War.

One wants France to be very French: an unshaven man on a bicycle with a beret carrying a string of onions while eating a snail and playing an accordion – that kind of thing. I'm a little hungry and should have eaten earlier – but it is less than an hour to the hotel and I want to save myself for something authentic.

We enter the small town near Abbeville, at twilight and the bus bobbles across the cobbles of the main square, which is dominated by an ancient, ornate and impossibly white abbey. There are no other cars and the few figures we see are making off purposefully, as if observing a curfew. The hotel is small, of the same white stone as the abbey, and casts an inviting lamplight through sash windows. The manageress is crisp but friendly and we are soon decamped to our white linen-scented rooms. While the façade of the building is vaguely Georgian, the interior has odd ells and ends, patches of old brick, arches and oak beams that argue an earlier date. The dramatically uplit abbey forms the only view from the bedroom, so the general air is of delicious monastic voluptuary.

A quick freshen-up and we are off in the old jalopy to a traditional restaurant recommended by the ever-helpful manageress. A short drive in the fading light through undulating fields lined by poplars and we are in Abbeville proper. Vin rouge is drunk, glasses are clinked and we unwind from the day.

The other members of the band are all taking different flights at different times to Barcelona, where we will meet up to do the show. I'm the only one doing it the old-fashioned way: it's good to be back on the road and not actually that different from other tours. Everyone likes to have a 'bad boy' image but, if truth be told, Pulp spent much more time in strip clubs and brothels shooting videos than as punters. What differs about this tour is that it won't be a frenetic dash: we're not doing press, so the times between shows will be spent essentially as tourists. The mood is more relaxed than it often was because there are only three of us and everyone seems to rather like each other.

Jolly and expansive, we head back to the hotel. Unravened by hunger there is time to take in the charming detail of the place. The boulangerie advertising '*tarte au myrtille*' (bilberry tart), the *fin de siècle 'Boucherie'* sign in black with gilded edges peeling to reveal mottled mirroring, distressed louvered windows. French France *par excellence*.

A stroll to the van parked outside, where bad reggae and worse herbal tobacco mark the entrance to Garethworld – a happy place to chill, kick back, sink down into the settee and ponder this best of all possible worlds.

Me: 'What mineral do you think the abbey's made of, then?'

Gareth: 'I was wondering that, it's too pale for limestone, isn't it?'

We go and have a look and the only thing we can think of is chalk – but that would be daft, chalk dissolves, doesn't it? Might as well build it out of cheese and be done with it. I go inside to find Ralph, sitting alone on a high bar-stool, sipping an absinthe and chatting to the manageress who, it turns out, is called Tatyana and is not French at all, but Russian – oh, Ralph, what are you like?

I ask the manageress what stone the building is made of and she immediately becomes very animated, clicking off briskly, beckoning us to follow. She scratches a long red fingernail down the screeching wall, turns round to face us, purses her lips and blows the dust off, like Marilyn Monroe blowing a kiss.

Tatyana: '*Craie!*'

Me: 'Chalk!'

Tatyana; 'Like zis, you see!' she mimes the action of writing on a blackboard and peers back over her shoulder in half-moon spectacles like a school ma'am in a porn film. 'And it is soooo sooooft, but zese, zee little stones inside zee *craie* are sooo hard!' Wide-eyed she scratches a nail on a flint nodule. 'So hard and so soft togezzer, but zee soft one is *so* dirty, look!' She waves chalky minstrel jazz-hands, puts them on her hips in indignation at the naughty soft stone making hand prints on her black skirt. 'Ohh! I have done it again, I am always brushing past zis stone and dirtying my dress, look!' She turns around slaps her thighs making a cloud of chalk dust 'Pff, dirty again, I must change!'

She returns in a shorter skirt with higher heels, redder lips and a décolletage-revealing top. So Ralph was wrong: minerals *are* a fanny-magnet.

It's time for another drink and I ask if there are any regional specialties. No, not really, it seems – well, that's a first and I'm not sure I believe it, the French will make a regional speciality out of almost anything. But there are Russian specialties, which she is very happy to make for us. These are all vodka based, brightly coloured and sickly sweet – lasses' drinks. They appear in quick succession and, when we politely refuse, they're suddenly on the house.

The last cocktail I remember is a 'Bloody Russian' – which is basically a Bloody Mary with an extra layer of vodka floated on the top. You are supposed to down it in one, thus avoiding the neat vodka. Ralph falls unconscious in his chair; Tatyana stomps off and returns in a frumpy cardigan, gets me a coffee and bids me good night.

Woken early Sunday morning by the bells I hate everything and everybody.

Outside in the village square, the war memorial is surmounted by an outsize rampant coq, beneath which I espy Gareth's distinctive barnet. He's sitting on a bench, with his back to me. I creep stealthily up behind him, dodging behind trees like an assassin and plonk my panama hat on his head, ducking in case he is a martial arts expert.

'Chapeau!' I cry.

'Oh, noooo, you got me there,' says Gareth.

'Chapeauing' is to become a sport. The rules are as follows: the player with the chapeau must place it on the opponent's head and shout 'chapeau' to receive a point (or 'chapeau'). If the opponent sees the player intending to place the chapeau and calls out 'chapeau' then they have gained a 'chapeau'. Ralph could never be chapeaued because he always wore a chapeau.

We buy a coffee from the café-cum-post-office-cum-bookmakers and watch the little town come languidly to life. People buy their fat baguettes from the *boulangerie* and wander off chatting, or get pastries and sit playing dominos. A man goes round the tables, showing people something in a fine wooden box with dovetail joints and a sliding lid, which he reveals to gasps of admiration. What could it be? Perhaps a clutch of delightful little goslings?

Still, never mind all that, it's a long way to go and there's no time Toulouse.

It's over 500 miles, so we take the beastly toll roads rather than the scenic route. The French build these in a V-shaped depression in the land wherever possible and when the roads are at ground level they put up fences so as not to ruin the look of the countryside. So it's like driving down a long claustrophobic tunnel.

The Russian cocktails have given me a terrific hangover and I look out miserably at the identical hypermarkets, retail parks and intersections. God, it's boring, we could be almost anywhere. Well, anywhere where the passenger has an inexhaustible supply of questions about minerals and the driver has an inexhaustible supply of bad reggae.

Don't get me wrong, I like most reggae. I've got the Trojan boxset and most Jamaican ska. I wouldn't mind anything from eighties Bristol either, Black Uhuru, Aswad, Misty in Roots, Musical chuffin' Youth if you really have to. I wouldn't even complain about a bit of 2 Tone 'wedding special' ska revival: The Specials, The Selecter, The Beat, Madness or Bad bleedin' Manners. I didn't realise that there was this much bad reggae in the world. I'm talking about 'lover's rock' and cod-reggae, and even that I bear with fortitude. But then, and you might have guessed what's coming next, when *all* the bad reggae in the world has been played, there's only one thing left …

UB-fuckinfortyforfucksake.

'Turn it off! Turn it off, you're doin' me head in!'

I gaze at a small furry figure on the table in front of me. He looks a bit like Ralph but he's called 'Slowpoke'. He's a mascot of sorts given to me by my mother, who thought he was a hedgehog, but actually he's a Pokémon. She also thinks I still *like* hedgehogs. God, Mum, I'm not five any more! I'm a middle-aged man: I want some horse brasses, a lovely old map of Derbyshire or a Haynes manual for a 1963 Alpha Spider.

The time estimates on Google Maps prove more relevant to a *Top Gear* challenge than actual motoring; with its meal stops, toilet breaks, missed turnings and traffic. So we run late and the arrival time on the sat nav keeps slipping back towards midnight, the latest check-in at the apartment. There is a lot of graffiti and a sign saying 'Periphique', which means we are still (and seemingly eternally) skirting Paris. In the time we've spent on this bloody ring road I could have got to London.

ENGLAND 1991

21
The Fall for Children

Our promo packs described Pulp as 'a cross between Abba and The Fall', so imagine our excitement when we got to support The Fall. Mark E. Smith was in the process of splitting up with his wife and clutched a bottle of whisky as he staggered down the dressing room stairs. When asked about Pulp he said: 'It's The Fall for children.' Mission accomplished then – even an insult from that man is flattering. We weren't the only band to attract Mark E. Smith's disdain; a Fall lyric said, 'It was the fault of Suede-uh.' Emerging scene-band Suede were flattered to be name-checked by this icon too, but Mark E. Smith said he was talking about suede the fabric and had never heard of the band.

Coming back from France as part of a movement that no one quite had a name for, we were a lot more confident. We got our first London headline shows at venues familiar from the press and we'd go into dingy little back rooms and think we'd got the wrong place, but we hadn't. Slowly we gained a following in the dimlylit dives of Camden and beyond. Some people who came to see us came to see us again and brought their mates. We probably met most of our 'fans' at the time; they were our kind of people, weirdo outsiders often doing something interesting and arty.

Sheffield label Warp released our stylophone-driven single 'O.U. (Gone, Gone)' on the same day as Nude Records released Suede's 'The Drowners' and the bands got joint 'Single of the Week'. We headlined a tour of small venues, kicking off with a launch of five hundred balloons in the centre of Sheffield. Island Records had been taking an interest and funded the local label Warp in a 'development deal' whereby they got to try working with us without the commitment of signing us up proper. One of the perceived advantages was that the band could grow organically and not be pushed too fast too soon.

The first show after signing the deal, at The Powerhaus in London, had a guest list populated by journalists, our new mates from the shoegazer scene and Island Records, who saw the audience going mad for their new protégés.

But not everything was quite as smooth as it appeared. Although the single got good reviews, it was actually, in our estimation, the fourth best from our current material. The idea was that we would build up to the standout 'baggy' track 'Live On' as our profile grew. But our old record label opportunistically released the album *Separations*, which they had sat on for years, to coincide with the tour, so we were effectively promoting old material.

At the second concert, we headlined Sheffield's Leadmill, supported by a local band. This ought to have been great but somehow it didn't quite hit the spot. The support band had younger and more enthusiastic skatepunk fans. Afterwards, I heard one of them say they had 'blown us offstage'. Now, this was an outrageous boast but obviously not so far off the mark that he couldn't conceive it. We were used to being the plucky underdogs who blew other people offstage. The support band's small but dedicated group of teen fans had no interest in us and it was concerning that we couldn't win them round: skatepunk's a different genre, but in the past we had ended up winning Hells Angels round. Somehow this night felt a little 'safe' – maybe it was just an off-day? These things happen. But you are only as good as your last concert and what should have been a triumphant homecoming was strangely lacklustre; there was no roar as we came onstage. We won most of the crowd round, but it was hard work, perhaps we were getting too old for this newer, grungier world?

The next concert was away from the media buzz in out-on-a-limb Hull, where we played The Adelphi again – to an audience no bigger than we had years previously. This was depressingly advertised as the return of 'eighties favourites Pulp' – we clearly weren't getting anywhere fast. This was ridiculous, we'd done everything right this time, the publicity was perfectly timed – we'd had a balloon launch for goodness' sake! It was a scrappy tour, attendances were patchy and a couple of the shows were cancelled. We might have been big in France and hanging out with the right people but we weren't big enough for a headline tour. We had fun though and visited cathedrals, castles, viaducts, markets, waterfalls, bridges, power plants, famous greasy-spoon cafés, gorges, Neolithic monuments and any conceivable point of interest that lay in our path.

On one of our few days off, we did a quick Radio One session. Utterly exhausted, we fell asleep on the studio floor afterwards. You'd think it would sound tired as a result, but it sounds great. The effortlessness of not giving a damn and just wanting it to be over with lends immediacy and it's the standout version of 'Live On'.

Back in London we played a festival in Finsbury Park headlined by goth band The Cult. We went on in the afternoon as a new band with a lot of buzz about them and pulled a more enthusiastic and sexier crowd than the bands either side of us. Underdog status suited us.

Damien Hirst was there with a giant record player onto which he put sheets of paper and threw tins of paint to make a spiral effect. The emerging music scene had its counterpart in a similarly unique Britart style. Fortunately, our hip supporters, the press and our suitors at Island Records hadn't seen us grinding away in the sticks and we felt like bright young things again.

My daughter Sophie was obsessed with Vic Reeves from almost the first time she could walk and talk. She once toddled in from the kitchen saying 'I've done a terrible thing!'

'What is it, darling?' I said.

'I've put a spoon in the knife drawer!' she said and burst into giggles. This was a Reeves and Mortimer gag and she did 'man with a stick' and variations of her own such as, 'What's on my finger?' which I won't go into. Sophie was beside herself on seeing Vic Reeves, who was hanging out at the festival, in the flesh and ran through a barrier to speak to him. But Vic was engrossed in conversation with Miles Hunt from The Wonder Stuff and didn't pay her any attention. Bob Mortimer bobbed down to talk to her and she transferred her affections to him. Which was a shame, because I'd got her a full-sized cutout of Vic Reeves for her birthday. My two-up two-down *Coronation Street*-style terraced house didn't have a lot of room for full-sized cutouts, so I put the thing at the top of the stairs to scare burglars. Almost every day this bloody thing terrified me when I got up in the morning or, worse, in the middle of the night after hearing a noise.

We played another show in Sheffield: in the City Hall ballroom, which had a dance floor that lit up with alternating squares of light. This was very Pulp in an end-of-the-pier way and inspired a later video. Our love of vintage equipment, combined with an inability to afford newer stuff, often resulted in technical breakdown. Jarvis's equipment was playing up and he ended up throwing his amplifier across the stage, destroying it completely. Avoiding projectiles from the audience was one hazard; avoiding the toys thrown out of Jarvis's pram was another.

Despite this, in a very Sheffield spirit of Dadaism, I put random objects on top of Jarvis's amp, which sometimes ended up as props for the show: a piece of fruit, a bottle of water, a mechanical toy. He made an art of this and all kinds of things ended up there: a klaxon, an electric fire, goodness knows what.

Onstage, I liked to throw contorted shapes and allowed myself to lean over then fall and manage to stagger upright. If there was spilt beer to skid on this only added to the challenge.

At the last concert, at Halifax's Piece Hall, (capacity 15,000, attendance 150) there was liquid on the stage. I got it wrong and fell offstage and badly injured my pride in a fitting end to a wobbly tour.

22
Suede the Fabric

Suddenly there was a huge buzz about Suede. They supported us at a venue in north London and there were more movers and shakers on their guest list than ours. The singer Brett Anderson personal style had a lot in common with Jarvis's but was more toned-down and sexy, without the ever-present hint of irony. Bernard Butler was a maestro on the guitar, a guitarist's guitarist – there was a clamour to sign them. They were managed by Ricky Gervais, if you can get your head around that! His David Brent persona was fully formed and we were all puzzled that such a naff, if strangely likeable, character managed such a cool band.

Suede played a tiny venue called The Elephant Centre in Brixton, which held about seventy people. Hundreds were turned away, including lots of journalists. This was a masterstroke, because everyone wanted to know what all the fuss was about. I saw them at The Duchess in Leeds and you could feel the wave of euphoria as they took to the stage. It didn't matter what they did because people were so excited to be one of the chosen few in the room. They were our biggest rivals and were rapidly overtaking us in popularity: after only a few months on the scene we supported them at a venue in France.

A common situation occurred – they refused to move their drum kit. Small venues have small stages and there is often not room for two drum kits. The headline band sets up first and gets the microphones placed round their drum kit. Then the support band has to cram their drum kit in wherever they can, and often there just isn't room. So they move the headline band's drum kit, at which point the headline band objects and pulls rank. A solution is to share drum kits, but drummers don't like this; the headline act may get theirs trashed and the support drummer doesn't like it because he isn't using his own kit. There are compromises, which need cooperation on a fast turnover in a darkened club and often result in flared tempers. The job of roadies is to bat for their team, so there is often a tense stand-off, which happened in this case. Suede wouldn't budge and there was no room for our drums. So we went to the promoter who, much to our delight, told Suede it was a co-headline and they'd better move it. I added to their discomfiture by telling them that there'd been a typo in the advertising and the only reason they were headlining was because people thought they were Slade, and there were fans outside with mirrored top hats. Suede might have taken London by storm but France was our patch. There's a lot of this kind of jostling and I'd always rather be the underdog blowing someone offstage than headlining when more people have come for the support.

There was an article in *Smash Hits* magazine that asked who had the sexiest fans: Suede or Pulp? And it really was true, the fans for both bands were notably attractive. The first five rows at the front of our concerts would be 90 per cent female, fashionable and dressed-up under twenty-fives. The guys were cool too. The lonely hearts small ads in *Select* magazine were something I watched avidly: 'Smiths fan wishes to meet similar', '"Suedette" wishes to meet similar' then, finally, 'Pulpette' appeared and we ran neck and neck with Suede for quite a while.

23
Professional Bridesmaids

Jarvis knows more than any man on earth about pop culture and has used a vast array of it in crafting his personal style and the music of Pulp. He was the first in the band to discover French music and pass this glorious knowledge on. Other influences were many and varied, and often naffer than the final result. Some of these I would have shared but others, like ELO, were beyond the pale for me. Gypsy music, Wagner, glam rock, and Hi-NRG all worked their way into Pulp from my end. Nick had a feel for ska, mod and northern soul that I shared; and a wistful regard for jangly indie pop that I didn't. I think he might have been listening to The Cranberries when he came up with the part Jarvis plays on the song 'Babies'. I hated 'Babies' when we first did it. It was everything the record company was trying to make us be; sub-Smiths, sub-Orange Juice, polite, twee, jangly indie froth.

I snarlingly put a saccharine lead line on top, in an attempt at mocking pastiche. Jarvis sang comedy lyrics, coming up behind Nick and fondling him. For a number of months, the song was called 'Watching Nicky Grow' and referred to Nick's weight gain. But it was a catchy little number and I attempted to come up with something more serious than my initial pastiche of a guitar line, but could never quite get away from it. 'Babies' was one of those annoyingly catchy tunes that you can't get out of your head (the Germans call it an ear worm). But I grew to love it because other people loved it, it was the first Pulp song I ever heard a stranger humming.

The B-side of 'Babies' came directly out of a mood-setting experiment. We'd been talking about how rubbish it was that Americans could glamourise their world, but when you did it in a British context you were always obliged to make it comedy. Instead, we wanted to express the beauty and the horror of the everyday world around us. So we dimmed the lights, lit some incense, imagined we were in a seedy little club and tried to channel the underbelly of Sheffield, in which porno movies are made in council house garages and 'Sheffield: Sex City' popped out the other end.

It is ironic that, when we were all living in Sheffield, we didn't draw direct inspiration from its music and Jarvis hardly touched on the subject of the city in the lyrics. It was only when everyone apart from me moved to London that Sheffield became a big part of our identity. Prior to that we were keen not to be a parochial 'local band', with all that implies. I can relate to this: I get most of my best ideas in transit and there is a long and distinguished history of artists only being able to clearly reflect upon a subject when they are outside it – Alan Sillitoe and Alan Bennett come to mind. There is a sense of capturing what has passed, of maintaining roots and, in our case, of focusing on a narrative the press were picking up on. Getting all dewy-eyed about northern life didn't really grab me; I was still living in the bloody place.

From the inception of the technology in the early eighties, I was making videos for ourselves and others cheaply and quite effectively, given the resources. When Jarvis and Steve went to art college in London they used the facilities, and the resources and quality upped, although the videos still remained decidedly home-made and low budget. Steve, as well as playing bass, was a 'grown up' and did most of the work getting the 'Babies' video together. It was set against a completely white background, which is deceptively hard to achieve. A white floor with a white wall makes a line at the junction between the two. In the sixties, when this look was in vogue, some studios were kitted out with a floor that gently curved into a wall, so that the result was seamless. We found the only extant one of these, gave it a lick of emulsion and shot the video there, using a shopping trolley with a cameraman in to get dynamic motion shots. These are small details that were important to us and made the video look distinctive. It was cheap, made in a day, fun to do and it shows.

The only problem was that there wasn't anywhere to show the video. Then MTV came along and they loved us. The first VJ, Paul King, and his mates were already regulars at our concerts and were keen to champion us in this new media. MTV had standards for format we didn't meet, so we copied our video onto the higher format. The quality was even worse but they turned a blind eye and showed it anyway. The 'Babies' video looked refreshingly different and innovative set against the ubiquitous dreary concert footage or endless homies with endless bling in red sports cars. Ours were sexy but not sexist. And they were influential – much of the style and technique was copied to the extent that they look rather clichéd nowadays.

Babies got tantalisingly close to the Top 100 – 101 in fact – very Pulp in an almost-made-it kind of way. A perceptive reviewer described us as 'professional bridesmaids'.

It seemed that Pulp would somehow go on forever playing quirky little clubs, but never really getting anywhere. We played a small venue in north London and the audience of a couple of dozen was smaller than we were used to. The cost of performing in London far outweighed the thirty quid we were getting paid and the big break looked ever further down the tunnel. After the show the journalist Jon Wilde, who wrote perceptive things about us, really ripped into me, saying 'What on earth are you doing, playing a venue like this?' and his article was no kinder. There was a meeting and grievances were aired: my main one was that Jarvis messed about too much, playing it for laughs; or got petulant and turned against himself, the band, the equipment or the audience. I made the point that you should never slag off the people who *had* come just because others hadn't. Something definitely changed after this; Jarvis could see defeat staring us in the face and acquired the desperation of a man who knows that every show might be the last. We had lots of rows, but that was an important one, our one great champion in the media had rightly turned on us and for this we owe him a debt of thanks.

Jarvis had a penchant for seventies suits and my Aunty Val (who had a penchant for spivs and conmen) rather took to him. I'd known Jarvis for many years and never met a woman who said they fancied him before. People liked him, but he was considered an awkward, nerdish type. So that was the start and it just snowballed from there – by some strange miracle, the gawky weirdo transformed himself into a sex symbol. We'd come offstage and see Jarvis getting dressed and possibly cutting his toenails and burst out laughing at the idea of him as a sex symbol, so it was a big laugh at first but soon it became reality.

The other big element upping the sexiness quotient was Steve, who was actually genuinely 'get given cards by model agencies' good looking. His recruitment had occurred across a supermarket car park when he was pushing a trolley. We didn't really know him but he was in a band called Trolley Dog Shag and I shouted oafishly, 'Where's the dog, mate?' He smiled and we asked him if he could play bass. Now, with Steve and myself standing super-cool never-smiling either side of Jarvis, there was little room for clowning around: we were a serious prospect.

24
Modus Operandi and Body Disposal

Suffering fools gladly does not come easily to me but it seemed to be my lot in life. We took on shows and lost money, basically for the thrill of going to a new place for a day. But when I figured out that I could have had a nice fortnight's holiday with my family for the price of one of these chaotic Pulp minibreaks, I became more circumspect about such ventures.

Our old bass player Manners continued coming to concerts and reminded me of something I said that stuck in his mind but didn't stand out to me at the time. When he was late for a practice I said 'Why didn't you at least have the decency to ring?'

Well, he 'had some shit on'. (On where?)

I said: 'If my father died, I'd at least have the decency to let you know that I might be a bit late.'

This was absolutely true and I think this anecdote is supposed to reflect badly on me, but I just don't get it – manners cost nothing, although Manners cost us a fortune and he wasn't the worst of them.

Jarvis *was* the worst. His peccadillos and perpetual tardiness created constant crises and wasted endless time and money. On concert day, when time was already tight, he would always need to go via Mexborough to pick up a kennel for his auntie's dog or some other such mind-numbingly tedious diversion. Then his auntie would be round at a neighbour's house and it turned out that it wasn't a dog kennel but a fish tank and did we have time to mend her flat tyre so she could get the missing pump for the tank?

Candida did her bit to make my job as a tour manager difficult by always inviting guests to squeeze into the already unsafe van. She had a seemingly endless supply of cousins visiting from Shetland, often bearing gifts of fish. All of Candida's cousins were very nice, but they all took up space. She had quite a lot of mates who turned up at service stations to meet us, whom the rest of the band referred to collectively as 'Scuzza' and 'Ragga'. All of these people would need toilet breaks, big rizlas, extracting from toilets and dropping off at 7 a.m. at the end of a very, very long hard day and I could have done without it.

If you take all those contrasting and clashing personalities and put them in a small tin box on wheels; rattle it around and force them to spend time in greater proximity than they would naturally spend with their loved ones; and there is no getting away from the sights, sounds and smells of the others; tension will inevitably result. This is where the ability to take the piss is a great safety valve.

There's a million and one annoying little habits that people, myself included, will have that get on other people's nerves. One of Nick Banks' was eating a lot of crisps, and then folding the packet very carefully before blowing it up and bursting it very loudly.

Candida's slender frame would twitch like a startled meerkat.

'Oh God, Nick. Do you *have* to do that?'

Nick would laugh.

I would say: 'Fuck you, Nick!'

Nick would laugh again, he thought his crisp-bag joke was hilarious and made him the toast of the town. 'Fuck you, buddy!' he would say, putting up one finger in a good-natured parody of a husky American redneck.

'Well, Nick, that's a very interesting point you make but might I counter it by saying: FUCK YOU!'

'No, fuck you!'

'*Au contraire*, Nick. I think you'll find that it's: FUCK YOU!'

'No, buddy, fuck you!'

'No, fuck you!'

And we'd bang the walls of the van and scream; having a whale of a time, finding it very funny and Candida would say, 'Can't you two just give it a rest!' and somehow this took the heat out of the situation.

But when everyone else moved to London, things changed a lot and I found myself retreating to an 'off the peg' northern stereotype to keep things real and swim against the tide of pseudiness that others were washed along with. I'd been the weird one, the intellectual, the reader of highbrow literature, the European, the cocktail drinker, the holder of masked balls; and now here I was having to play the gruff, flat-capped, Henderson's Relish-swigging Sheffielder – just so Pulp had some semblance of roots.

It takes a lot of courage and drive to uproot and make a new life elsewhere. Those who do so tend to assume that the only reason anyone would not follow suit is a deficiency of drive. But there are other reasons for not getting swept up in the rootless and ruthless world of ambition. It's entirely possible to *choose* to live up north, to find there to be something more wholesome and desirable about it. It has its charms, it's less false, people are friendlier, there's more of a sense of roots and the steel is very cheap.

I'm a great believer in taking the piss and really don't mind having it taken out of me quite mercilessly. As we got more famous and smooth, a day came when some people in the band didn't like this childish banter any more and it became difficult to alleviate the tension in this way. And that's when it got really tense – when we stopped taking the piss out of each other.

Hip bands will find themselves surrounded by flatterers that a Tudor monarch might find unctuous. Some people like this and it doesn't make them bad people. It's nice to be complimented and valued, but after a bit it just makes me uncomfortable. My contrarian reaction was to find people who take you down a peg or two refreshing. So that was a thing that happened: a kind of north–south divide within the band that just got worse over the years.

There were different camps at different times and I can honestly say that everyone has, at one time or another, been my favourite and least favourite member of the band. That's understating it: it goes from soulmate through to contemplating weapons, *modus operandi* and body disposal.

2011
FRANCE

25
An Overrated Kink

So here I am, my teeth grinding in irritation at the mere recollection of being on a bus with Pulp. And you can probably imagine that others of a less rational, intelligent, handsome, noble and quiz-loving nature might have found me irritating too.

Me: 'What blue mineral, occurring in Afghanistan, was much prized as a pigment by Renaissance painters?'

Gareth: 'Is it lapis lazuli? All right, I've got one for thee: what mineral, when added to an axolotl, turns it into a newt?'

Me: 'What?!' I'd bought an axolotl as a teenager, they are albino amphibians with freaky external gills – this was preposterous. Gareth: 'Ahh, I thought you'd say that … it's iodine, if you add iodine to axolotls they turn into newts.'

Me: 'Oh, give over.' But now I come to think about it, the axolotl *did* mysteriously disappear and I *was* in the habit of adding salt (which contains iodine) to the pond (not out of cruelty or surrealism but to prevent fungal diseases in koi carp) … and there *had* been a newt … could this really be the case? 'Gareth, you're doing my head in, put the bad reggae back on!'

The sun slowly sets and little glimpses of La Belle France appear, shadows of chateaux and scenes of rural simplicity. France seems leisurely and untouched and now dark, so there's nothing to see for hours and hours and hours.

Travel offers the ancient thrill of exploration: the promise of riches, mystery, and romance in the lands beyond the green door. The possibility that around the river bend might be something unexpected, something better. Better in a way we may have imagined or, better still, in a way we'd never imagined – something off the map. But more than this, there is something imperative about travel.

Light travels at 186,282 miles per second and time slows to zero as you approach the speed of light: so presumably it slows by a tiny bit, even if you are just walking. I figured that if you travel 186,282 miles it doesn't really matter at what speed you go: you will have gained that second and cheated time. You just need to go round the world eight times and you're more than a second up on the deal. So I reckon it's in our DNA to try and avoid death; and in a very small way we are doing so every time we move. Somewhere inside is a biological urge, like the need to procreate. So there's this extra little thrill to it, you are getting something for nothing – in this case time – and everyone loves a bargain, even if they hate a tourist.

Back on earth, wanderlust is an urge that can be fulfilled by touring. But it's not ideal because you get it as a by-product and might not have the time or energy to fully enjoy the places you go. There are places where the main thing I saw was a road, a hotel and a dressing room. It's such a shame to do all the travel and not see the place.

For this tour we'd had an offer to play Moscow – which would involve about a week on the bus each way, with only one night in Moscow. If one builds in the normal contingencies and doubles it to account for the Pulp 'fuck-up' factor, then I could really do without the hassle of dashing all the way to Moscow, only to not see the place properly – so, very reluctantly, I said no. It would be pointless to go all that way just to feel hurried and hassled and perhaps not even see the Kremlin.

When we needed to schedule a secret warm-up show I had only one thought – a club called 'Le Bikini' in Toulouse. The other alternative, favoured by our ever-earthbound drummer Nick Banks, was a former steel factory in Rotherham. Rotherham? Toulouse? Toulouse? Rotherham? Hmm.

Toulouse seems very French, but in a slightly different way. This is the Occitan, a region of history and mystery: where a jumble of shadowed back-alleys escape the scorching heat to lead past antiquarian booksellers, where one might come upon a lost incunable. Down to the vast Garonne river and the pink-stoned Ville Rose, where swallows circle, giving scale to the Cathar temples in an air heady with linden blossom.

I scrape away at the violin in a last-ditch attempt to familiarise myself with a repertoire that has shrunk to a mere fifty songs from an original 130 – none of which I'd played, or listened to out of choice, for fifteen years. It's the equivalent of learning four concert symphonies. One of the sentimental reasons for doing these shows was the opportunity to give some songs one last airing – the songs are our offspring and it's not their fault that the parents are estranged: the songs are innocents, they shouldn't suffer from the break-up.

Rehearsing and trudging the cobbles has made my back hurt, so I take a codeine.

The funny thing is that, after spending so much time making the songs, I never listened to them. I hear some of them on the radio and it is quietly pleasing to know that something you have helped make is still part of the culture. But now bittersweet, half-forgotten but freshly familiar tastes are coming back and haunting me. The songs come through a time warp and evoke different places and times, different versions of myself. There's a melancholy in knowing that this will be their last chance to breathe – and they won't all make it. I feel protective towards these lost children. There's a sense of loss and evaporation and relief at getting a monkey off my back and a concertinaing of time and just too many damn things to hold in your head at once. It's like falling off a cliff and having your whole life flash before you and it's hard to keep a lid on it. And there's no one I can talk to about it because I don't know anyone who is in the same boat and could possibly understand – apart from maybe Candida.

Candida and I have been a mutual self-help counselling service during the run-up to the tour. So I ring her, and the fact that she has her own jitters, and can share this strange sense of dislocation helps bring me back down to Earth and France and Toulouse and Here and Now, and now I think that it might even be a blast.

We have invited a young chap called Jack Clayton to come and stay with us in the apartment in Toulouse. He is suitably wowed by this ... as well he might be!

Picture the scene: you are playing a concert to a few mates in Sheffield and a former pop star invites you to hang out in an apartment in Toulouse, come to a secret gig (at a club called 'Le Bikini' no less!), then hop on the bus to Barcelona and check out the show along with Nancy, the rather beautiful daughter of Pulp's accountant . . . Okay, 'accountant's daughter' isn't exactly a cool tag – though it might make a good limerick. But the general package has a beguiling ring, especially when offered with such studiedly casual insouciance.

Jack wants to go to a strip club and we intend to oblige him. But, as neither Ralph nor I are great habitués of such places, we don't know the form. One imagines a French strip club has more pizzazz and is less seedy than one back home. There are a couple advertised in the hotel brochure but it's all in French and we can't tell whether the Pink Palace is a gay club, so we opt for the one with the classiest models, which is called 'Galleries Lafayette' – but the lighting is too bright and the girls turn out to be surprisingly coy, though they do spray you with perfume, which is an overrated kink.

FRANCE
1992

26
The Great Make-up Rebellion

Island Records finally took the plunge and signed us up for five albums – a major champagne corks moment. After many years in the wilderness, I got my priorities right and went straight to a theatrical outfitters to buy the biggest stage-mirror money could buy and every conceivable accoutrement a professional make-up artist could own. Over 10 per cent of the band's advance was spent on make-up and the glitter mines of Moldova cancelled all leave.

If you are in a band in your thirties and don't wake up in the morning looking meltingly gorgeous, then make-up is a very good idea for photographs. It is the same on the TV and even truer onstage, where you need a lot of slap to make sure your features don't just disappear under the stage lights. I'd been on a theatrical make-up course and was a firm believer in its benefits. This was not immediately apparent to other members of the band, particularly Rotherham's finest, Nick Banks, who tended to regard make-up as a bit poncey. Nick and I had many enlightening debates in which he called me various euphemisms for gay and I said that, from ten rows back in the audience, his mouth looked like a crack in a pie and generally mocked his lack of confidence in his own sexuality. In the end, he gave in to this bludgeoning and took to it like a fish to water.

For some reason, make-up artists loved working on Nick and were always complimenting him on his bone structure – I didn't think he'd even *got* bones. Nick was photogenic and, with a bit of slap, went from looking like John Prescott's dad to a young Jack Nicholson. But when you think about it, saying someone is photogenic is a bit of a back-handed compliment. Basically it means that you look worse in the flesh than your photos. Well, I comforted myself with this thought while Nick was getting fawned over. And make-up really *is* a fanny-magnet. Women love it: it makes you Byronic, dangerous, unconventional and exciting.

That oversize travelling star-mirror, with rows of bulbs down the sides and plug points for shavers and lava lamps, was the best money we ever spent. When a band sets that up in the dressing room, you know they are somebody. All the world's a stage, you see, including backstage. With our new deal and kit we walked a couple of inches taller. We expected to be taken seriously – and we were. 'Who are this lot, with their big mirror?' promoters would wonder. 'I wonder if you might have any fresh towels and perhaps some ice, my good man?' – 'Certainly, sir, would there be anything else, may I make so bold as to recommend the lager?' – well, not quite, but more in that direction than formerly.

This produced some resentment in the crew and there was the 'Great Make-up Rebellion of 1992' shortly thereafter. The crew didn't mind lugging the heavy black boxes that make lots of noise about. But they did mind lugging a heavy pink one marked 'make-up' around in front of their laughing peers. So they refused to move it and a couple got the sack for this mutiny. These guys were 'graduates' of some kind of council-funded roadie school that had given them really inflated ideas about what the job entailed. I don't think anyone had thought to mention that shifting gear was part of the job, so even that they did rather grudgingly. They'd swan about onstage, large Maglites dangling from their belts, occasionally saying 'I'm not doing that, I'd look a dick!' at some request they felt was beneath their dignity. So we got in more professional roadies after that, who did shift gear, including pink boxes, but had Maglites smaller than their dicks.

The other Britpop bands didn't wear make-up, it wasn't very 'for real' or 'streetsy', but Pulp were all those things and we did wear make-up. After seeing us look like a bag of spanners backstage then look better than them in the photos, with their undisguised spots (try a bit of *green* concealer, it works wonders), the habit spread and I got to do a bit of make-up for many of the bands. So this was a way in which the Pulp, shall we call it glamour, spread into the body politic of Britpop. Best to point out that this didn't include Black Grape.

I'd bought a nice pair of silver sunglasses by Charles Jourdan in the style originally made for and called 'Jackie O' for 50p in the local cat shelter charity shop. I wore them clubbing in France and found that it was possible to gain free entrance to nightclubs by use of the following phrase: '*Bonsoir, je suis un rock star Anglais . . . je joue un concert dans cette ville ce soir, je voudrais entrée votre club libre avec mes amis.*' ('Good evening, Me English rock star . . . I play concert in city tonight, I like penetrating your entrance free with my friends.') And, if all that failed, '*Je suis Bono!*' I never got refused and once got fifty people in free. At a very cool underground club in Nancy I was offered £20 for the sunglasses – a princely sum – and it wasn't the only offer! So, back in Blighty, I set about raiding the charity shops for sunglasses and amassed enough to fill a suitcase. I affixed numerous pairs to the inside of my jacket the next time I went out clubbing in France, ready to whip it open to reveal my wares – but no one ever asked again, so that was the start of my sunglasses collection. Friends passed on interesting ones, fans sent them in the post and a Japanese company brought out a 'Pulp' brand of sunglasses.

I've got quite an intimidating stare and found that wearing sunglasses made me much more approachable. Paradoxically, people's first line was often: 'You look so unapproachable.' I also got a certain amount of stick along the lines of: 'Who the fuck do you think you are wearing sunglasses in a dark club, you ponce?'

It's nigh on impossible to see with sunglasses onstage, so I only really made use of them for making an entrance and would take them off halfway through the first song. Rover used to mark a line using fluorescent gaffa tape so I could feel my way to the guitar without bumping into too many things. At small venues souvenir hunters invariably nicked these glasses, along with plectrums and set-lists.

There was a distinct look to Pulp and, as an antique dealer, I provided props for photo sessions: seventies rugs, sixties Scando Holmegaard bottles, Czech drinking glasses. It was an odd kind of antique business, though, because I bought stuff from charity shops and car boot sales round the north and took them to swanky parts of London to sell. Then I bought stuff in top London auction houses and sold them on Barnsley market, which is a contrary way to do things and perhaps explains why I didn't make much money. But why shouldn't people in Barnsley have art deco lamps? They make excellent coalscuttles. I got some amusing things into auction; including Bay City Rollers shoes into a modern design sale. The Sloane Rangers who populate the lower echelons of top London auction houses can easily be fooled. Across the road from one auction house was a trendy cappuccino bar – biscotti, that kind of thing. But just round the corner was a greasy spoon café that the Sloanies never went to. The cruet sets they used were from the 1950s and I had found a reference to them in a coffee-table design book. So I tried to put some of these into the swanky auction sale – and to my surprise and delight they illustrated them and put a high estimate on. I don't think anyone ever found out that they were selling the same cruets as the greasy spoon café across the road used. There's quite a lot of chippy class revenge going on here – and, if you are familiar with Pulp's music, you can probably find a bit of that there too.

Nick was always keen to snaffle Pulp souvenirs. You have to admire his faith in the band and pre-eBay forward thinking. Nick's pre-eBay forward thinking was less in evidence when we were kicking a football around and I noticed some scuffed signatures on it: they were familiar names, so familiar I presumed they were fake.

'Where'd you get this ball from, Nick?'

'Uncle Gordon.'

'Might be worth something one day, this!'

Nick's uncle was Gordon Banks the goalkeeper and we'd rendered almost illegible a signed football from the 1966 World Cup squad.

Although I was tempted, I always stopped myself from keeping souvenirs due to the following incident.

In a top auction house I witnessed a tragic scene unfold. A man in tight leather trousers with big hair, shades and the ubiquitous Stevie Nicks-type girlfriend in cowboy hat and boots strode confidently up to the appraisals desk. He handed over a bass guitar. The correct expert was found and through half-moon spectacles he said, 'Might you be a rock star, sir?' 'Yes', said the fellow, puffing himself up in front of his bird, 'I played bass for Kiki Dee, this bass was actually played on "Don't Go Breaking My Heart"!' Oh no, this wasn't going to end well – memorabilia sales throw up some high figures for Marilyn Monroe's dress or Jimi Hendrix's guitar but there are remarkable bargains to be found outside the headline items. I've seen Frank Sinatra's trilby or Tommy Cooper's fez go for £200, so what price Kiki Dee's bass guitar? 'Weeeell, sir, I'm afraid that, in today's market, it would be unlikely to fetch more than its intrinsic value as an instrument.' Which meant *fuck off and take it to the pawn shop, you 'orrible little man.* Seemingly by way of compensation but *actually* by way of further stabbing him repeatedly in the balls, the sneering toff added; 'But magnificent machine heads, sir!' (Machine heads are the knobs at the top of a guitar, before you get to the knob playing it.) Well, that was a salutary lesson: the poor chap had been demolished and slunk off, several years older. I pictured the hope with which he must have entered the auction house; imagining it to be an affirming and uplifting thing to hand over your treasured instrument to the admiring gasps and curatorial reverence of a grateful expert. A scene so ego-enhancing that you and your partner would get dressed up in your finery, the better to savour it.

So, when any potentially saleable items that I might have wanted to hang onto came my way, I treated them as if they were radioactive and gave them away, pronto. My future self had come back to alter the course of the universe and prevent my younger self from ever acquiring the items that would have resulted in such a humiliation – so I don't have much Pulp memorabilia. I've got to say though, they were *truly* magnificent machine heads.

27
Feather Boas and Lovehearts

We moved into a rehearsal room under a railway arch above Nick's parents' pottery warehouse in Catcliffe near Rotherham. It was flanked by pot-bellied brick kilns and rumbled by overhead trains. Alongside ran a malodourous sewer called the River Rother which, in the past, allowed fragile merchandise from Staffordshire to be brought safely on barges to the pottery.

Choosing between the Scylla of hypothermia and the Charybdis of asphyxiation by carbon monoxide gas heater, we wrote songs amidst maudlin ceramic clowns, garish jardinières and thimble sets of the counties of England. And we knew if a song was catchy when the youths outside throwing stones up at the corrugated iron walls started singing mockingly along.

The youths rode mopeds down slagheaps and shot air rifles at fish saying 'Stitch that, you bastard!' when they hit one. They more or less kidnapped Jarvis one day and forced him to drive then to a reservoir, inspiring the lyrics to the song 'Joyriders'.

Imagine our joy when the youths began to sing 'We can't help it, we're so thick we can't think!' to 'Joyriders'.

We set off on tour to promote the single 'Babies' and headed for Scotland. After the snarl-up of Leeds intersections, it all got rather lovely. We played a game called 'spot the Scottish thing' and points were had for heather, gorse, highland cattle, broom, thistles and the low barns we counted as 'crofts'. As it turned out, we were still seventy miles from Scotland. Gosh, if Yorkshire looked this Scottish, imagine how

Scottish Scotland would be! We awaited lochs, bagpipes and haggis, but sadly as soon as we crossed the border it flattened out and started to look like the Midlands.

The venue King Tut's Wah Wah Hut had a mirrored back wall. This was handy for practicing moves during the soundcheck but made for a rather self-conscious performance. A lot of local bands, including Teenage Fanclub, had come to see us and it felt like a showcase where we were being appraised rather than a vibrant gig. But we held their attention and they applauded politely between songs and enthusiastically at the end.

We were in the habit of writing to the local indie bands and asking if we could stay at their houses. We stayed with The Blue Aeroplanes in Bristol and Chumbawamba in Leeds – my God, can those guys eat lentils! When we played Glasgow we'd written to The Pastels and they'd made their excuses, so Jarvis made the announcement that we were looking for digs. But The Pastels relented and invited us back, so at least we had a bed.

We played Cardiff University in a room that held 800, which was a very big audience for us at the time. Earlier in the evening, in the 2,500 capacity main hall, the Manic Street Preachers played a triumphant homecoming concert and it was a sight to behold. I hadn't taken the Manics very seriously before, regarding them as a poor man's taffy Clash. All that over-the-top posturing and 'for real' stuff had a sensation-seeking media slavering, but left me cold.

The audience went over the barriers in impressive sacrificial waves. The Manics had a lot of really good songs, and could they move! Nicky Wire was slinky and bounced off the monitors like a lizard. They really were inspiring and I can say that with no fear of contradiction because, although the Manics are snidey about many bands, they reserved a special contempt for Pulp and always said perfectly beastly things about us.

Seeing the Manics gave us all a swagger. Nick Banks, when refused entry to the concert by student union security, said 'Do you know who I am?' We mocked him mercilessly, changed it to 'Do you know how much I weigh?' and ran a 'guess the weight of the drummer' competition at The Leadmill show.

Seasoned road crews don't rate student union entertainments committees very highly. The stereotype is of a bunch of officious jumped-up patronising little Hitlers who don't know their arse from their elbow – clueless yet supremely arrogant students with bags of attitude.

When it came to our turn to play, I tried this monitor-jumping lark and found it great fun, though the ents committee were none too pleased. We were brilliant, the most energetic we've ever been and an initially hostile crowd was won round. Some of the people who'd been to the Manics' show saw us too and we went back to the Manics' hotel with a gaggle of these kids. It was the first time we'd really seen that kind of scene – the band lounging around in shades and feather boas – it was really showbiz. The Manics didn't talk to us. Why should they? They probably didn't know who we were at this point, or how much Nick weighed, and made themselves scarce fairly sharpish. But we hung around – carousing with five girls who all wore white fluffy jackets, white sunglasses and white feather boas. There were two tiny blonde ones who were in a band called Shampoo, who used to follow the Manics round: they came to our concerts after that, adding to the feather boa and glamour count.

We went back to our more basic hotel with about fifty people, but the staff were having none of it. So we strode the streets, keen to keep the aftershow alive. We tried other hotels but none wanted this lively or, as they might have seen it, rowdy bunch. We went into a hotel, which was clearly very shut and made to leave, but the night porter was able to offer assistance for a small remittance and showed us to a large unused ballroom, which we could have a party in.

There is an old party game and it goes like this: names of animals are put into a hat and each contestant picks out an animal, which they have to impersonate until the others guess it. This can be funny and alluring. There was a German girl who got something that no one could (or would) guess and she writhed around on the floor in reckless abandon; slinking, slithering and flicking her tongue to bemused appreciation. Somehow or other, Rover ended up spending time with her. She also had that Germanic finger-clicking bossiness and had him running around after her. 'Rover, come to my room!' she announced and he went after her, winking, to many a raised eyebrow. In the morning I was very curious as to how it had all gone. It had all seemed very promising, they had a drink and a chat and suddenly she ordered him to … 'Get on your knees!' Crikey, this was looking good. 'Now, close your eyes!' Even better! And he waited … 'Now, put your hands together!' Alas, she was a born again Christian and Rover had to spend the night praying.

We played Manchester, which has possibly the best musical heritage of any city in the world and spawned its own sound: the slowed down form of funk called 'baggy', which was a prime component of the emerging scene. Pulp's take on Isaac Hayes and Barry White wasn't a million miles from baggy. People in Manchester had seen Pulp on TV – something we hadn't done ourselves. It was a place where we sold records and could pull in 150 people when we struggled to get fifty elsewhere. The audience at The Boardwalk was a who's who of those in bands or about to form them.

When living in a monotone world, there are two possible artistic reactions. You can hold up a mirror and reflect it – and with Joy Division, The Smiths and many more, Manchester had cornered the market in grey alienation. The Sheffield way had often been to go the opposite direction and revel in contrary glamour – put on an angst-fuelled Busby Berkeley spectacular. The Human League did it, ABC did it and Pulp did it. But now Madchester was starting to party too.

I might not be much of a guitarist but I can work a mean wah pedal – which I acquired in an attempt to replicate 'Silver Machine' by Hawkwind, and it does this surprisingly well. At the time, wahs were seen as cheesy seventies items, best left to working men's club turns with Jason King perms, aviator shades and droopy moustaches – very uncool – but not in Manchester, where they were all at it too, though probably more influenced by 'Theme from Shaft' than Hawkwind.

They play in a different way on the wrong side of the Pennines. They walk in a different way and they smoke roll-ups more furtively. I've watched The Farm, Happy Mondays, Cast and The Stone Roses at close quarters and they have a way of stomping about to keep time that, as a Yorkshireman, is as alien to me as doing a salsa. They have more rhythm.

Our label Warp was a joint Sheffield–Manchester venture. One of the guys who ran it said that he could tell immediately which of the cities a band was from. Sheffielders came in apologising for cluttering the office up with carrier bags, 'Is it okay to sit here, if it isn't putting you out too much? A cup of tea? Oh, yes, that would be lovely.' Manchester bands swaggered in, grabbed a can of Boddingtons, put their feet up and acted as if they owned the place. *Vive la différence* I say, but the difference is huge. They are funky, we are not.

Things were snowballing now; we had a few days off and rushed to record another single before the next London show. Saint Etienne DJed and members of Lush, Blur, Kingmaker, Suede and My Bloody Valentine were amongst the audience. Joe Strummer of The Clash congratulated us and comedians Vic and Bob, Eddie Izzard, Newman and Baddiel, Sean Hughes and Jo Brand (whom Rover flirted with outrageously) were among the audience. We couldn't release songs fast enough and fitted in filming videos and interviews in a frenetic whirl of activity.

No one was selling many records or making any money though, so after the Sheffield show the boys from Saint Etienne stayed at my house. I'd forgotten they were there and, after my customary morning shriek at the Vic Reeves cutout, I went into my infant daughter's room, to find her face hidden behind a picture book called *Baby Animals*. 'Hello, darling,' I said, then screamed as I saw her hairy face. It was only then that I remembered she was away and Bob Stanley of Saint Etienne was staying in her nursery. 'This is a really good book!' he said. Bob and Pete Wiggs had a great love of and knowledge of French pop: France Galle, Françoise Hardy, Jane Birkin. They were always aiming for this red balloon, light-as-air, artless French coolness – and they achieved it.

We got better value for money when we played Paris and crashed at Bob's girlfriend's flat on a quaint corner of Montmartre, outside of which two of the saddest old trannies since Les Dawson plied an unlikely trade; smoking drooping Gitanes in their wrinkly stockings. We were filming a video for the single 'Razzmatazz', which we intended to be extremely glamorous, and booked the Moulin Rouge and two crocodiles. Although the record company had sent a stylist and racks of clothes, we still wore our jumble-sale clobber, which the staff at the Moulin Rouge took one look at and refused to let us in. We improvised some scenes back at a seedy hotel, which had cockroaches and, much to Jarvis's delight, brown walls.

We shot more scenes at Sunset Strip, the oldest strip club in Soho – which had plenty of razzmatazz. Adrenaline and an on-the-road diet is very slimming and we had the fashionable 'Junkie Chic' look, even though none of us were junkies.

We'd had so many false starts that we didn't get carried away with it, but there was an emerging theme in reviews of: 'Catch this lot now, they're going to be huge'. The 'Babies' tour went well, instead of chairs we got bombarded with underwear, feather boas and lovehearts – which were worse than the chairs – a full packet end-on at impact velocity leaves a nasty bruise.

'Razzmatazz' got to number eighty in the charts – our first Top 100 and we supported friends Saint Etienne, who were the first band from the scene to get UK chart success.

The tour started off in Scotland – as many do, which gives an opportunity to iron out teething troubles before becoming subject to the Sauron gaze of the English music press. Apparently, when they go mad in Scotland they really go mad, but they never had for us and they certainly didn't for Saint Etienne.

Bob Stanley and Pete Wiggs of Saint Etienne come across as cool dudes but are at heart music fans, spending a lot of time in small rooms with big records. Obsessed as they were by French cool, they sought a chanteuse and when Sarah Cracknell (ex-model and ice-cool Hitchcock blonde) walked in, they were reduced to nudging, sniggering and going 'grrrl', like a rainy afternoon crowd in Games Workshop might do if Angelina Jolie suddenly appeared. So there they were, they'd got the songs, they'd got the singer, they'd been working in the studio and now the record company needed them to tour the album. But they were more of a studio project and although they put a band together hurriedly they never quite took to playing live.

We often went down better than they did and it wasn't an entirely happy time for Bob. Roadies don't much care for non-proper bands who use backing tapes and, for all our foppishness, Pulp were a real band and commanded a grudging respect. Not so Saint Etienne. A recalcitrant roadie inserted 'Is it real or is it Memorex?' amongst the list of hipper slogans that were flashed up on screens behind them. When their backing tape played up, they had to do the same song twice, looking round in uncomprehending panic at each other. This was funny but also distressing if you wished them well. Sarah Cracknell used to say rather reprovingly, like a prissy governess: 'We're *not* a rock band, we're a *pop* band and we *don't* do encores!' which was disastrous for the vibe. An audience that has paid and clapped wants an encore. Saint Etienne drew in quite a few from the hip dance scene, but they didn't deliver anything in the way of big sounds for that crowd (their PA was paltry) or rawness for the indie kids. So they fell between two stools and we were the beneficiaries of better reviews, accidentally piggy-backing on our mates' higher profile.

Not that Pete Wiggs minded, he was a party animal and we added a lot to the party. There was always an impromptu aftershow because both bands were small enough to be approachable and were well plugged-in to underground culture. So backstage was a riot. We usually shared a dressing room with Saint Etienne, which Jarvis was always drying washing in and generally turning into a squat, much to Bob Stanley's consternation.

It's great supporting, you play then you can go and watch the headline and meet the kids, then pile back to the headline band's dressing room for a party. His patience stretched to breaking point, Bob Stanley freaked out and wailed in despair: 'Who are all these people?'

It really was all our fault and, if the boot was on the other foot we'd have been the same, but the phrase stuck and was jokingly reused.

Sarah Cracknell, unapproachable ice maiden onstage, was fun offstage and affectionately referred to as 'Crackers'. After a show, as I was heading off into town to go out clubbing, Rover lazily said 'Bring us back a supermodel, would you?' Sarah gamely agreed to play along in a wind-up on him and, at four in the morning, he was woken by her, resplendent in gold leather jacket, angelically purring 'Rover, oh Rover'.

28
Fifty-franc Whores

After the support tour, we played some of our own shows. London was always a big deal because that was where the press was. We could play to 500 people in Sheffield and go down a storm but it was the concert at the Dog and Duck in Islington with thirty people that got the reviews. My memory of these venues has blurred into one: we played them all, from pubs and clubs to colleges and large theatres. One show that stands out was when we were supported by Daisy Chainsaw at a venue under a flyover – either Subterranea or The Underworld. Singer Katie Jane Garside writhed around in a tattered dress drinking orange juice from a baby's bottle. She kept wrapping the mike lead round her neck and ended up choking, which ended the concert.

Things had been going pretty well for us live, we were headlining a London pub and, with many hours to kill before the show, we'd filled the time drinking. Jarvis asked me what I thought of his trousers, which were yellow with a black grid. Very nice I said (it just made life easier). And the red polo-neck jumper? Also very cool. The concert was shambolic and at some point in it Jarvis must have realised what the audience already had – that he was dressed as Rupert Bear. It's funny now, but, for a band trying to shake the comedy tag, it was not wise to be doing this in front of half a dozen journalists and, more importantly, people who'd paid good money to see us.

We weren't exactly ecstatic to be on the same bill as comedic act Cud, who we supported at Blackpool Tower. We saw ourselves in the same bracket as The Fall and Joy Division but we'd often been understandably, but lazily, lumped in with bands like World of Twist, The Wonder Stuff, The Sultans of Ping FC and now Cud. We were determined to hate them but, as it happened, we clicked. Carl Puttnam was a kindred spirit, but we weren't going to admit it or play any more concerts with them.

Chasing more wild geese we went to Ireland in response to a massive petition to have us play. We went on a zany car-crash of a television show in Dublin, where we walked on one by one. As I came down the steps they put on 'This Town Ain't Big Enough for Both of Us' by Sparks. I'm reckoned to look like Ron Mael out of Sparks, so this was taking the rise, and the rest of the interview was in a similar vein. The anticipated adoring crowds never showed up and we found out the reason when we met a competition winner, who had won the dubious honour of meeting us. It was a fourteen-year-old girl, who readily confessed to having faked the entire competition. She was our only fan in Ireland and had contrived to get us to do the show there, basically for her own amusement – which does show some enterprise. It was a frustrating time in other respects and everyone we met seemed to want to waste our time on some fool's errand. Temple Bar, the supposedly bohemian area, seemed like a big show put on for the American tourists, with locals milking the 'old country' shtick. Our guesthouse had pictures of potatoes on the wall – it all seemed like something from a comedy sketch and failed to win me over. This is purely personal, I'm sure there's more to Ireland than this, but the trip cured me of any whimsical notions I might have had, and when some bearded old wiseacre said 'Would you like a drop of the hard stuff, sir?' I was tempted to say, 'Look, mate, you can drop all the blarney now, I'm not American, so it doesn't wash.'

We played a television show called *No Stilletos*. Legendary Irish folk band The Dubliners were playing, with Shane McGowan of the Pogues guesting on vocals. As a violin player, I was concerned that, set alongside these people who presumably had learned to play their fiddles at the age of six on their grandaddy's knee, I might be discovered for the bluffer I was.

The dressing room had live CCTV images from various parts of the building beamed into it, which allowed us to clandestinely watch a simulacrum in miniature of events unfolding on the stage. There was panic amongst the show's organisers because The Dubliners were late, having discovered the duty-free shop at the airport with Shane, and were still holed up there. They eventually arrived, but I thought to myself

'Whiskey just makes fiddle players better, right?' Not so: the band struck up 'The Irish Rover', very badly, and Shane started singing 'Whiskey in the Jar', very badly. The Dubliners started playing 'Whiskey in the Jar' and Shane started singing 'The Irish Rover'. They argued amongst themselves with Shane saying something vehemently in an incredibly slurred brogue – but presumably understandable to a fellow Irishman, you might think. Much to everyone's delight, one of The Dubliners turned to another and said in a thick, but entirely comprehensible accent 'I can't understand a blind word the man's saying!' When we went on, I held my head high, I was the best violinist in the room – if only for that night ... and unlike the rest of them, knew the difference between 'The Irish Rover' and 'Whiskey in the Jar'.

Back in England, Nick Banks and I hung out with Irish band The Cranberries when they were just bursting onto the scene and he was first in with the slightly dodgy Irish jokes. But their singer Dolores O'Riordan loved Irish jokes and we walked around London shouting 'Tatoe!' and 'I'm just a simple girl from the bogs, might you know where I could get a tatoe, sir?' as if it was the funniest thing in the world, which it kind of was. At their hotel the night porter made the rather insulting assumption that she was a prostitute, even though it was her staying there, not us. He kept finding excuses to burst in, hoping to have his suspicions proven correct. So we played along and put the suitcase stand on the bed, strapped a banana to it with a belt. Then we bounced up and down on the bed smoking cigars, moaning and going 'Yes, yes, tatoe, please, tatoe sir!' I'm not sure exactly what particular form of deviancy this might facilitate and how it might be enacted, but it confirmed the porter's suspicions and he threw us out, which we were very proud of. Look, I know this is nauseatingly infantile, but it's what happened, don't shoot the messenger.

At the same time as this colourful new British collision of indie, dance, baggy and quirky pop was forming, grunge, which was the complete grey antithesis of that, was becoming popular in the UK.

We supported a grungy band at The Leadmill who were flavour of the month with the *NME*. The place was full of pissed-up, shoddily dressed students. We saw ourselves as Michelangelo supporting the hod carriers in our home city – a humiliating indignity. But grunge was getting the kids moshing and British variants of the common or garden shed variety seemed to be eclipsing the rebirth of glamour. Mark Goodier introduced us as 'The Status Quo of Sheffield', which we didn't appreciate. It seemed that every step up the ladder was followed by a slide down a snake. We were often being nudged into one camp or another but saw ourselves as something different – something that didn't have a name.

Select magazine got this new thing though and did an edition with Brett Anderson of Suede sexily posturing on the cover against a backdrop of the Union Jack and the words 'Yanks go Home! SUEDE, ST ETIENNE, DENIM, PULP, THE AUTEURS and the Battle for Britain.' *Select* saw it how we saw it and the term Britpop came into common coin. This vastly influential edition of *Select* crystallised and gave a name to the nebulous strands that had been coalescing to form this new constellation. It may or may not have been influential with the public but it made all the bands sit up and take notice, especially those not on the list. John Robb, a fanzine writer with whom I'd been in correspondence, had been using the term Britpop before there was the music to fit the label, but now the label had a music.

And all the disparate bands that had had the Britpop label attached to them ended up knowing and socialising with each other. At Sheffield's Pond Street bus station Nick Banks and I saw a forlorn figure sitting on the ground. Nick nudged me, 'I'm sure that's Luke Haines from The Auteurs' he said. So we went over and offered consular assistance. Luke was very dejected as he'd attempted to buy something to eat at a kiosk and had found the accent so incomprehensible that he'd given up. We translated and wandered around with him bitterly moaning about The North. So we played up our northerness: 'Tha't in't "Otter's" in't tha? Is tha wi thissen?' In a Yorkshire accent The Auteurs would actually be pronounced ... The Auteurs, but we stuck to calling them 'The Otters' to compound his sense of otherness. Oh, heartbreakingly lovely Auteurs, I'd always assumed they'd be much bigger than Suede and us, they just seemed in a different class, surrounded by stardust.

Another of the bands name checked on that seminal *Select* cover were Denim. We met Lawrence of Denim, who was an odd character but had a lovely name, so I called my newborn son Benjamin Laurence. He inspired earnest French people to buy Chicory Tip and Lieutenant Pigeon albums and was obsessed with unpopular musical forms, particularly from the crushingly unfashionable eighties – which would have been funny if Lawrence hadn't taken it so seriously. He was certainly fastidious and focused and was said to be obsessive compulsive. So the fact that he flat-shared with wildman rocker Bobby Gillespie, from Primal Scream, was even odder. Apparently they used to get on each other's nerves quite a bit, because Bobby would make an awful mess but Lawrence was the type who would number tea bags and fold the corners over at the end of toilet rolls like they do in hotels. There's a sitcom based on this unlikely pairing crying out to be made.

Pursuing obscurity almost for its own sake, someone put together a tribute album to an unknown (outside France) musician called Michel Polnareff. Pretty much all the Britpop bands were invited to contribute a cover version and all the best songs were snaffled before we got to them. We were stuck with a daft song called 'Les Roi des Formis' (King of the Ants), which we recorded with Blur's producer Stephen Street. It's an abiding regret that our only foray into the studio with such a great producer was on this fool's errand.

So what did Michel Polnareff do when the cream of the crop of the emergent Britpop scene revealed this touching tribute to his genius? Did he do a little jig? Did he invite us all over for dinner round at his *maison*? Did he kiss us on both cheeks? Did a tear slowly roll from an old man's eye on receiving the international validation from a new generation of admirers? Did it heck as like – he said: 'Who are all these people? I 'ave never 'eard of zem, where eez Whitney Ooston, where eez Michel Jackson, zese nobodies cannot presume to cover zee works of the maestro.' Well, something like that (allegedly) and he refused permission for its release: in perhaps the uncoolest act of a not particularly cool career, he told us to Polnareffoff.

Shortly after that we supported Scottish band Teenage Fanclub in Paris. I like them for three reasons:

1. Lovely people.
2. Their music isn't my genre but still leaves you with a lovely warm glow.
3. They take a pot of white emulsion round with them to paint over graffiti-covered dressing room walls, which is a great service to mankind.

Teenage Fanclub and The Pastels, who'd been at our Glasgow show, were part of a whimsical, jingly jangly, lo-fi, indie guitar movement called C86 that revered an American band called Big Star, who in turn revered a man called Jad Fair, who was also on the bill for his first-ever European show. Pulp's rhythm guitarist Mark Webber, who was a fan of the C86 movement and an inveterate taper of rarities, was keen to capture this historic moment on tape. This was ruined by our lovely Geordie driver who loudly 'Why-ayed' throughout, interspersing the gentle stylings of Jad Fair with such gems as 'Hie away, Rover, and gan us a beer!' and 'There's fifty-franc hoors outside, man!'

29
Lipgloss and Cigarettes

We began work on the album *His 'n' Hers* in Britannia Row studios in Islington. Nick, who by that time had moved back to Sheffield, and myself were billeted in a lovely Georgian terrace.

The song 'Live On' was, in both the band's and our audience's opinion, Pulp's best song for a period of time. When we came to release singles, we ranked them in order of strength and popularity: 'Live On' was best and 'OU' was fourth. We were persuaded to defer releasing 'Live On' and work up to it, but when it came to recording the album *His 'n' Hers*, Jarvis had gone off it. We organised a showcase of the songs in front of the record company and others and the universal view was that 'Live On' was the strongest song. But Jarvis just couldn't bring himself to sing it. I was furious; but his point was kind of a fair one – that eighteen months down the line it was sounding a bit derivative of baggy. Nonetheless, it's the best song we never released. When we played the City Hall in Sheffield for our triumphant homecoming someone had made a banner saying 'Don't drop "Live On"' – they were right.

Vic Reeves and Bob Mortimer used to hang out at the studio. Vic's real name is Jim and Jim, like most comedians, was a maudlin and tormented chap when offstage – though a thoroughly lovely one. Bob's real name when offstage is Bob and he was indistinguishable from his onstage persona. At first I thought Bob was doing an act and laughed at the things he said, but he was just being himself. Once Jim and Bob were sitting on the settee in the studio and Bob was squirming about. 'What is it, Bob?' said Jim. 'Anal hair entrapment, Jim' said Bob.

Away from the creature comforts of home, especially books, I crawled up the walls if I stayed in, which I only did on two nights of the several months we were recording *His 'n' Hers*. Home life was nappies and sleepless nights, but in London we were invited to an endless stream of live shows, parties and launches and released a guitar-driven single called 'Lipgloss'. This was lyrically louche and glamourised the adrenaline-fuelled Britpop lifestyle. The video was filmed in a multicoloured inflatable Verner Panton art space. It got to number fifty in the charts and, all of a sudden, it was all happening so fast we couldn't take it in.

We kicked the 'Lipgloss' tour off at The Leeds Duchess, supported by our Sheffield mates The Longpigs. No empty rooms now, it was the place to be for a new generation of jumble-sale kids in feather boas. I was espied choosing a pair of sunglasses from the immense suitcase by a journalist and referred to as 'The Imelda Marcos of Sunglasses'. At Manchester University we got mobbed for autographs going to the venue. At King Tuts in Glasgow no one was taking notes, they were dancing to us and support band Elastica.

Elastica singer Justine had been out with Brett from Suede and Damon from Blur and was the androgynous femme fatale of the Britpop scene. Then there was their guitarist, Donna. Great guitar players like Bernard Butler or Richard Hawley don't intimidate me because we do a different thing. They may be able to play 'All Along the Watchtower' better than Hendrix but they can't do spare and spiky and proddy as well as me. But Donna was like a more aggressive form of me, with breasts. And there was a general air of violence surrounding Elastica, reminiscent of the early days of punk. Someone once threatened to throw me off a balcony at one of their concerts for being too smart.

Justine's dad was a big-shot in business so they never shook off the 'rich kids slumming it' tag. But where would the sixties be without rich kids slumming it? – minus Mick Jagger, for a start. Decadence and excess surrounded Elastica. Half-remembered nights sitting around in hotel rooms with people shooting up as a couple of girls lazily snogged, not remembering whether they were gay or doing it to impress the boys, and the boys too far gone to care.

Heroin is a bad drug. You'll have heard tales of, 'Do you remember that time we got stoned and ended up ordering three pizzas each, then gave them away to a hedgehog called Mr Spikey?' You'll have heard tales of, 'Remember that time we did mushrooms and thought there was a gorilla trapped up the chimney?' Or, 'Do you remember that time we did speed and stayed up dancing all night with some Albanians?' 'Do you remember that time we did coke and ended up ...' Well, there are fewer good coke tales. But I've never heard an amusing heroin anecdote. Never ever. And I've known at least ten junkies and liked them – though most are dead now. Just before it all kicked off for Elastica, Justine said she felt 'like I'm about to get on a rollercoaster and don't know where it's going'.

The rollercoaster took us to a very strange concert in Aberdeen, where the November wind whipped off the North Sea and howled down the granite streets. With hours to kill, we huddled on sticky sofas in the black-painted and very cold dressing room. I noticed a draught that seemed to issue from behind a poster. I looked behind the poster and saw a panel, which once removed revealed a cold darkness beyond. I shone a torch down and peered into the Stygian Gloom (that would be my stage name if I was in a goth band). There was a large subterranean chamber about twenty feet high, with passages leading off. At the side, but tantalisingly just out of reach, was a roughlyfashioned wooden ladder. We couldn't get down but made enquiries. Apparently, there was an immense network of tunnels that led all the way to the sea, but by then it was time to go onstage and we never explored this mournful necropolis. There it lies behind the panel, awaiting more adventurous and well-equipped children.

During that tour we did our first big television appearance. We'd done a few regional television shows, sandwiched between 'Fear stalks Heckmondwike as local thieves steal bag of potatoes' features. But the first national telly was a programme called *The Word*, hosted by an in-yer-face Mancunian called Terry Christian. *The Word* was an early foray into the Japanese world of humiliation TV and was always trying to shock, but they had the best bands and we did a version of 'Lipgloss' that stands the test of time. Nick must have been very excited: if his heart rate was the same as his bpm he'd have been rushed to hospital. It was comically hard to keep up with his cartoon-chase pace, but it was an edgy performance.

On the Sheffield leg of the tour, The Leadmill was packed to greet the conquering local heroes. The upfront fee was small but the venue held 800 and, if they sold more than 500 tickets, we were due to get a lot more money. My trademark laser stare must have been particularly disconcerting for the audience that evening as I was attempting to count them, one by one.

I calculate large crowds in the following way: I divide the audience into sixteen sections, choose a section, count the number of people in it, then multiply by sixteen. I did this several times and there were always fifty or more in the section I was counting – so there were 800 people in.

When I went to receive payment I was told that there were 499 people in. I was outraged that, not only had they seemingly robbed us of our fee, but also not even had the decency to come up with a plausible lie – 499 was a slap in the face. In France and London we were treated with respect but here in our home city they were taking the piss – for the last time. I went down to the dressing room and started smashing the place up with my briefcase. I was taking a swing at a row of lightbulbs on the dressing-room mirror as security walked in. This was the eighteenth time we'd played The Leadmill and our last.

I was very embarrassed and came back the day after with lightbulbs to replace the ones I'd destroyed. I got ridiculed in the *NME* for this; not for the vandalism, but for being so un-rock-and-roll as to replace the lightbulbs.

30
Small Room, Big Records

I used to go in a pub in Camden called The Good Mixer, which was the haunt of mods, Graham Coxon from Blur and some old punks including Steve Diggle of the Buzzcocks and Knox from The Vibrators. A guy called Chris Gentry was lolling about like a big puppy dog in a tailored suit. 'Do you wanna fight?' he said. He was smiling as he spoke and that was it, somehow we were friends.

Chris and I went to a disco in the upstairs room of a pub in Camden called The Laurel Tree. This was just down the road from The Good Mixer and around closing time the pub would decamp to The Laurel Tree where a night called Blow Up was getting increasingly popular. The DJs played a mix of mod, with quite a bit of French stuff thrown in. You'd get 'Green Onions' by Booker T. and the M.G.'s and 'Keep On Running' by The Spencer Davis group alongside 'Mini-mini-mini' by Jacques Dutronc and 'Contact' by 'Brigitte Bardot'. Blow Up got even more popular and there were long queues outside on some nights, they were victims of their own success. People were let in according to the coolness of their attire, and many were turned away, including people in established bands who thought they ought to be able to get in. But Blow Up wanted the acest faces and would favour a dressed-up unknown over a dressed-down minor celeb. So, in a way, it was a private club for an extended group of friends. This was fine by me: at Sheffield's Limit Club on a Friday night I felt like an exhibit in a zoo, with squares coming to point and stare. Here a straight man could wear eyeliner without getting hassle.

Things were looking good for Pulp: we were signed to hip-but-big Island Records and getting to make videos with decent production values. When we were filming the video for the song 'Do You Remember the First Time?' a girl was dispatched to 'find some cool kids' and she came back with Chris Gentry and some of the lads I already knew from Blow Up. The video was a laugh and the four boys got on well. The girl said, 'You look like a band, you lot. You should call yourselves "Menswear".' So they did, and wrote four songs – heavily influenced by Blur and Elastica – and got signed by Island Records for three times as much money as Pulp had – everyone wanted a piece of this new Britpop craze and were prepared to pay for it.

This caused huge resentment amongst bands that had been paying their dues and struggling their way up the ladder. I commented to an Island Records executive that, 'It wasn't bad money for a band with only four songs.' We'd got albums and albums worth, had toured extensively and actually had a fanbase. But such was the feeding frenzy that no one wanted to miss out on Menswear, it was a bit of a bubble.

Menswear bassist Stuart Black said: 'I know people hate us, I'd hate us if I wasn't us. I know we're not the best band in the world, but we're all right and we've just been offered a deal, what are we gonna do, turn it down?'

Menswear had a song called 'Daydreamer' and a mod got beaten-up by some yobs singing this song. There's a pause where the lyric goes 'Breath deeper …' then a martial drumbeat, then, '… daydreamer', which the attackers chanted whilst delivering blows to the tune of the music. Such was the venom.

Menswear were being feted by people with power and hated by others for it. And people really did hate them. Chris was always doing his 'cocky little git' act and not everyone got the joke. I stopped going out with them after a week in which, during five evenings out, they managed to get into a fight four times. It all sounds rather glamorous, but fights are actually horrible and best avoided. I never saw them actually hit anyone but they got hit themselves and didn't exactly tone it down to avoid it, in fact they turned it up. The final straw was when an evening out ended in a large brawl – which was pretty much Chris's fault – and some of their friends got hurt. I wasn't one of those friends, as I'd scarpered out the door as soon as it started turning nasty. I was used to them by now and had no intention of getting hit just because they didn't know when to shut up.

Johnny Dean the singer was imploding almost before it had begun. He was a striking figure and the Japanese loved him – he looked like a manga hero. He cut a dash but never quite looked comfortable in his own skin. He had to cope with all this adulation and hate and just froze like a rabbit in the headlights.

Knowing Menswear to be a bit of a handful (to say the least) a legendary tour manager called Scottie Jobson was hired. He was the brother of the granite-faced singer from The Skids and was a hard but generally good-natured Scotsman who didn't suffer fools gladly. To an awkward promoter he said: 'I'm six foot three, I'm Scottish, I'm coming down with a cold and *yoor* startin' on me?'

We toured with Menswear and they were a delight, as was the long-suffering Scottie Jobson, who used to arm wrestle Menswear to wear them out – like taking an excitable dog for a run. Stuart said, in his Cockney accent: 'He's jast a laverly ma-an.' He said that about a lot of people, he liked the world and saw it in a simple and humble way and boy, was he cool. The only time I've ever gone into a hairdresser with a picture and said, 'I want my hair like that,' I was holding a photo of Stuart.

Chris Gentry was always cracking up, spurting his beer out, laughing and falling over sideways. My daughter, who was pre-school at the time, absolutely adored him. And Menswear adored Graham Coxon of Blur – who had taught them how to play 'There's No Other Way'.

After spilling out of a nightclub somewhere, maybe Smashing or Madame JoJo's, some insistent German women wanted to take Menswear home with them. Chris wasn't that impressed, but the Germans were most persistent.

'Have you got a big room?' he said, sceptically.

'No, no, we have small room!' they said.

'Have you got any records?' he said.

'Yes, yes, we have records, big records ... small room, big records!'

We were pretty much dragged off by these women but when we got back to their flat we ran off, scared but laughing at the thought of the small room with the giant records. It's just one of those daft things.

When touring with Menswear we found on the dressing room wall a map with directions of how to get to Topshop, for Menswear, and Marks & Spencer, for Pulp. The previous occupants – the irrepressibly scruffy Levellers, who were the last people one would expect to give out sartorial advice, had left this for us.

Menswear got all their suits made at Tony the Greek's, a little tailor in an upstairs room on Carnaby Street who did 'a special price for the modernists'. Mod was a component of the Britop style, attitude and, to some extent, music. It was by no means straight modernism and would certainly offend a purist. I was sitting in Britpop hangout, the downstairs bar at Shuttleworth's on Shaftesbury Avenue, when an immaculate mod gave me the traditional compliment: 'Well suited-up, mate.' But when I got out a spaceship-shaped lighter he shook his head sadly and said 'The lighter's wrong, mate.'

We had a launch for 'Do You Remember the First Time?' at the ICA and I guess it was a very romantic night: I know of three married couples who met there.

We'd been told by the record company that the single should get into the Top Forty and listened to the chart rundown. As each song was announced we cheered, knowing that it meant ours would be higher up. But after several tracks had passed we began to have doubts as to whether it had made the charts at all. When it finally came in at thirty-three there was huge relief and great celebration: our first Top Forty hit, a decade after I'd first started; as long as The Beatles's entire career.

31
Le Bikini, 1994

The album *His 'n' Hers* went in at number nine. The whirr got faster but I must have been having a good time. We did some signing sessions in record stores notable for the amount of underwear brought in to sign, but of the UK tour I have no recollection. In light of our higher profile the record company re-released the single 'Babies' and we made a new video with a professional producer – in the same style as the original version, but with higher production values. Then set off on a French tour.

After our first Parisian headline show we went out clubbing and, not wishing the evening to end, I had gone on my own to a club called Les Bains, a jet-set place in an old public baths. The French may have better lives but they can't dance for toffee. So, I was strutting my stuff on the dance floor to 'Harley Davidson' when this tall, immaculately dressed black guy said, 'You're English, aren't you?' and we got chatting. He was buzzing because he'd just shown at the Paris Fashion Week for the first time. It had been a triumph and he wanted to share it with a fellow Brit. We discussed details of suiting and tried to spot any Brits, just from their dancing. Ozwald Boateng gave me his card and said, 'Come and see me in London, I'll make you a suit.'

I told the rest of the band about the interesting chap I'd met with the unusual name, and the free suit he'd offered me. Steve, who knew about these things, told me he was quite famous and was I *sure* the suit would be free as he was Savile Row and usually charged a lot? Well, the impression I'd got was that the suit *would* be free, but it sowed the seed of doubt in my mind. How crushingly embarrassing it would be if I was faced with a bill

I couldn't pay, so I never followed it up. In his own way Ozwald Boateng was a child of Britpop himself and his very individual styling owed a lot to the mod revival element within it.

We pitched up at a venue in Toulouse called Le Bikini, which was run by head chef and force of nature Hervé. Hervé served us a meal on a long trestle table by the banks of the Garonne – a trio of sublime sorbets assuaging the blazing heat of the day. I played him at chess: though I'm not a good player, I look like the kind of person who would be and lose with such bad grace that I'm satisfying to beat. He gave me a bottle of Bison Grass Vodka as a consolation prize.

In many ways, our French audiences seemed to have a clearer sense than elsewhere that they were witnessing something new and special. The audience was up for it, we were the coolest thing in town and the show was electric.

Afterwards, in the balmy evening, we all ended up in the outdoor swimming pool. Yes, a backstage with a swimming pool! We sat in the shade of Hervé's pride and joy, the Palme D'Or – the largest, oldest and most splendid palm tree in all of Toulouse. We asked if it would be okay to set off some fireworks. Of course, said our ever-accommodating host, who went inside to get more titbits for our delectation.

In a bid to impress the lissome lovelies gazing at our antics, Jarvis set off a Catherine wheel, which he nailed to the Palme D'Or. It whizzed round, emitting sparks that set the tree on fire. A sober man would not try and douse a fire with Bison Grass Vodka, but I was not sober and – in a scene reminiscent of *Apocalypse Now* – the palm crackled, then roared in a blazing fireball, before turning black with a small mushroom cloud hovering above it, just as Hervé emerged to see what all the commotion was about.

In cartoons, people jump up and down and shake both fists in rage. I had never seen anyone do this in real life, until now. We ran, all of us, from this bull of a man and left in the van, with him running down the road after us – still jumping up and down and crying.

We thought we'd never be able to go back but, a couple of years later, a bottle of Bison Grass Vodka arrived in the post and it seemed we might have been forgiven. Then the offer of a contract came, with the unusual stipulation that I play Hervé at chess. We had some trepidation about returning, fearing that it might be a ruse to lure us back and extract some shocking revenge for the loss of the Palme D'Or – perhaps involving fireworks and arses. In an attempt to placate him, I had taken the precaution of bringing a small palm tree with me as a peace offering.

But all was fine: Hervé and I played chess; I lost, and ran around shouting '*merde*', jumping up and down shaking my fists; and we enjoyed Hervé's copious hospitality once more.

FRANCE
2011

32
Le Bikini, 2011

Hervé is delighted to see us and, after a rib-crushing hug, takes me to see the palm tree I had given him almost two decades before. It has grown to adulthood, in the fertile soil with the warm sun and his tender care in the kitchen garden he uses to supply his table. It bears the legend: 'No fireworks please.' He serves us succulent and gargantuan steaks and is laying into a huge hunk of meat with a cleaver when our friend Nancy arrives with her parents. They are vegetarian, which only encourages Hervé: 'What we do is we cook everything in the blood of the cow,' he says. They go to get something more acceptable ... 'Including the fruit salad!' he shouts after them.

We sit, chill and play chess by the swimming pool, drinking red red wine. Word has got out that we are playing this secret warm-up show and some people have come a long way. Here, at this intimate venue, probably more than anywhere else we will play, the fans are aware of my particular role in the proceedings. That the difference between this tour being a comeback tour of a band whose star had waned but now waxed and what this is – the reformation of a classic line-up, was me. A large number of people who had tickets for the tour wouldn't know my name and wouldn't care two hoots whether I was playing or not, but here many did and knew it was significant. There were fans from the old days and a new generation of aficionados. Pressure.

People have been queuing round the block for hours, so we will be facing a forgiving public. If you think that's a reason to treat it casually, then you would be talking about a different band to Pulp.

I go and attempt to chill and lose myself in company and banter; putting off thinking about the almost unfaceable reality of actually going onstage. There's such a lot riding on this and the great unknown is: how we will fare? We're all knocking fifty and have not done this for a long, long time – the others for several years and me for almost two decades. But really, what is the worst that can happen? The worst that can happen is that we perform badly, are a great disappointment and really embarrass ourselves. Then are stuck grinding our way through a tour as a bunch of washed-up old has-beens that ought to have known better. That the kudos I had (if only in my own head) of having foregone the easy and lucrative option of staying in the band when it was past its sell by date will be totally trashed and I will be somewhat financially better off but spiritually much the poorer, and feel like a fifty-franc whore – other than that, not much.

Pulp are a terrible example to other bands. We paid our rock and roll dues for a decade and in the end it came good. We epitomise the belief that, if you stick at it long enough, then you'll make it. This gives false hope to many to keep on plugging away when they really shouldn't bother. If you are in any doubt and you ever think, 'Well, Pulp were in the wilderness for years and they made it, so why shouldn't we?' you are clutching at straws and should just jack it in. We are the exception that proves the rule. Being in a struggling band is a vale of tears and should not be the career choice of a rational being – the only reason you should do it is if it's a compulsion that you can't help. Perhaps this struggle makes the music better. It certainly supplies more source material for the second album than the overdone and hard-to-relate-to pressures of coping with fame that bedevils those who find instant success. But it also feeds into the anxiety of performance if one is dropped in at the deep end without the incremental build-up of success. In short, it is a damn sight easier to go onstage to 1,500 people when one went on to 1,400 the week before.

No one could ever have accused us of over-rehearsing in the past. But this time was different; we'd put months and months of very hard work to hothouse ourselves back into the zone – but would it work? I have my first drink, unless you count wine. To drink too little is bad: three drinks are the best, takes the edge off, allows you to relax, let go, and live in the moment.

We have formed a method, after many years of getting it horribly wrong, to try and make sure we peak at the right time. If three hours before a show you are counting down in eager and frightened anticipation then you will go off your head with nerves and sag when you should be psyching up – so you need to distract yourself and avoid thinking about what is ahead. It is also bad to not have enough time to get ready and be panicked and forget to tie your shoelaces, or be on the loo with someone screaming at you to get onstage. By tradition we clear the dressing room of non-combatants half an hour before showtime to get changed, put on warpaint and effect the transformation from mere mortal into performer. This is a subtle and mysterious metamorphosis and must be very like a football team in the dressing room or even, in some regards, a battalion about to go to war. I always referred to it as 'going over the top' and in many ways it was what I lived for. There seems something noble and brave about it, it's scary and exciting at the same time.

We had looked at this rickety rollercoaster and bought a ticket. Now we are strapped in and it is starting to move. At the sound check I feel a numbness spreading through my ear and the side of my face. A stroke! I'm having a stroke! I take out my earplug and discover that I have somehow contrived to insert codeine into my ear – what a dick. This doesn't help my jangled nerves.

And here it is, the engines are running, we are standing on the runway waiting for take-off. It's ninety degrees in the dressing room; goodness knows what it is under the stage lights. A packed house, the noise of the crowd, five minutes to go. All the lapsed smokers restart. The call comes, nervous looks all round, Steve sounds calm but his hands are shaking and he cuts himself opening the door. Jarvis gives the executioner a wan smile.

House lights off, the crowd chants.

Is my collar straight? We primp and preen, more for distraction than anything else. Time slows and hangs in the air, the clock creeps on. But I just wanna get up there and blow, get it on. So, after remembered rituals and the few endless minutes of pre-stage hyperventilation, it's over the top, through liminal space, into the mirror and onto the stage.

Adrenaline.

Jarvis seems to really explode onstage; he appears so excited that it is all happening. We've had the rehearsal, we've had the dress rehearsal but this is no rehearsal and has a whole extra energy of its own. There are people here who'd been there in 1994 when we'd last played, people who know more about Pulp than I do. There are people shouting my name and calling out for early songs. I think the audience is happier to hear an obscure song like 'Countdown' than our big hit 'Common People' and we play by far the longest encore we've ever done, well over half an hour.

House lights on.

It is touching and warm and good but I don't remember much else. I go into a trance-like state. Often one comes offstage bleeding or bruised somewhere and can't remember how it happened.

After, I just lie down and can hardly talk, sagging like a deflated balloon, completely fucked and barely able to lift an arm to clink a glass with Hervé, who has prepared yet another banquet for us.

There is immense relief that we've finally got one under the belt but the big one is in less than two days – Barcelona.

They say you should never go back. Well, we have, but we won't be doing it again. Not least because after secreting the majority of the delectable but far too large steak lovingly prepared by Hervé in the fridge – wrapped in a napkin and hidden behind cans of Red Bull – in the post-match torpor I forget to retrieve it. I didn't want to offend him by not eating the steak. I'd said it was too much but he'd said 'You'll eat what's on your fucking plate!' – those were his exact words, delivered with such vigour that they are tattooed onto my cerebral cortex. So no doubt by now he will have found it. I may as well have slapped him in the face with it and burnt down his new palm tree.

FRANCE
1994

33
Mariah Carey's Biscuits

The French tour continued as we eagerly awaited the chart position for 'Babies'. We'd been assured that it would be in the Top Forty and as each position was announced we cheered; particularly at number thirty-one, which meant we were Top Thirty. As the countdown progressed and still 'Babies' had not appeared, the same trepidation that perhaps we'd missed out began to set in. When, after an age, it was at number nineteen we were ecstatic at being in the Top Twenty and feverish preparations were made to fit in a *Top of the Pops* appearance, even though we were still in France.

We did a television show called *Le Circle de Minuit* at midnight. There were two 'Russell clones' in the audience who had dressed the same as me and invaded the stage, putting a white feather boa round my neck, which I kept on as we headed over to the airport. This was the first time I'd been on a plane and I was looking forward to it.

At the airport someone furtively asked me to look in their case, 'I think I've done a bad thing,' they said. They had, there was a gravestone inside. 'Well that *is* a bad thing, a very bad thing.' Where had it come from? They couldn't remember – one of those mad nights in Paris – so what to do now? Is there some department of missing gravestones to contact? We needed to catch the plane, so we grubbed in the dirt at the side of a service road and with a little ceremony of apology – trying to show some remorse and respect – we buried it, then caught the plane. Still there probably, or baffling Scandinavian detectives.

As a kid I wanted to be an astronaut and, unable to make a rocket, built a primitive hang-glider, utilising the parts of a plastic gazebo. It was about fifteen feet long and red-and-white striped (come on, ye Blades). For extra support I'd used my grandfather's ancient wooden golf clubs. So I ran up and down our street with this contraption, to the bemusement of the other kids. The fateful day came when the wind was high enough to take it up for real and I went onto the school field, followed by an excited bunch of onlookers. I tilted it up, the wind caught and I could feel the lift pulling it off the ground. I ran off a small defile, took off briefly, then was swept into the ground, which shattered the glider and my grandfather's golf clubs, and left me bruised and bleeding. The crowd dispersed, muttering, and I had to limp back home, dragging the remains of my sorry-looking craft in a grim parody of the crucifixion.

But I'd always wanted to fly: I thought that airplanes would be sleek and smooth, antiseptically clean like Hawkwind's 'Silver Machine'. But this one rattled and shook a lot; there was clearly something wrong. Someone said of the Munich air disaster that they all knew there was something wrong but no one said anything because, 'It takes a brave man to be a coward.' I was that brave man. I screamed for the plane to stop, but it was too late, we were all doomed – and I spent the entire journey in white-knuckle terror, bracing myself for the deadly impact. I think I may have made some promises to take up religion. It was a pledge made with the best of intentions but I shouldn't have made a promise I wasn't absolutely certain I could keep and for that I'm sorry.

When we set down safely I kissed the tarmac in relief and this may have been the start of my patriotism. In subsequent flying I often did this and not just in dear old Blighty ... any country that was quality enough to have built a serviceable runway would do. I was told that I would lose my fear of flying with familiarity but this didn't happen and I didn't have the best of luck. Take-offs in snow, Aeroflot planes, planes with propellers chugging along hesitantly, turbulence so bad the stewardess hit the roof, fog, bumpety bump clouds, being struck by lightning, having a mysterious (and, in my imagination, flammable) fluid poured all over me from above – it was a constant source of terror.

TOTP is not at all like you'd imagine it to be: you are required to turn up in the morning and wait around all day in a small bare room, with only a trip to make-up to alleviate the boredom.

Make-up artists are great sources of scurrilous gossip and, presuming me to be gay – based on my extensive knowledge of foundation – shared juicy details:

'Well, apparently so and so likes to ...'

'Noooo!'

'... and is having an affair with so and so.'

'Reeeally? Well, I heard that ...'

There was a skinny boy fag-hagging around, doing jazz hands and adding extra sordid details, which largely amounted to almost everyone being secretly gay. As a make-up wearing lover of gossip and Hi-NRG music, who thought Kylie was simply divine, I was assumed to be one of the brotherhood, with full rights of access to gossip: I didn't put them straight. It never occurred to them that a straight man could like Kylie – which is pretty blinkered really, I mean you'd have to be gay not to, wouldn't you?

I wandered down a corridor and this little kid was coming the other way, so I lifted my arm to let her pass underneath and it was Kylie: she's so, so tiny. She went and sat down with Nick Cave, whose looming presence dominated the canteen. I'd seen him up close before, when he was in a proto-goth band called The Birthday Party. On that occasion he'd jumped into the audience and landed on my head, so I gave him a wide berth – he's a big feller. He did 'Where the Wild Roses Grow' with Kylie and their performance was mesmerising. Mariah Carey was on too and, despite, according to the make-up guy, having had a dodgy prawn sandwich, did an impeccable performance. As she didn't feel like eating, we ate her biscuits, which were specially brought-in American cookies. *Carpe Diem*: it's not every day you get to eat Mariah Carey's biscuits.

By show time we were bored out of our minds and just wanted to get it over with and escape. Rover had got me a shiny spangly guitar to mime with. 'You're a pop star now, that's a pop star guitar.' I was touched.

The audience of terrified teenage girls was herded around the huge hangar with megaphones and cattle prods from one stage to another and hectored to look enthusiastic. We'd managed to smuggle in some of our friends, who cheered us on, pretending to be teenyboppers in a post-modern, ironic kind of way and we made a decent fist of it with 'Babies'.

But big deal stuff like doing *TOTP* doesn't stay a big deal for long and it rarely sinks in in the way you might imagine. When I was little I was run over and sat at the side of the road looking at the tyre mark across my leg and thought, 'Hmm, so I've been run over.' Then I noticed a crisp packet and my attention shifted to that, 'What flavour was it? Are blue packets salt and vinegar or cheese and onion?' It was probably shock, but in a way there is the same anaesthetising effect with all these big things.

When you imagine finishing some big thing that has been hanging over you, let's say finishing your exams, you think that the world will open up and you'll be blissed-out and happy and will run to the top of a hill, twirling around with outstretched arms in unburdened joy. Well, this euphoria lasts for a bit, but it's surprising how little duration it has. Within the week, normality has descended and the big deal hasn't really changed much. If only you could bottle this conviction of certain happiness and keep sniffing it, life would be sorted.

My great ambition was to get on *Top of the Pops* and when I'd done it I was quite euphoric for a bit. People asked what it felt like and I said how amazing it was, but after I'd been asked a few times and having to whoop it up in the same way, it felt a bit bogus. But people expect you to be bowled over by it, so you fake it for their sake – it just makes life easier. Within a week, life feels very much on a level and the only way to get more euphoria is to get another hit of fame. So it's an endless mountain, that you pitch a base camp on and feel the satisfaction of achieving that, but you always know that you are only as high as your last base camp and you need to push on up to keep the adrenaline flowing. My trajectory of fame and achievement was always up – however slow and stationary it may have seemed at times. Then I voluntarily chucked myself off the cliff at the top, but it wasn't the absolute top – there is no absolute top.

I met Bryan Adams when he'd been top of the charts for fourteen weeks and the only thing to do was to cling on with fingernails, hoping for another week, because to have done otherwise felt like failure. But for him too it was more for other people; he thought it was mad that he'd been there so long, knew it had to end and was quite cool about that. However, many famous people cling on for dear life and will claw their way up; scratching people's eyes out, abandoning everything that makes them what they are in a desperate bid to get their next fix.

I cottoned on fairly early to the fickle nature of this fame thing and never really put that much store in its triumphs and disasters. I never much fancied the slow slide down, though, and got out well before that. But I can imagine that it doesn't feel very nice to have your freezing fingers lose their grip, one by one. You might cope with it by insulating yourself in a sycophantic bubble, fooling yourself that it isn't really happening, like a dictator in denial. As the realisation dawns that the troops being marched past you are just going round the block and coming back again for show you must convince yourself that you are doing something ahead of its time and vitally important, if misunderstood. There will always be those on your shoulder who keep telling you this.

It's likely that other people in Pulp had a greater addiction to fame than mine because they stayed for longer. I have felt the lure of fame and achievement very keenly and after *TOTP* I was pacing around, waiting for the next hit. Perhaps it's because I saw at this early stage quite how corrosive fame is that I decided to regard it as a dangerous whirlpool. I guess if you don't let it puff you up too high then the comedown will be easier.

34
Jumble-sale Chic

People think that if they've seen you on *TOTP* you must be a millionaire. In reality it only meant that we were finally able to pay ourselves the princely sum of £100 per week. So we still took our washing home to our mums and bought clothes in charity shops – but with £100 a week you can go mad at that.

Buying something interesting from a jumble sale imposes a new look upon you. Whether you like it or not, it says something about you, maybe something you weren't trying to say. When you leave home and start to buy your own stuff you can play around with identity: you can try new looks, new versions of yourself and this affects other people more than it does you because they are looking at you and forming an impression. I never set out to be a mod and only realised I might be considered one on bank holidays in Scarborough when rockers gave me dirty looks. I loved jumble sales and the endless possibilities they offered – getting excited about finding a rare button-down Ben Sherman shirt, a pair of Levi's Sta-Prest, a mohair suit, a pair of two-hole shoes, or a thin Trevira tie. Jarvis got excited about kipper ties, flares and velvet jackets with the widest lapels imaginable. Steve broadly cleaved unto the Jarvis direction but in a toned-down, sexier way and Nick cleaved unto the mod, with a nod to the football manager, Candida did her own indefinable thing. We sometimes found clothes that weren't our style or size and gave them to each other. We loved bargains and brought in our finds to a mixture of ribbing and appreciation. I can't think of a single garment that any one of us wore that anyone else would be seen dead in. So we had our own style, a mash-up of sixties and seventies and glam and mod, which ended up getting called jumble-sale chic.

The newfound riches enabled the drivers to buy a car each, which all cost a few hundred pounds and were quite old. Mine was an Alfasud Cloverleaf, with 'orange peel' finish, Nick's was a gorgeous old crimson Lancia Fulvia and we proud new owners of vintage Italian sports cars sniggered as Jarvis pulled up like Mr Bean in his tiny mustard-yellow Hillman Imp.

Pulp dressed up at a time when bands dressed down and got some funny looks and comments from passers-by. It was sometimes scary to walk about town in the stuff we wore, but our audiences dressed up too and ran the same gauntlet. Once safely inside a Pulp show, being different made you fit in. We weren't just offering songs but a lifestyle and attitude that, as we got popular, people increasingly related to. It fitted with the mood of the time – the song 'Mis-Shapes' best articulates this. In the video Jarvis machine-guns a group of 'townies' who have been harassing him – the perfect nerd revenge-fantasy. (Funnily enough, on that video shoot we got on better with the townie kids than the indie ones.) But, on the whole, our 'fans' were an exciting bunch and it was a joy to meet them. Some of my stage clothes were gifts from them.

We always tried to push what you could get away with onstage – but there was a line we didn't cross; it was always clothes and never costume. If you're a band with the aim of connecting directly with an audience, wearing costume makes it theatre and creates a remove. So we always wore something that could be worn out to a club, a bolder version of ourselves. Because there were clubs at the venues we played at, the clothes were often worn offstage. They were never some big contraption that had to be hoisted off between songs.

35
The Embassy Hotel

I was spending most of my time in London and stayed at The Embassy Hotel, as did Sparks. Ron Mael of Sparks was aware that he had a supposed doppelgänger in me and we had breakfast together, trying to avoid each other's eyes so as not to get locked in an eternal staring competition. Sparks had impeccable manners and breakfast with them is the most quintessentially English thing I've ever done, despite them being American.

Richey Edwards from the Manic Street Preachers also stayed at the Embassy and disappeared one day; he left the hotel and was never seen again. I've no wish to cause distress to those who cared about him, because I didn't know him, but it would be disingenuous to pretend that his disappearance didn't mark my life too. I got a spate of letters from people who had written to Richey and needed someone to talk to: I was the one in Pulp that this psychosis most attached itself to. I didn't really know how to deal with this and tried to be kind but I felt an imposter because I didn't self-harm, nor, despite being thin, was I anorexic. Richey would have known what to say, I didn't – I just used a lot of eyeliner.

36
Blur + Support

Before the first show of the USA tour in Boston we were queuing for food in catering along with the crew and Blur pushed in front with sheepish smiles. I suppose it was fair enough, but we wouldn't have done it. As Captain Scott said, 'That this action is outside one's own code of honour is not necessarily to condemn it,' so I didn't. Then Blur took forever at soundcheck and even ended up working out new material, so we didn't get a soundcheck. Scott would have decked 'em at this point.

It was drizzling, and there were lots of technical problems but the show went on. We played as well as we could and just about got away with it. Blur came on to 'The Self-Preservation Society' from the film *The Italian Job*, which was on constant rotation on their bus. I watched them from the mosh pit and they were great.

After two more shows with Blur we had our own show at The Howlin' Wolf in New Orleans. This involved extra flights (for those foolish enough not to travel on the crew bus) and many thousands of pounds of extra expense.

The Howlin' Wolf had the wrong kind of electricity, I think they were using protons instead of electrons, but we got it fixed by knocking a hole in the wall and running power in from outside. There were ten people in, none of whom had come to see us. They played pool throughout as the staff swept up and put chairs on tables. New Orleans was fun though, especially the voodoo shop where we got essential supplies of alligators' heads, voodoo dolls, gamblers' lucky room-spray and a large and impressive tribal fetish.

It was so hot that the driver had to turn the air-conditioning off so the bus didn't overheat, but we did. El Paso's parched oven-blast heat and pueblo noir gave the working title and spirit to the song that became 'I-Spy'.

Where were we? What did the itinerary say? 'Travel day'. It didn't matter where we were, we were going from somewhere to somewhere and we were in-between.

For the Hollywood Palace show in LA, some perfect mods had driven 600 miles across the desert on scooters without tickets or loosening their ties. I put them on the guest list, which a wily stoat from the record company had left pinned up in the dressing room. It had a host of important industry people and celebrities. Now it should be mentioned that, to amuse themselves, roadies often put *preferred* rather than actual guests down: often sexy ladies and sometimes dead people – Jim Morrison was on the list. Many clubs had permanent places on their guest lists for individuals they hoped might come, like Madonna – someone had ligged under that name.

It was a brilliant concert though, 1,200 people going mad. The real Uma Thurman was doing her *Pulp Fiction* dance at the back and Johnny Depp invited us to go and play an impromptu set at The Viper Room.

On the way we called in at a condo with lots of black leather and chrome where there was a Latino guy in a white suit with a Hawaiian shirt and lapels so wide they were illegal in several states. It was a coke deal and coke deals are much heavier than dope deals. (You've seen the films, right? Well, it's like that.) We sat on a squeaky white leather sofa while the man made sweaty hysterical phone calls. He kept turning round, grinning like a crocodile, to inform us that it was all very cool and, had we got the money? I didn't even do coke and kept making to leave and getting told to sit down because the man would be here in a minute. So, waiting for the man, we missed The Viper Room.

We were in San Francisco for a show at The Fillmore. We went into the hotel and the guy on the desk was a real slacker and looked at us gone out and said: 'What do you want?' and we said 'Rooms' and he said, 'Oh, rooms, to like sleep in and stuff? I don't know if we got those.'

Then the manager came and he was well turned out and sprightly and as big a fan of *The Wizard of Oz* as Candida. Steve put the fetish from the voodoo shop, which was stuck with nails and had a large erect phallus, on the desk. The manager raised an eyebrow and lisped 'Mmm, I see Pulp have arrived'.

There was a swimming pool and our chums Blur were there, so we all ended up in it. Blur did a radio interview where they *jokingly* ribbed Oasis, who were also playing in town, because they'd picked up from us that this was how working-class chappies talked to each other. But Oasis didn't see the funny side and one of them said something nasty in their interview about Justine from Elastica, who was going out with Damon from Blur. This was fighting talk and Blur were cocky because they'd got security. We went down to see Oasis play at a pub in town, where there was a comical stand-off because Oasis had also got security – from the same firm – and the security guards held back the bands. I think Blur were still hoping it was going to end up with them all being friends, but it didn't. So the Blur versus Oasis thing started on that day and in that place, wherever it was.

A visiting member of Blur's crew sociably racked out some lines of coke. Some of our lot took a toot with gusto and others did it because they didn't want to appear like bumpkins in front of the big lads. There was a line left for me. It was generously meant but coke wasn't my bag so I said: 'Nah, mate, I'm cool.' No one called me names for not doing it, but it almost seemed rude not to when someone had so kindly offered. This is how peer pressure works. Dope is better for this than coke, you can take a sociable puff and unselfishly not hog the joint if you aren't into it, but a line of coke is a line of coke and you either snort it or you don't. Thing is, this guy had paid me the compliment – and it was a compliment – of assuming I was an up-for-it fast cat, so it didn't occur to him that I wouldn't want any. So I liked him and we got on, all the more because he didn't ostracise me for not doing coke and I didn't ostracise him for doing it.

By the end of the week there was a two-grand order arriving. Those who were into it huddled together, sharing the diamond pure insights they were microscopically focused on, and talked a right load of fevered nonsense. The lingo of coke was relished and the knowing code phrases got on my nerves: 'It's snowing tonight,' 'The doctor is arriving soon.' A 'doctor', i.e. a coke dealer, arrived, taking the guest-list place of someone else's family member who had travelled to see us.

Coke is a great party drug, it adds sparkle, but it's a terrible habit. I won't say coke turns people into knobheads, but it does release their inner knobhead. There are two kinds of tours; dope tours and coke tours, and dope tours are better.

Canada had very strict entrance checks and for an internationally touring person to be convicted of a narcotics offence was an effective end to their career. As we approached the border the crew set about cleaning the bus of any trace of drugs – they emptied the ashtrays and the bins – then phoned a dealer to score some more once were in Canada.

In Toronto a couple of very determined girls who were watching from sidestage, whilst provocatively doing their lipgloss and talcum powdering their underpants, had succeeded in making friends with the crew – not a difficult task for foxy chicks who boasted of intimate tattoos which they promised to reveal in a more private place.

When we got on the bus, the back room had the general air of a western saloon – with cigarettes, whisky and wild wild women. The tour manager interrupted the reverie with the unfortunate phrase: 'Excuse me, ladies, but we've got to shoot off now.' This had the desired effect, however it was interpreted, and the girls left, having tried vainly to befriend Candida. This was all splendid stuff and everyone was a winner. The girls could hold their heads up high because all their mates would have presumed they were up to no good, because anything *could* have happened. And no one had to have a shag in a toilet looking at the 'No Solids' sign and wake up in a strange town feeling like yesterday's fish and chips.

Although it will disappoint people terribly to learn this, the encounter was our first with 'groupies' as such. The groupie phenomenon really had nothing to do with sex – sex was the ticket price to ride on the bus and everyone wanted to be on the bus. Lots of girls had been interested in us, but they wouldn't and we wouldn't have called them groupies.

There was a horrible thing in the world of seventies rock that I didn't observe in Britpop. Bands onstage would hand out backstage passes to attractive ladies in the audience. Backstage passes in a different colour were obtainable from roadies, in return for bestowing perhaps the flash of an ankle or a fluttered eyelash upon them. These passes were referred to as 'boiler passes' and marked the unknowing girls as second-hand goods. Ugh, men can be so vile.

Peculiarly, there seems to be no male equivalent of the groupie. Many a young Frenchman confessed to having a soft spot for Candida but they would hardly dare talk to her, let alone make a pass or plight their troth and I'm pretty sure it is the same with other female artists, none of whom would garner as many propositions as the most ill-favoured hobbledehoy supporting Shed Seven.

Back in Blighty, we played some more shows supporting Blur – building up to a massive show at Alexandra Palace. There was a warm-up show in Blur's hometown of Colchester in Essex – notable for the number of white stilettos. The Ally Pally show was the zenith of the mod revival and immaculately customised scooters with multiple mirrors, tiger tails and targets promenaded in front of the steps. The world record for the number of fishtail parkas in one place must have been smashed on that day.

Later we played at the London premiere of *Pulp Fiction*, which had a star-studded audience who weren't the least bit interested in us. We were just the house band who happened to have an apt name and I've never felt more like a working-men's-club-turn than at that glamorous occasion.

37
Good Grief Christina!

We went into London's luxurious Townhouse Studios to record the album *Different Class*.

A suave man wearing a long frock coat, with a neck brace covered by a very long, multicoloured woollen scarf turned up. Well, that's the new Doctor Who sorted out I thought.

It was the producer Chris Thomas, who is the greatest genius I have ever had the privilege to work with. He was a big fish and had an infinitely higher profile than Pulp at the time. Landing him was a catch and turned out to be a seminal point in our ascent. His previous album had been with Elton John, but he liked to slum it every now and again and work with upstarts like ourselves.

His method was sympathetic and inspired. If I may draw a dental analogy ... other producers were happy to extract flawed teeth but Chris drilled and filled and straightened and scraped the cabbage off and found the beauty in gaps and crookedness. Previous producers had spent a lot of time trying to get Nick to drum in time. Chris Thomas was the first producer to see a real strength rather than an inconvenience in Nick's tempolexia and took weeks and weeks finding out where the natural rises and falls were. He didn't replace all the imperfect snare hits with copies of the best one but painstakingly took out the worst and replaced faulty ones. He got us all to play together and create something organic if imperfect. To paraphrase Hawkwind he rejoiced in our uniqueness and considered every weakness something special of its own.

I've always avoided influence like the plague, especially contemporary ones. We'd been compared to The Velvet Underground for years before I listened to them. I avoided them like that friend of a friend one is assured one has much in common with and will absolutely love. But I did love the Velvets, especially the violin, and spent many hours trying to figure out how the screech on 'Venus in Furs' was made. I never discovered how to do it but found a lot of interesting screeches along the way, most familiarly at the start of 'Common People', which Chris augmented with a cocktail of fizzing keyboards.

There's a section at the end of 'Common People' where the violin is technically out of tune, it gives a queasy and disquieting feeling to the song. I didn't relish playing it in front of a producer because I'd had run-ins about this kind of thing before. In deference to the man who had produced *Never Mind the Bollocks, Here's the Sex Pistols*, *Let's Stick Together*, played keyboards on *The White Album* and made the first record I'd ever bought ('Good Grief Christina' by Chicory Tip) I'd prepared an alternate version in standard tuning. But Chris would have none of it; he liked the out-of-tune version.

This contrasted to a previous producer who had said of my violin playing: 'If you don't play it better I'm going to go and find the nearest tramp on the street and get him to play it.' He sent me away to rehearse for a week. When I came back, not in a great mood as you might imagine, but prepared to redo the offending part, he said 'There's nothing wrong with the original – you know your problem, you're too much of a perfectionist!' This and other things didn't endear him to me and produced the discontent that lead to us looking for a new producer in the form of Chris Thomas.

Chris was an equally hard taskmaster and often kept me in the hot seat for hours redoing a part, but always to improved effect. He noticed things about my playing that I wasn't aware of, like little halts and slurs that gave a dynamic which I lost when under the pressure of trying to get things down mechanically. We all took a lot more out of the studio than we came in with.

When we first went into the studio 'Common People' was over seven minutes long and sounded like a poor man's Stereolab. But pruning is painful. Luckily Chris, as an artist himself, empathised with our pain and anaesthetised us with honeyed words for the necessary surgery. Authenticity was everything with him and he laboured for six months to produce the album rather than taking any shortcuts. He liked the fact that we brought in lots of crazy ideas and outré instruments and compared it to working with the early Roxy Music.

He had a method rather than a formula and treated every artist with respect and curiosity. For Elton John he conjured up cinematic lushness and for the Sex Pistols he conjured up raw power. He loved the fact that Steve Jones played with such regularity and attack that the guitar could be multi-tracked without creating an excessive chorus effect – I'd pogoed to Chris's sounds. And he knew absolutely everything about everything: the joy of massive rotating Leslie speakers for monumental reverb – but also how not to overuse them; that the cheaper Vox AC 15 amp made a punkier sound than the generally preferred Vox AC 30; that Czech valves made prior to the fall of the Iron Curtain give a warmer sound than the post-communist ones.

He took on board new ideas with gusto, even managing to get some 'jungle' beats onto the song 'Feeling Called Love'. And he could add these seemingly incongruous colours to the palette without jarring the overall tone.

But Chris was no techy nerd and moved in elevated circles way beyond ours. There's an awful lot of hanging about in studios and one day we were watching a documentary about a sculptor whose major work was a life-sized elephant carved out of granite. Chris liked it, got on the blower and got his people to sort out getting it helicoptered into his garden. He had a chauffeur on hand at all times, just in case. The model Helena Christensen would turn up for lunch, Elton John would ring up for a chat (we also learnt that he gave a car as a present to a sound engineer to make amends for shouting at them). A girl I knew called Dylan rang up the studio about something, Chris asked if he could have a word, I didn't know he knew her: 'Hi, Bob!' he said.

Later I answered the phone and a sonorous German voice said: 'It's Nico, is Chris there?'

'Chris, it's for you,' I said, handing the phone over but there was no one there when he answered.

'Who was it?' he said.

'Nico.'

'I doubt it, I went to her funeral.' An odd crank call.

Chris would turn up at small shows when we were playing somewhere glamorous like Marseille in a red boat-backed Alfa Spider with a couple of old-school hippie mates from the sixties who looked like Roman Polanski and Julie Driscoll.

Chris Thomas made us pop stars. He was different class.

FRANCE
2011

38
Minstrel Mayhem

Chris Thomas turns up at Le Bikini and it is lovely to see him and such a shame to not have the energy to carouse with him until dawn, but it's 2 a.m., I'm knackered and have to get my head down.

In the morning, Nancy's smiling parents wave us off from the hotel. Not many parents waving their daughter off on the road with a pop band would have been so relaxed. But Nancy's parents are used to rock and roll and know that it isn't all biting the heads off bats. They feel she is in little moral danger, unaware of the aphrodisiac effect of mineral quizzes on the fairer sex.

Now we are five: this is a good number. We take the long way round avoiding the toll roads, through timeless France.

Jack Clayton has heard tell of the mineral quiz and has prepared a few questions of his own, but the phone line must have been bad.

Jack Clayton: 'Who played Al Jolson in in *The Jolson Story*?

Ralph: 'Larry Parks'

Jack Clayton: 'Where does the sun shine best?'

Ralph (with jazz hands): 'The Swanee River.'

Jack Clayton: 'Who would Al Jolson walk a million miles for?'

Ralph (with jazz hands): 'Mammy.'

And so it goes on – by osmosis and dint of being older I can answer a few of these questions on minstrels, as can Gareth.

But Nancy is absolutely baffled; she picks up her book and reads Sartre in French rather than play this daft game – a sort of low-grade form of self-harm.

The black-and-white minstrels used to be on teatime telly and I just thought they were really boring black people. Later I became aware of their potential for offence and as a radical young man was happy to denounce them.

But these particular specimens of the younger generation have a completely different take on minstrels. Steeped in the post-modern irony that comes from being on a doss course, drinking vodka jellies and spending too much time in the university common room watching *Teletubbies*, *On the Buses* and *Up Pompeii!*, it seems they have developed a secret love for minstrels. As veterans of the 10p record box at charity shops, and having already acquired, *Manuel & His Music of the Mountains*, *No Jacket Required*, *Dare*, *Duke*, *Camp Granada*, *A Golden Hour of Max Bygraves*, Fritz Wunderlich's *Wonderland of Song 3*, Mantovani's *Moonlight Serenade*, *The Joe Loss Orchestra Goes Tropical*, *Top of the Pops Volume 17* and *This is Hardcore*, they ended up, out of curiosity, buying black and white minstrel albums. They'd never seen this stuff on the telly and it seemed surreal and compelling. Might there be an alternate minstrel reality out there – a failed minstrel mission to the moon in the 1930s perhaps?

In the back of a van things get quite surreal after a few hours. The quiz resumes, this time it is 'euphemisms for drugs': reefer, weed, smack, Bolivian marching powder, speed, charlie, snow, brown, skank, green, purple hearts, bombers, gak etc. etc. etc.

'I thought we were going to have a mineral quiz?' says Nancy, pouting. The mineral quiz had gotten quite hardcore, so Ralph goes the other way and asks questions to which the answer might be something lovely, like 'diamond'. This morphs into 'song or artist names with a mineral in the title': 'Ruby Tuesday', 'Gold' 'Diamonds Are a Girl's Best Friend', 'Karma Carnelian', 'Jet'.

It's amazing how few songs use minerals in the title. It's a rich vein to be mined. There's an instrumental concept album out there waiting to be made by some has-been rock star.

Opus I
Amethyst (a bit goth, video set in Whitby)
Beryl (about a girl)
Jade (also about a girl, perhaps a lovely Irish girl with green eyes?)
Emerald (pursuing the Celtic theme, big barnstorming *Riverdance* ending)

Opus II
Quartz (cool and technological, lots of bleeps)
Chrysoprase (bit sci-fi, about a naïve space girl)
Serpentine (meandering and slinky – could feature medieval instrument the serpentine?)
Garnet (also medieval, inspired by finds at Sutton Hoo burial mound, features sound effect of quaffed mead)

Opus III
Lapis Lazuli (arabic sounding, lots of wailing, they could all be girls these, really)
Citrine (harsh, cold and blonde – perhaps inspired by an ex-wife called Gwyneth?)
Onyx (funky, about brief rebound encounter with a mature black lady)
Talc (very soft and touching, homage to a lovely new young wife)

Back to the quiz and it's fictional colours for paint:

'Masquerade' (a subtle violet)
'Jazzdance' (a vibrant fuchsia)
'Poltroon' (an irreverent green)
'Mouse's Ear' (soft grey)
'Marmoset' (dark grey)
'Waltz' (dark blue)
'Brigadier' (pillar-box red)
'Brigadoon' (pillar-box green)
'Pierrot' (the softest of china whites)
'Mortimer' (black with a flush of purple)
'Burlesque' (purple)
'Piccadilly' (bright yellow)
'Marilyn' (pale cream)
'Harlequin' (not sure about this)

Then, it's fictional colours for paint that didn't quite make the cut:

'Buckingham Purple'
'Torpor'

'Gash'
'Rat's Tail'
'Albino's Eye'
'Harlot'
'Camel Toe'
'Clown's Pocket'
'Bogey'

It's a long journey to Barcelona but we've run out of ideas for quizzes now, so, like a gap-toothed gypsy uncle, I try to get Jack to take up a challenge called 'Archimedes'. This requires a water butt, a paddling pool and a lot of beer. The person taking the bet must immerse him or herself in the full water butt, thus displacing a volume of water equivalent to their own body into the paddling pool. The water is then measured and the person has twenty-four hours to drink his or her own body volume in beer. Jack isn't too keen: I can't say I blame him, it's probably impossible.

Then I try and get him interested in a bet called 'Bag of flour in an hour' (please, please, don't try any of these at home), in which the person taking the challenge has to eat a pound of flour in an hour, and then whistle the national anthem. I am explaining the rules to him when I notice he's asleep.

We arrive at the border and Jack wakes up, spluttering. In his dream he has been detained at customs in blackface: unable to explain himself, due to having his mouth gummed up with flour, he is dragged off, waving floury hands and gurning – which only makes him look even more like a minstrel.

We're in Spain now and look around for Spanish things to point at. Gareth puts the bad reggae on and Jack asks me how you get your band signed to a record label. It's a question I'm often asked and I don't really know the answer because it took us ages and we had years of treading water on a small label, which I can't tell you much about. I'd say they were litigious, but they'd probably sue me.

39
Alan's Big Bath

The last time I played Barcelona in 1996 was my final concert with Pulp. We had a great time playing a corporate event for a beer company. They'd pulled out all the stops for their most valued staff members and booked a hip band – us, and a load of models (Linda Lusardi comes to mind). It was well paid too and we were put up for three nights in the very cool Hotel Arts – which was the best hotel we'd ever stayed in and overlooked a giant copper sculpture of a whale. The first comment anyone made was: 'Have you tried the showers?' They were high-powered wet rooms, lined with travertine marble, and squirted water into quite unexpected places. You know you've arrived when you don't steal the toiletries and for the first time I didn't – but it was a pointless gig. We played an old amphitheatre to a happy, ebullient, but not particularly interested audience. It was the first time I'd not given 100 per cent to the performance, but why bother? And if you feel like that, why be in a band at all? I was romantic about Pulp, it'd taken a lot of struggle to get here but I felt pretty cheap playing something like that, it felt like a sell-out.

But Barcelona is a great city: it gives so much and deserves the best anyone can give it back. Part of the allure of doing these shows was the appealing poetic circularity of atoning for ever having taken my foot off the gas enough to become a corporate whore, however unwittingly, just for one day.

Barcelona oozes style at the worst of times and this is the best because Ralph and I are staying in a very swanky hotel. Not only does the hotel look like something from a mojito advert, but the clientele do as well. It manages to be friendly and not at all intimidating, so you can hang around taking an hour over a half of lager – or green tea in Ralph's case.

The rooms are immaculate, but a triumph of style over function. I can get the television to rotate but not come on. And there's the bath: it's immense, the sides are a good foot across and the shampoo comes out of a square chrome Philippe Starck dispenser that holds half a gallon and weighs a stone. When I get in I find myself sloshing from one end to the other, struggling for a handhold. Cursing, I get out to answer the bloody doorbell. It's Jack Clayton. He marvels at the sophisticated gadgetry in the room and I show him the bath, 'Hmm,' he says, 'Alan's big bath.'

Nancy arrives and sits smiling sweetly, twiddling her fringe. A friend from Barcelona called Spanish Anna, who used to live in Sheffield, takes us through a maze of back streets to a little square, which we'd never have found without a native guide. She likes it because, being the haunt of local bands, it reminds her of Sheffield. We have tapas, it's famous for it, and this is where the locals go. I love the idea of tapas and its evolution from bars competing with their free nibbles to attract customers. You can get good tapas in Sheffield and I like to cook it at home but have *never* found anything decent in Spain. This is no exception: there are some croquettes with a sloppy grey filling that mum could have got from Iceland, and a few eggs with piped salad cream and gherkins stuck in that you would have praised a child for making at a party, but diplomatically chucked away afterwards. There is a florid little diced-vegetable salad of the kind illustrated in Marguerite Patten's post-war austerity cookbooks, and a bunch of unhappy cephalopods – which should come under the category of 'creepy crawlies' rather than food.

A man comes round selling bright plastic sunglasses with flashing lights on. I haggle and buy a pair in each colour. Make a nice present for the kids I think, before remembering that my kids are actually grown-up.

Back at the hotel I have chicken tandoori – but somehow, with garlicky tomato sauce and sliced olives, they manage to turn that into tapas.

The show coming up is huge: the waters have retreated, leaving gasping fish, and the distant shadow shakes the ground as it gains strength, looming on the horizon dark and unknowable.

How did I get into this? I'd never so much as tapped the word 'Pulp' into the Internet before this tour. I didn't know how many albums they'd done since I left or even if they'd split up. People were always asking me what Pulp were doing, but I'd really no idea. I knew Jarvis was still one of those annoying pundits on the box, but other than that, I was in the dark.

You know how when you go back to a place that you are familiar with from your youth and everything looks small because you remember it from when lampposts were ten times as big as you? Well, it's the opposite here, because most of my Pulp shows were in transit vans – most of my memories are of us being a small band. There was a short, rather unreal, period at the end when we were playing arenas, but that was quite forgettable. So, in my head, Pulp are a small band.

The pre-production rehearsals for this tour were in a huge purpose-built hanger, the same kind proper big acts use. We'd never done anything remotely on this scale before; we'd never had pre-production rehearsals before. The light show cost ten times as much as anything we'd used previously: it was all a bit unreal, was it really happening, had someone made a miscalculation, was it an elaborate practical joke?

Jarvis is practicing his patter. Some of the stuff he would never really use was a parody of the pig-ignorant rock star trying to connect with the kids. We were offered a show in Singapore: 'Awight, yuh know, when I first came to Singapore, the only fing I knew about it was that you 'ave fackin' great noodles ... yeah? But we've hung around with some *really* cool people and they've shown us some amaaazin' places and I've come to realize that there's so much more to Singapore ... you don't just have fackin' great noodles ... you've got fackin' great rice as well! Awight!'

Jarvis's patter was a big part of the appeal for the audience. When he got it right it worked very well, which was most of the time. But he was always grasping for something connective to say and didn't always have anything. So, rather than just sing he foundered around. In France he fell back on saying; '*ambiance très espéciale*' (very special atmosphere) quite a lot, to the point where I challenged him. What if someone had seen us at another show – wasn't it a bit bogus? Now it's become a joke and he says it in rehearsal quite a bit, though hopefully he'll desist from doing so onstage. It's important not to just trot out the clichés. I wonder what Spanish for 'very special atmosphere' is?

We meet up before the show in Jarvis's seventies wood-panelled hotel. We'd heard that there had been secessionist riots in the city that day, with 100 people hospitalised. They looked pretty much like peaceful protesters on the news and that was the view of the promoters, who ask us to say a few words in support of the demonstrators. Now, we are ignorant about the political situation in Spain, so have a strategy meeting to compose a statement that avoids any nauseating and ill-informed 'If the Basques cool it and the Catalans cool it, it's all gonna be groovy, awight!' nonsense and come up with something that feels apt.

At the venue I see our booking agent Jeff Craft for the first time in many years. We all love Jeff: let me tell you why. He's got a bit of an East End gangster look, with slicked-back hair and he owns racing dogs. He doesn't mince his words either. He was always our sternest critic, seemingly never happy, always pulling a face. After a show I'd ask him if it was all right and he'd wince as if he had toothache and say 'Weeeell, it was okay but, but, but, but, but': there was always something missing for him somehow. I once watched PJ Harvey with Jeff from sidestage. The guitarist scraped his guitar with a steak knife and Polly was Boudicca, Brigantia and Sheela-Na-Gig: Jeff was enraptured. 'This is what's missing from you lot,' he bellowed in my ear. And I think I know what he meant – the transcendental edge-of-madness stuff. That was what I wanted for Pulp but hadn't quite got yet – the kind of concert where it feels appropriate to take your clothes off.

When things were happening for Pulp a friend of ours wanted to promote a festival with us headlining. Jeff's reaction was: 'And where was this friend when you actually needed concerts?'

I was prone to coming up with fanciful ideas for shows that Jeff relished shooting down in flames. For instance, I wanted to tour Russia. Jeff's reaction was apoplectic: 'No, no, no, no, no, no, no. Bands have this patronising idea that they are bringing culture to the poor deprived Russians. Have you ever thought that they might not be that bothered about you? Anyway, if your idea of a good time is losing money while watching your few fans get bludgeoned by riot police, then I can look into it; but I warn you, it's usually something that I resort to at the *end* of a career, not the start.'

He wasn't exactly keen on the notion of a tour of forests either (although the buggers got to do it after I left – one of the few times I had a wisp of regret about leaving).

Then there was the idea of taking a boat round as a venue that concertgoers would come onto at different ports. Many cities are accessible by boat: Manchester, Liverpool, Bristol, London, Edinburgh, Glasgow, Portsmouth – the list goes on. It was deemed impractical:

Top: The swivel-eyed hitcher you don't want to pick up. My passport photo from the early 80s.

Bottom left: Never one to avoid advancing the greater glory of Pulp by resorting to bad taste, I cut out a picture from a Romanian magazine of a man wired up with electrodes – onto which I drew broken glasses to make it look like Jarvis.

Bottom right: From left: Jarvis post-geek, now proto sex symbol; Nick and Candida fighting anorexia with Dairy Milk; me holding a mirror in a Bavarian beaver hunting jacket (why?); Steve pre joining the floppy fringe brigade.

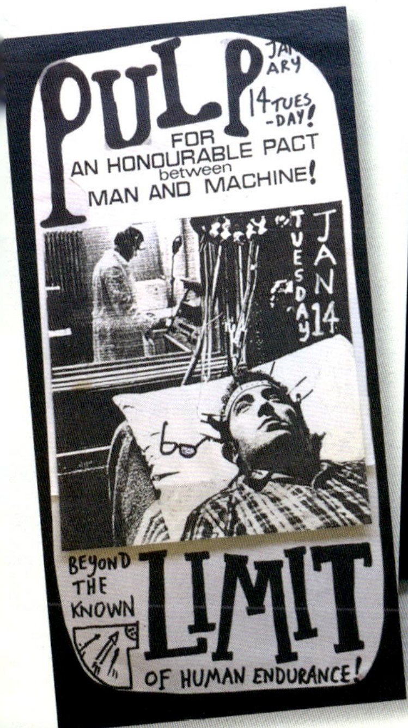

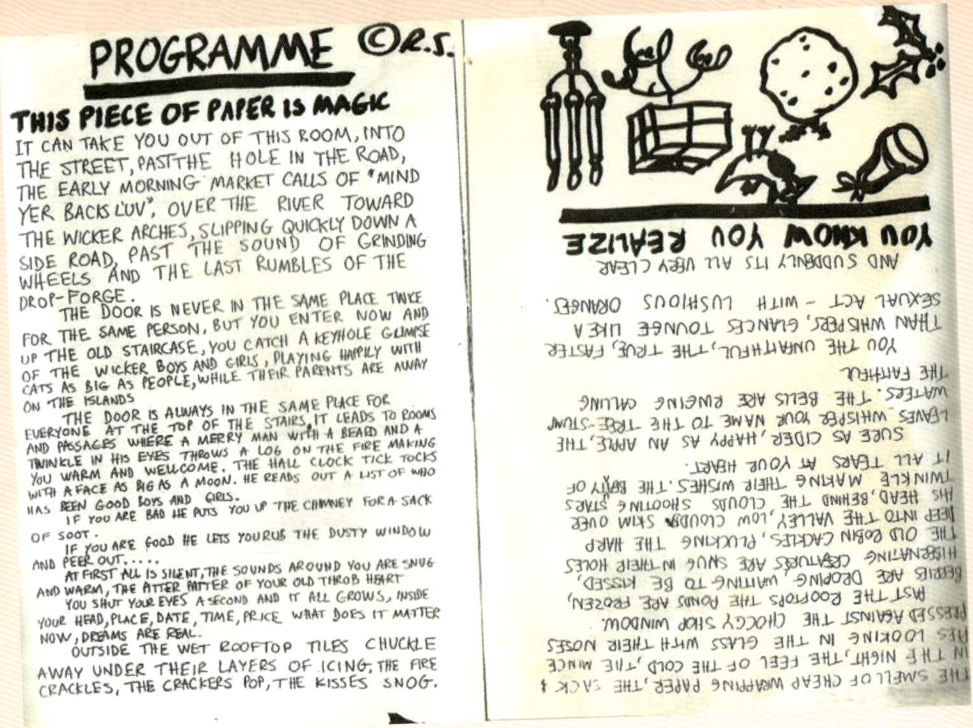

PROGRAMME ©R.S.

THIS PIECE OF PAPER IS MAGIC

IT CAN TAKE YOU OUT OF THIS ROOM, INTO THE STREET, PAST THE HOLE IN THE ROAD, THE EARLY MORNING MARKET CALLS OF "MIND YER BACKS LUV", OVER THE RIVER TOWARD THE WICKER ARCHES, SLIPPING QUICKLY DOWN A SIDE ROAD, PAST THE SOUND OF GRINDING WHEELS AND THE LAST RUMBLES OF THE DROP-FORGE.

THE DOOR IS NEVER IN THE SAME PLACE TWICE FOR THE SAME PERSON, BUT YOU ENTER NOW AND UP THE OLD STAIRCASE, YOU CATCH A KEYHOLE GLIMPSE OF THE WICKER BOYS AND GIRLS, PLAYING HAPPILY WITH CATS AS BIG AS PEOPLE, WHILE THEIR PARENTS ARE AWAY ON THE ISLANDS

THE DOOR IS ALWAYS IN THE SAME PLACE FOR EVERYONE AT THE TOP OF THE STAIRS, IT LEADS TO ROOMS AND PASSAGES WHERE A MERRY MAN WITH A BEARD AND A TWINKLE IN HIS EYES THROWS A LOG ON THE FIRE MAKING YOU WARM AND WELLCOME. THE HALL CLOCK TICK TOCKS WITH A FACE AS BIG AS A MOON. HE READS OUT A LIST OF WHO HAS BEEN GOOD BOYS AND GIRLS.

IF YOU ARE BAD HE PUTS YOU UP THE CHIMNEY FOR A SACK OF SOOT.

IF YOU ARE GOOD HE LETS YOU RUB THE DUSTY WINDOW AND PEER OUT.....

AT FIRST ALL IS SILENT, THE SOUNDS AROUND YOU ARE SNUG AND WARM, THE ATTER PATTER OF YOUR OLD THROB HEART

YOU SHUT YOUR EYES A SECOND AND IT ALL GROWS, INSIDE YOUR HEAD, PLACE, DATE, TIME, PRICE WHAT DOES IT MATTER NOW, DREAMS ARE REAL.

OUTSIDE THE WET ROOFTOP TILES CHUCKLE AWAY UNDER THEIR LAYERS OF ICING, THE FIRE CRACKLES, THE CRACKERS POP, THE KISSES SNOG.

THE SMELL OF CHEAP WRAPPING PAPER, THE SACK & IN THE NIGHT, THE FEEL OF THE COLD, THE MINCE PIES LOOKING IN THE GLASS WITH THEIR NOSES PRESSED AGAINST THE CHOCCY SHOP WINDOW.

PAST THE ROOFTOPS THE PONDS ARE FROZEN, BERRIES ARE DROPING, WAITING TO BE KISSED, HIBERNATING CREATURES ARE SNUG IN THEIR HOLES THE OLD ROBIN CACKLES, PLUCKING THE HARP DEEP INTO THE VALLEY, LOW CLOUDS SKIM OVER HIS HEAD, BEHIND THE CLOUDS SHOOTING STARS TWINKLE MAKING THEIR WISHES. THE BEAUTY OF IT ALL TEARS AT YOUR HEART.

SURE AS CIDER, HAPPY AS AN APPLE, THE LEAVES WHISPER YOUR NAME TO THE TREE-STUMP WATERS. THE BELLS ARE RINGING CALLING THE FAITHFUL

YOU THE UNFAITHFUL, THE TRUE, FASTER THAN WHISPERS, GLANCES TOUNGE LIKE A SEXUAL ACT – WITH LUSHIOUS ORANGES.

AND SUDDENLY ITS ALL VERY CLEAR

YOU KNOW YOU REALIZE

Top: A flyer for a Leadmill Christmas show in the mid-80s.

Bottom left: A poster in bold council-house door colours.

Bottom right: A hand-drawn flyer in oil pastel – it was the 80s.

Left: At this stage in our career I produced more promo material in Serbo-Croat than English.

Right: Yet more Serbo-Croatian promo.

Bottom: My ridiculously over-complicated stage notes with directions for various smells and costume changes accompanying songs for a show preposterously conceptualized as 'The Day that Never Happened'.

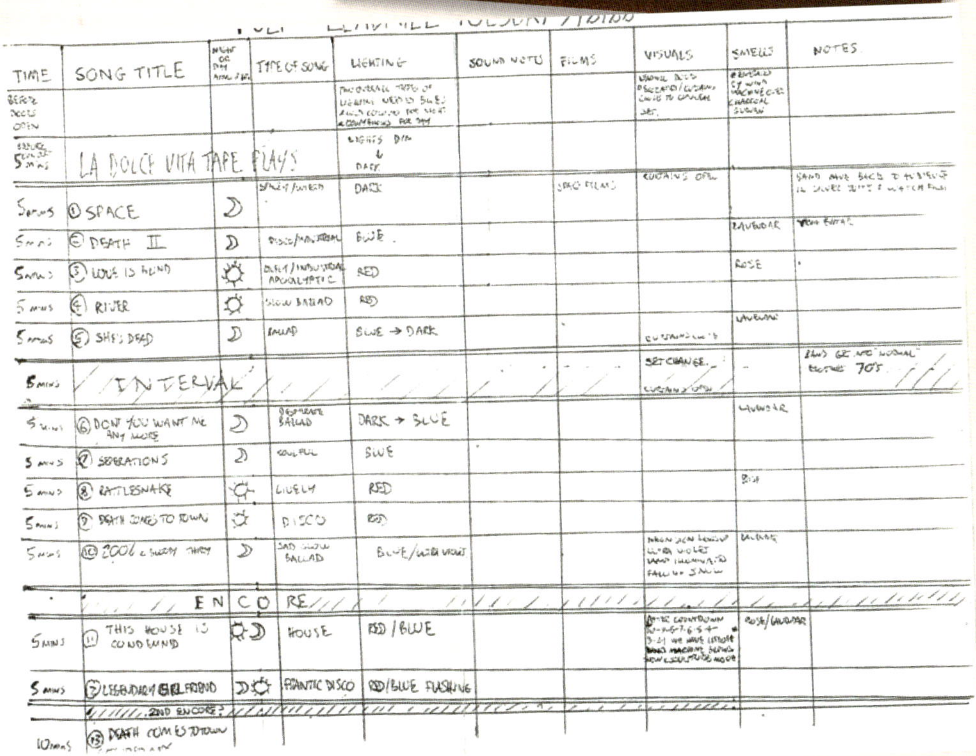

TIME	SONG TITLE	NIGHT OR DAY	TYPE OF SONG	LIGHTING	SOUND NOTES	FILMS	VISUALS	SMELLS	NOTES
BEFORE DOORS OPEN									
5 MINS	LA DOLCE VITA TAPE PLAYS			LIGHTS DIM ↓ DARK					
5 MINS	① SPACE			DARK		SPACE FILMS	CURTAINS OPEN		
5 MINS	② DEATH II		DISCO/[illegible]	BLUE				LAVENDAR	
5 MINS	③ LOVE IS BLIND		[illegible]/INDUSTRIAL APOCALYPTIC	RED				ROSE	
5 MINS	④ RIVER		SLOW BALLAD	RED					
5 MINS	⑤ SHE'S DEAD		BALLAD	BLUE → DARK				LAVENDAR	
5 MINS	INTERVAL						SET CHANGE. CURTAINS OPEN		BAND GET INTO "NORMAL" CLOTHES 70'S
5 MINS	⑥ DON'T YOU WANT ME ANY MORE		DESPERATE BALLAD	DARK → BLUE				LAVENDAR	
5 MINS	⑦ SEPERATIONS		SOULFUL	BLUE					
5 MINS	⑧ RATTLESNAKE		LIVELY	RED				ROSE	
5 MINS	⑨ DEATH COMES TO TOWN		DISCO	RED					
5 MINS	⑩ 2006		SAD SLOW BALLAD	BLUE/ULTRA VIOLET					
	ENCORE								
5 MINS	⑪ THIS HOUSE IS CONDEMNED		HOUSE	RED / BLUE				ROSE/LAVENDAR	
5 MINS	⑫ LEGENDARY GIRLFRIEND		FRANTIC DISCO	RED/BLUE FLASHING					
	2ND ENCORE?								
10 MINS	⑬ DEATH COMES TO TOWN								

Top: From left: Me, Jarvis and Steve. The craving for baggy in Manchester produced such a shortage they had to import it from Sheffield. I think this may have been from the 'New Sessions', a regional Manchester-based late night music show in 1991.

Left: Signing records or possibly underwear.

Top: Immediately after Le Circle De Minuit in Paris, 1994. Despite appearances the other chap is not in Pulp – we missed a trick there.

Bottom: At home with my daughter enjoying a huge haul of charity shop finds including: sunglasses, *The Egyptian Book of the Dead* and the jacket of a small town American mayor – a polaroid from a session for *Select* magazine c1992.

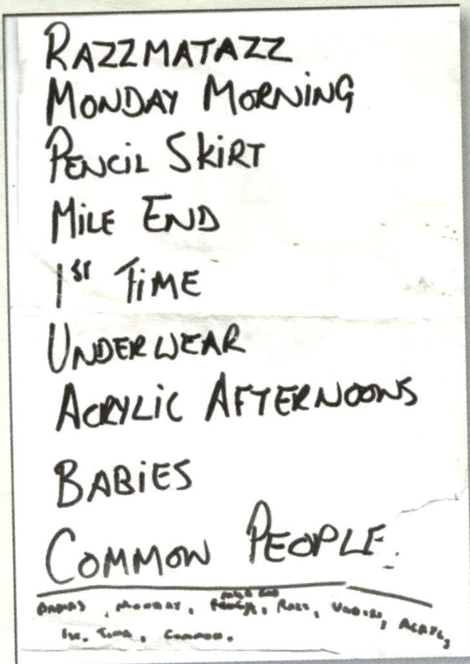

Top left: Set list.

Top right: We are the mods.

Bottom: 90's Candida, Nick, Steve, Jarvis and me.

Top: From left: Candida, me, Jarvis, Mark, Brian Eno (giving us the Mercury Music Prize) and Steve. Free champagne really screws you up.

Bottom left: Slowpoke enjoying the tour in 2011.

Bottom right: The English 1933 Rules of Poker that I insisted be printed in our itineraries to stop brawling.

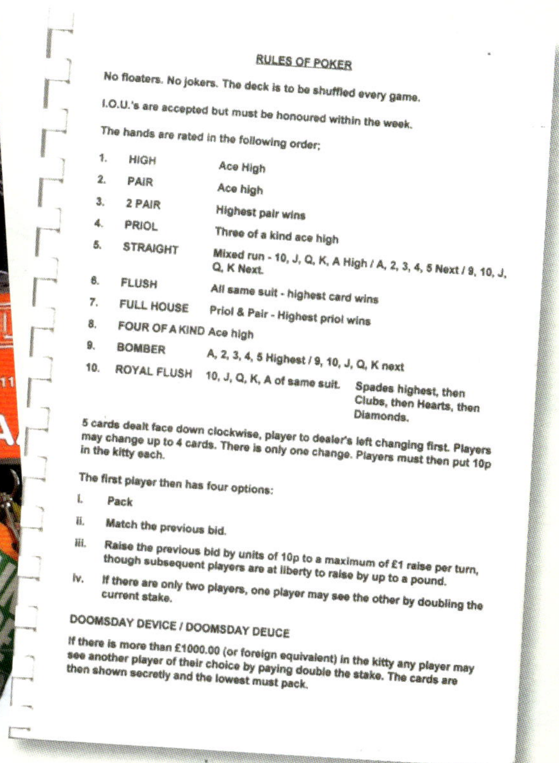

RULES OF POKER

No floaters. No jokers. The deck is to be shuffled every game.

I.O.U.'s are accepted but must be honoured within the week.

The hands are rated in the following order;

1.	HIGH	Ace High	
2.	PAIR	Ace high	
3.	2 PAIR	Highest pair wins	
4.	PRIOL	Three of a kind ace high	
5.	STRAIGHT	Mixed run - 10, J, Q, K, A High / A, 2, 3, 4, 5 Next / 9, 10, J, Q, K Next.	
6.	FLUSH	All same suit - highest card wins	
7.	FULL HOUSE	Priol & Pair - Highest priol wins	
8.	FOUR OF A KIND	Ace high	
9.	BOMBER	A, 2, 3, 4, 5 Highest / 9, 10, J, Q, K next	
10.	ROYAL FLUSH	10, J, Q, K, A of same suit.	Spades highest, then Clubs, then Hearts, then Diamonds.

5 cards dealt face down clockwise, player to dealer's left changing first. Players may change up to 4 cards. There is only one change. Players must then put 10p in the kitty each.

The first player then has four options:

i. Pack

ii. Match the previous bid.

iii. Raise the previous bid by units of 10p to a maximum of £1 raise per turn, though subsequent players are at liberty to raise by up to a pound.

iv. If there are only two players, one player may see the other by doubling the current stake.

DOOMSDAY DEVICE / DOOMSDAY DEUCE

If there is more than £1000.00 (or foreign equivalent) in the kitty any player may see another player of their choice by paying double the stake. The cards are then shown secretly and the lowest must pack.

Top: After multiple pileups with time's winged chariot, make sure you always have a guitar redder than your face. Glastonbury, 2011.

Right: The Werewolf hotel, France, 2011.

Bottom: 2011 – The Palm Court Orchestra entertains.

apparently the only viable way to do it would be to have the band travel by boat and then play the concert in a normal venue, with the crew travelling separately. This negated the whole whimsical point of it. But the thing is, despite the initial hurdles he threw up, Jeff always looked into the ideas to see if it was possible. He was up for doing things differently but was just practical and honest about it, which is all you can ask.

When we toured Europe in the nineties we were going on in the afternoon, fifteenth on the bill. This time we are the main attraction. Barcelona was the first show announced, it sold out fast: setting a record for the festival. The main reason most people are coming to Barcelona is to see us, so no pressure then.

It's headline-act treatment too, something we are largely unaccustomed to at festivals. There is a catering tent and a chill-out lounge but the nerves are still there, no matter how nice the vol-au-vents.

We are going on after Belle and Sebastian, a quiet introspective outfit who won't drain the audience of every emotion left in their souls – yippee!

So we pace and hyperventilate and shout and do our warm-up routines and very late, after an age of tension, walk towards the stage. Are we conquering heroes or condemned men?

It is a charged atmosphere in Barcelona tonight. After the riots, which seem to signal a new push in the historic aspirations of the Catalans, not to mention the fact that Barca are playing Man U in the Champions League final tomorrow, the air fair crackles with static.

Words flash up on the screen, concealing us from the audience and the audience goes mad, even to that. To say this is an eagerly anticipated show would be an understatement.

The opening bars of 'Do You Remember the First Time?' start and we have a little look round and give a nod of acknowledgement to each other and prepare to strike.

Bang! We're in: the audience bounces and heaves, they know all the words. And we're good: no, sod that, we're brilliant, really on it. I'm no longer fifty with a bad back. I do some rather elegant kicks but as the monitors aren't rigged for jumping I fill in with some moves that I've nicked from Jack Clayton, who is standing stageside. I give him a minstrel jazz-hands in acknowledgement. There are banners saying '*Viva la revolución, viva los common people*' waving as Jarvis delivers the well-measured piece we'd composed earlier – along the lines of, but more eloquent than: 'We've been asked to say something about the trouble in town today and I don't normally get involved in things I don't know much about … but I do know this … when 100 peaceful protesters end up in hospital there's gotta be something wrong … so this song's for them … it's called "Common People".' He's got the tone spot on … and it explodes. We play all the big hits, they love it: we connect and come off in buzzing triumph. All the hard work, all the turning over of stones-best-left-unturned, has been made worthwhile by this one show. We're like a team celebrating winning the FA Cup and I'd venture to suggest that, in many ways, it's much deeper than that. All those years coming round on themselves, all that doubt, all gone in an instant of euphoria drenched in revolutionary glamour. Wow.

I ask Jeff Craft how it was: 'Weeeell,' he says, 'it was great, you know, obviously the audience loved it but, but, but, but, but … and the set list isn't *quite* working and, and, and, and, and … ' (all things he was right about by the way). But I saw the same look on his face that I'd seen as he watched PJ Harvey, and knew that we'd nailed it.

So that was an up. No sleep then, but so what. We 'liberate' the remains of the complementary food and drink for the long journey back to Blighty but Jack and Nancy don't want to come. They want to keep the party going and stay to check out the vibes. The vibes are that the audience left hours ago, the venue is shut and the only people that remain are sweeping up, so they have a long walk back, but such is youth.

40
Werewolf Hotel

During the planning, we'd attempted to leave as much open to chance as possible and had no accommodation booked for the long drive back to England. The route doesn't take us through any population centres and lacks hotels beyond the alienating travel-tavern type. The camper van affords us the luxury of being able to do this as, at a pinch, we can sleep in it, though it would feel pretty rum to do so after headlining a festival.

We bid a fond adieu to Barcelona and – on the advice of a truck driver, who tells us that this is a scenic route, with a bridge worth seeing – head north towards Millau. Out of Spain and into the Midi, on an empty road that sweeps past limestone gorges riddled with caves. The drama of the landscape increases as the road winds through the Massif Central, under crag and over ravine, until the Millau bridge takes our breath away: arching gracefully beyond the precipices it spans, immense tapering pillars throwing down spidery stays that hold the whole improbable edifice as it curves lightly in the air.

There is one hotel vaguely en route, with a strangely antiquated-looking website. Ralph seems to think he might have accidentally booked it. There is no confirmation email, as is usual, but a grandiloquent and courtly request for us to await a telegram pops up on the screen before fading out. So it's all a bit up in the air.

A stop at a complex that specialises in candied angelica, where Gareth wanders off to collect brightly coloured flints only to receive a vigorous chapeauing. Another shop that makes a big to-do about cassoulet, displaying it in jars – assuring content and quality by revealing the oddments of dismembered fauna, snouts, wings and webs pressed distorted against the sides of the glass. At twilight the proprietor of a small petrol station fails to answer the bell, leaving me to peruse a wall dedicated to postcards featuring only bilberries and wolves.

Small deer skip off into the undergrowth, birds of prey circle in the spiralling updrafts over volcanic peaks. Gareth says that you never catch up on lost sleep, you never get it back, but Gareth says axolotls turn into newts.

We enter the decaying spa-town – whose ornate cornices, oval windows and porticoed doorways are decorated with recumbent putti, bundles of lictors, swags of husks and bursting baroque pomegranates – and drive between stone pillars, down a gravel driveway to the front of the hotel. It's late and we don't want to make a commotion in this silent town, so tiptoe whispering along the crunching gravel and tip our hats to a grande dame who greets us outside: it seems we are expected.

Now this is the truly strange bit. Everyone is in clothes at least a century old. A monocled man who looks like the Kaiser wears a cummerbund and monstrance-like medals on a silk sash. Women in ballgowns and tiaras float through the foyer. There is no wedding, the people are old and it is quite late, no mobile phones go off, there are no keycards, no signs of modernity whatsoever.

The porter is a lupine man who stays uncomfortably long, gazing at me with piercing blue eyes, lolling his head inquisitively first to one side then the other until I gave him a tip. There's a full moon and I hurry out to find Gareth and Ralph but get lost in the narrow creaking corridors and have to squeeze past an ancient crone in a ballgown, who smiles through flaking make-up as she lifts up her hooped skirt, showing her bloomers. In the foyer a woman, also in a ballgown, suckles an infant on her exposed breast. I ask the grand dame where the others are and she says that she has directed Gareth to a nearby park to spend the night in the van. She leads me to Ralph, who is sat alone eating at a table laid with ornate silver on a white linen tablecloth in a vast banqueting hall where every table is set for dinner, with huge floral displays. Four liveried waiters dance attendance.

Me: 'What's all this for? We're the only diners and it's almost midnight.'

Ralph: 'We're the only guests, apparently, the others are the townspeople … and they've invited us to "join their little gathering".'

Me: 'It's funny, isn't it?'

Ralph: 'Yes it's very funny, I've tried ringing Gareth but I can't get through, I thought it might be better for us to sleep in the van too.'

We go to our rooms, which are on opposite sides of the hotel. I try to put the strange hotel out of my mind as the wind brings a distant howl from the volcanic hills. Not having slept the night before and having drunk some wine, I nod off. It was as if the hotel had been waiting for us; poised immobile, only springing into a jerky clockwork dance at our arrival. Was I already dead; was this some anteroom to hell in a portmanteau horror film?

I'm relieved in the morning to be still alive; the hotel, while certainly old-fashioned, has a less sinister air. The company of revellers has departed and people in at least twentieth-century clothes have returned to the world. In the warm light of day, the travails of the night before seem comic. At the time it was genuinely disturbing, only ameliorated by the ever-present sense of surreal absurdity. It strikes me what an excellent horror short it would have made if we had joined the 'little gathering' as honoured guests, or perhaps 'main course'. The *Our Man in Havana* attire Ralph and I were wearing, while not as antiquated as the others, was certainly old school and didn't jar with the mood. We were also travellers from another era. It was just a moment that happened, will be there in the past for ever, but now is gone, evaporated by the morning sun.

We wander off in search of Gareth.

Gareth's pay, like most professional drivers, includes a stipend to cover accommodation and he could have stayed with us. Most drivers spend about one night in three at a hotel to freshen up, thereby boosting their income considerably. Gareth likes sleeping in the van though; there are washing facilities and an endless supply of bad reggae, so he's happy.

And there he is: I reach for my chapeau but he's seen me, one chapeau to Gareth.

He's sitting in the town square with his shirt and cap off; the cap is full of money. It turns out that as he was sitting there, with his forlorn puppy face, a well-to-do local, mistaking him for a beggar, had thrown some coins into his cap. Gareth said '*Merci*' and another local, moved on this fine morning to charitable competition, had outdone the first. Gareth made to remove the money, but its jingle attracted others, who added to the haul. After a while he ceased trying to explain and sat there allowing his wages to be topped up.

Unlike most professional drivers, Gareth smokes relaxing herbal tobacco. This is banned in the van and he periodically goes off for a crafty toke. At first I'm a bit nervous about his smoking habits, as well you might be, but Gareth, who doesn't drink, explains that 'It's like my Ovaltine.' Hang on, doesn't that send you to sleep? I've given up on safety and taken to lying down in the back, listening to him regaling us with tales of derring-do in caves as we head north.

In need of a less frightening nocturnal adventure, Monsieur Ralph rings Tatyana to see if there are any spare rooms for us. There are and my favourite green leather armchair has a '*Réservé pour Monsieur Russell*' sign on. It seems another lifetime ago that we were last here and it's good to be amongst friends. Somewhat to my surprise, hotels are very accommodating to the louche group of people from our party, who drape themselves nonchalantly around their communal areas. You see, people don't dress up much these days and you are much more likely to see a tracksuit in the lobby of a high-class hotel than anyone in a suit and tie. So, despite our slightly disreputable air, we count as welcome glamour.

41
Kate Moss Pulls it Off

Some days later, we're stuck in traffic on the M1 on our way to the Isle of Wight Festival. A chap comes over and strikes up a conversation; he's the typical 'gift of the gab' salesman type from Leeds, friendly but on the make. We await the inevitable pitch for life insurance, timeshares or health supplements, but it turns out that his wife needs the loo. Oh dear, how awkward. You see, to put none too fine a point on it, shit smells and what goes in the loo stays in the loo and you really don't want to have that in your cramped living room. We show him the loo, which is piled up high with instruments, so he doesn't feel too bad about it, but there you go. The bushes are over there, mate.

The news comes round the cars that the delay will be three hours. Some lads start a game of football, we offer water to people with kids and a beer and some bog roll to the chatty Leeds chap. So it's the spirit of the Blitz. A camper van is absolutely the best vehicle to have in such an event; you can make a beverage of your choice and lie on the settee, looking at the sun through the overhead window – a very English form of bliss.

It's a longish way to the New Forest, where we are staying, but after the drive to Toulouse it's nothing really. I like wildernesses, and forests in particular, and this is one I've never seen. As we enter, it promises to deliver but never quite does. After an appealing stretch of woodland there is always something a bit pedestrian round the next corner: a golf course, a stolid five-bedroomed retirement dream with stone-effect cladding, a country club Alan Partridge would like to join.

Things improve and trees of notable stature line the route. We turn into a long gravel drive (always a good sign). The hotel is a manor house of the 'not quite as old as it appears' type from the late nineteenth or early twentieth century. The former pile of some magnate made good with a penchant for the Gothic. I like these kinds of places, but wouldn't want to be a caretaker in the winter. There is a lot of oak panelling and a teddy bear on the bed, which is for sale at an exorbitant price. Many hotels do this shameless form of emotional blackmail. Try telling a five-year-old that the bear they have named and fallen in love with can't come home. Try telling Ralph!

The grounds are rambling and appealing in a melancholy kind of way. Such places seem to sigh with the memory of a time when people did things properly and befitting of their dignity. The staff are polite and all call me 'Mr Senior', even when passing in the corridors. Good hotels pride themselves on this kind of personal touch – electrocute their staff until they can do it. But it's utterly bogus, this isn't the 1920s: I haven't struck up a rapport with the commissionaire, formed whilst trying to smuggle a showgirl out of my room; nor had my monocle retrieved from an errant dachshund by Betsy the parlour maid. I wish it were the 1920s.

Ralph and I take a stroll over the croquet lawns, get lost in the overgrown maze, and follow a green woodpecker through the forest. But, through the redwoods thick, we espy the smoking Gareth's shining eye. He's home alone, well off the main drag in a sylvan dell. This is a bonanza, a chance for an unprecedented double-chapeauing. We sneak through, hugging the trees 'Nam-style, and come up behind him. 'Chapeau!' he cries four times, banging his hat down on each of us in turn. He'd circled round the van and not only foiled our chapeauings but got two of his own. Damn you, Gareth! Damn your woodland skills.

Me: 'Gareth, are you "hard"?'

Gareth: 'Not at the moment.'

Me: 'No, I mean, we've been offered concerts in South America, I was wondering if you could double as a bodyguard?'

Gareth: 'Well, yeah, I suppose so … I've put a couple of guys in hospital for trying to nick me chain.'

This is a surprise, there's not an ounce of aggression in him. It transpires that it was all a terrible misunderstanding and something of an aberration. A keener observer of social signals might have already noticed the chunky gold chain round Gareth's neck which says: 'I'm confident enough to wear this, you might be able to get it off me, but you won't find it easy because it's still there and so am I.'

On show day we pick up Rover, Rover's mate and Rover's mate's girlfriend at the port. Innsmouth is an old-fashioned port sinking into the sea, which runs a small wooden ferry twice a day in the summer months. We chug past creek-wound mudflats, where lonely whippoorwills keen at sun-bleached crabs trapped in the samphire marshes by the receding tide.

The part of the Isle of Wight we pass through lacks any discernable magic or mystery, the towns are decidedly no-frills suburban in architecture and more likely to boast a Lidl than a blacksmith.

A lot of the bands playing the festival are doing an almost endless round of touring. It must be hard to make it special and unique when you have the name of the place written on the back of your hand so you don't forget it.

The backstage area has Seasick Steve, Foo Fighters and Iggy Pop, so it's all 'Hey, man, how ya doin'?' Yank stuff. I've seen Iggy play a few times and he's definitely in the top-ten hard acts to follow. All those songs that I've danced to, and now here he is saying 'Hey, man' as we squeeze past in the corridors. I'm not sure whether the correct form of address for such a legend is the presumptively familiar 'Iggy', or the preposterously formal 'Mr Pop'.

I'm always outraged when my punk rock heroes do adverts. If I have been sold a dream of freedom and rebellion, I don't want it cashed-in to sell me a product. 'I am the passenger and I ride and I ride – if you've been a passenger injured in an accident that wasn't your fault then don't hesitate to call … oh, what, you don't insure musicians?' I have no lust for life insurance: neither, I suspect, does Iggy. But then he never pretended to be anything much and doesn't really give a damn. I go and watch him from the crowd and he's ace as ever. I sing along to 'Search and Destroy' with the hairs on the back of my neck standing up.

It's a really nice atmosphere at the festival; the fad of the day is daisy-chain flowers in girls' hair. People sit picnicking on the floor in what for a moment feels like a new Summer of Love.

There are quite a number of areas set aside for corporate hospitality that my pass won't get me into. Inner sanctums always inspire curiosity – 'I don't know what they've got, but they're laughing a lot behind the green door.' Clubs with those roped-off VIP areas make you wonder what kind of delirious excess goes on there to make them so worth paying for.

Here's the truth: it's all a great big con. The best parties are outside the inner sanctums. The inner sanctums are solely for the kudos of depriving others of access, feeling good by making others feel bad. It's a form of segregation and snobbery that was abolished centuries ago in other walks of life. There is such a thing as a good party you might not be able to get into – but if that party has some special area that is denied to most people, then I've never known one to be better than the party outside; there are fewer people for a start.

At a huge venue there were no fewer than five layers to this onion – and, out of curiosity, I made a point of getting through them all. So the final VIP platinum-pass-only area had two burly security guards outside and inside was one middle-aged man sitting at a bar crying into his beer: possibly the Ghost of Myself Future, if I kept pursuing this kind of exclusivity. I went back out through the layers, without having found Prester John or the Holy Grail, and ended up at the swinging party I'd left. People were still hustling to get a pass, and I didn't blame them, I'd been the same. There's a moral in this maze somewhere.

One of the imagined horrors of embarking on such a reformation was the prospect of middle-aged ladies who ought to know better wearing feather boas reliving the glory days of Britpop. Kate Moss, Sadie Frost and their mates are celebrating a hen-do by going round the summer festivals in a pink stretch limo. They ask if they can come and dance on stage while we're playing. We say no and in the end I'm glad because a more biddable band say yes and it's a bit naff to see them all carrying infants in arms and staggering drunkenly about waving feather boas in the air – completely upstaging the band and shattering any willing suspension of disbelief that might otherwise have been conjured.

I don't remember any details about the show other than that it was good: if you were there then we shared that.

On the way back, Rover and guests are 'ver ver' drunk. At the ferry port some piss-taking youths are mocking our camper van – the very idea! Rover's mate's girlfriend tells them to piss off: oh dear, I really can do without this. They go outside and slag each other off for a bit but thankfully it ends in camaraderie. It is revealed that a member of Pulp is on the bus and there is banging on the walls and a chorus of 'Common People', which is fortunately the only song they know – cheers guys. Flushed with the success of the conflict, Rover makes increasingly obvious passes at his mate's girlfriend. Uncomfortably, a hand-on-posterior incident is observed in the appropriately named 'rear view' mirror. Rover's mate has his head in his hands when they come back onto the bus; he is not a happy camper. But Rover is oblivious, homing in for the kill with his you-know-you-want-it-you-dirty-cow-type comments. By adding a homeopathically small drop of irony to a gallon of such innuendo, he can just about get away with it in his own addled head.

The piss-taking youths, who are now Rover's bestest-ever mates invite us to spend the night on their yacht (kids have yachts here?). On the ferry, Rover manages to split his head open, he doesn't remember how but seems rather proud of it. He's still being a complete bastard but, sad to say, some ladies, especially when drunk, like bastards.

The main thought on Ralph's mind is: how on earth do we get rid of them? We don't want to turn up at that hotel with this lot at four in the morning and dump them and their shenanigans on Gareth for the night. But Gareth's okay, he's had his Ovaltine and can sleep through the inevitable coitus.

For Rover, the morning brings headache and remorse. His friend is so irked with him that he has not yet dared to return to his hometown.

So that one got a bit messy and I'm in no hurry to repeat it, it was something of an aberration compared with the general tone of the tour. Onwards and upwards to the next show: a secret appearance at Glastonbury.

1995 GLASTONBURY FESTIVAL

42

No, Friends Are *Not* Electric!

In the middle of the recording of *Different Class*, the headline act at Glastonbury that year, The Stone Roses, had to pull out and we were offered their slot. Crikey! There were only days to go and we bashed out a few quick rehearsals while continuing work on the album. We weren't a big band at the time and would have otherwise warranted an afternoon slot on one of the lesser stages. In a studio you are hermetically sealed from the outside world like a *Big Brother* contestant; living on a diet of takeaway food, Sonic the Hedgehog and ping pong. We'd got reports that 'Common People' was doing well but, used to the hyperbole of the record business, hadn't really given it much mind. What we were only too aware of was that The Stone Roses were *huge* and most people had paid their ticket price to see them. We fully expected to get bottled off by irate Mancunians. We were also pretty convinced that we weren't really an outdoor band at all, being more suited to the intimate surroundings of a small seedy club, preferably one with no windows.

And things can go horribly wrong at Glastonbury. There is footage of our mates The Boo Radleys playing their hearts out to 'Lazarus', unaware that their bald heads were steaming twenty-foot vapour trails into the air like hot Christmas puddings. The morning when they woke up and watched that playback would not have been a beautiful one.

Backstage we met Robbie Williams, who had just left Take That. My daughter was at an age where she might have been expected to be rather wowed by him. She wasn't and he was a bit crushed. More excitingly, we met our punk rock heroes Rat Scabies and Joe Strummer, who knew and liked our music. Gary Numan was there too and Rover, who had been watching him from stageside and rolling on the floor with laughter said to him: 'Gary, in answer to your previous question, *no*, friends are *not* electric!' But this was and we had to go on feeling like lambs to the slaughter.

It was all a bit unreal and, as we took to the stage, we kept a wary eye out for projectiles: an art in which Pulp were well practised. The lights shone in our eyes, so we couldn't see the audience and a strong wind blew any sound away, so it was hard to keep in time and in tune. We didn't play terribly well and thought we were absolutely dying. But years of playing small venues with bad sound had taught us to at least be able to suppress the internal wince and go through the motions convincingly. So we strutted and postured and Jarvis gave it out to the audience as only he knows how, but there was a horrible sinking feeling. I thought I knew the difference between a good show and a bad show and that was most decidedly a bad show. The wind occasionally brought a little ripple of polite applause but not the roars we were used to when we played to 600 people. There is a huge gap between the band and audience and we were accustomed to playing off intimacy and direct eye contact. Which is why, when at the end the lights were turned on the audience, and we saw the ecstatic multitude going mad and singing along with 'Common People' it just didn't compute. It was unreal, like a slow-motion car accident.

We came off and everyone was slapping us on the backs, saying how amazing it was. But as a band on the up you get used to sycophancy and Jarvis and I were very down – we got quite angry with the people bulling us up. Only when the normally undemonstrative Jeff Craft came and raved about how fantastic it was did we believe it really *was* amazing, at least for the audience – and there was no refuting the reaction to 'Common People'.

So there it was, a legendary concert. We were the perfect underdogs to melt the hearts of that crowd and the music we were making perfectly encapsulated the zeitgeist of the moment, so it was a triumph. This isn't false modesty: I think Pulp are definitively one of the best live bands of all time, I'd hold our live performances as our greatest achievement; far outweighing our recorded output, which never quite did it for me. After that show we were about three times as big as we were the day before and the whole thing kicked into overdrive. But, honestly, we've done loads of better shows than that.

2011 GLASTONBURY FESTIVAL

43
A Man With a *Lot* of Piercings

We are making a surprise appearance at Glastonbury, the scene of our 1995 triumph – described by John Peel as 'the best concert of all time'. In the run-up it has been imperative that we keep the concert secret. We were contractually obliged not to advertise any shows before the Isle of Wight, and the Glastonbury show would have had to be pulled if news had got out. Of course, there has been speculation and rumour, but as long as it hasn't come from us, it remains just that.

I drive Ralph and myself to Bath, where we are staying. The journey has become faster and one loses the sense of travelling through changing regions, from the grim north with its smokestacks and cooling towers to the bountiful south-west of thatched cottages, mistletoe decorated orchards and swanny rivers. Bath is as beautiful as ever.

Ralph and I try to scope out something that young people might like, as my daughter will be joining us tomorrow. We go under Pulteney Bridge and almost walk past a doorway leading down into dark vaults. Intrigued, we go back to the doorway and peer into what looks like it might be a kooky, but closed, shop. It's hard to tell what it is: there's a lot of detail, a boar's head with a top hat on, things in cabinets, the suggestion of a shisha bar. Unsure as to whether we are supposed to be there we prepare to leave and, as if by magic, a shopkeeper appears. 'What can I get for you?' he says. Amongst all the other things we'd missed the spirit bottles, it's a bar of sorts. There are further rooms, each with a different colour and theme. The genius that put this together must have been a fan of Edgar Allan Poe, Aubrey Beardsley and Lewis Carroll. Extracts from Milton's description of Pandemonium snake round the doorway in a psychedelic art-nouveau script. There are pouffes, and chill-out areas strewn with rugs and scatter cushions. Daughter will love this.

The day after, Gareth picks us up to go to the show and, after the usual Glastonbury inefficiency and mud, we eventually find our way backstage.

Word has got out that we are playing and the viewing area, which holds 40,000 people, filled up hours ago. Beyond that there are biblical multitudes watching from vantage points on the hills.

Sometimes bands take these mystery guest slots as an opportunity to inflict a lot of new material on an audience. This is a mistake we won't make, as we have not even spent five minutes jamming, let alone attempting to write. The task of learning all the old songs was just too big and I, for one, hadn't signed up to rejoin Pulp on a permanent basis. The last time we played Glastonbury most of the songs were unknown to the audience, but they knew the songs this time.

So, like a boxer warming up, or a tennis player shouting at themselves to gain concentration, I pick up my instrument, doing some robotic twitch-mantra of remembrance. And we're on.

I always used to keep a stern face onstage, not wishing to be one of those zany self-congratulatory, informal types – this was serious art. Whenever the temptation to laugh had come upon me, which was often, I turned my back to the audience until I could regain my composure. But somehow this time it seems okay. Someone holds a sign up saying 'Srpski Jeb', which is a very, very obscure song and I crack a smile. So it is more matey and warm and it doesn't seem to matter. We are great, the audience is great, we have swag and bluster, raw emotion, angst and whatever else you want. Jarvis leaps about like a dervish on speed. Like a cat he's very good at climbing up speaker stacks but not so good at getting down and there are a couple of ungainly dismounts, but on the whole he gets away with it and has a level of energy surpassing almost anyone. I think Jarvis is the best frontman since Mick Jagger. His ability to connect with and hold an audience is unequalled. Usually when watching concerts there is a drift of attention after three or so songs, but with Pulp it just builds: it's a special band to be in for that.

To the casual eye, Pulp's great virtue is the perfect pop timing, the ersatz just-so-ness, but this is superficial gloss. There's a lovely moment, improvising on the violin, when beauty balances on the blade's edge of ugliness. I love this moment, seek it out by sticking my finger at some random point, plough down into the dissonance and sweep out into a glissando, way beyond the ability of my mind to calculate. Jarvis feeds off these rises, swells and contrary counterpoint punctilios. He dances to the tune and the violin answers back, it's something we've never discussed, calculated or worked out, but it happens. It's that and the many other interlockings which make the engine of this band so organic. As people we have little in common, but as a unit we work. There's an alchemy that makes Pulp brilliant which manifests itself in rare moments like these and makes it all worthwhile. Nick's drumming is often erratic, if they gave out speeding tickets for alterations in tempo, he'd have lost his licence years ago. But it gives something frenetic and excitable, chaotic and unpredictable to the mix, reminiscent of a Hungarian Czárdás. It is raw, visceral, cathartic, warm, touching; all those journalistic words that you'd wish to hear. And there's the rush, that pure adrenaline high that makes you want to cry in the shared moment of connection. All artists have something missing in them that can only be completed by such a ritual of communion with the audience, the jigsaw piece that makes them whole. And all great shows channel this act of mutual vampirism into a mutually elevating cycle. You think that's pretentious? You weren't there, man; you don't know what it was like. I remember the first time and this is better.

My daughter loves it. She had been here the first time in 1995, on someone's shoulders, but at too early an age to take it all in. Her early life had been an odd one, with a father trying to make ends meet by dealing in antiques while pursuing the feckless dream of being a pop star. Hippies brought their kids to festivals but my daughter was the first child of Britpop and was made quite a fuss of. The main thing she would remember from us playing T in the Park would be the ladybird sunglasses someone gave her. The main thing from Glastonbury was the raspberry ice cream, and so on. Then it all stopped and I led a normal life and all she had were disconnected memories that might have seemed like something from another life. There were dips back into a glamorous showbiz world every few years with, say, going to Jarvis's wedding, or meeting The Strokes, but by and large it was very much something of the past.

You might think that having been in a fashionable band would garner some brownie points with your kids – forget it. When I took my daughter to school I had to drop her off enough yards down the road that her friends would not catch a glimpse of the leper that all parents become. It didn't matter that when shopping in town, a man with a *lot* of piercings would give her a discount on earrings because he recognised me.

After I'd left the band and was watching The Strokes from sidestage with my now-teenage daughter, The White Stripes were moved aside so she could get a better view. This wasn't because I pulled rank or made a fuss, just out of a respect I had earned amongst my younger peers ... and still at home the rolling eyes and 'whatevers' persisted. I may as well have turned up at her school wearing odd shoes and glasses repaired with Sellotape for all the good it did me.

So there you go, parents, if you want your kids to stop thinking you are a dweeb the trick is to wait until they're twenty-three and then play a secret gig at Glastonbury.

1995
ENGLAND

44
Sorted

I knew 'Common People' would be a hit because when it came on the radio my seven-year-old daughter started jumping up and down. I thought it was cute that she was dancing to Daddy's song, but she didn't know it was Daddy's song, it was just infectious and lots of kids were jumping up and down.

'Common People' was selling well midweek and someone in Island Records's marketing department dreamt up a radical new strategy: take the records *out* of the shops. We went into the offices and an enthusiastic young man with beef-coloured spectacle frames explained this counterintuitive plan using lots of buzz words, but we really couldn't understand it. We'd spent years trying to get our records *into* shops. So the question was asked: 'Have you ever tried this strategy before?' They hadn't. So we were to be the guinea pigs. We didn't like it, Island listened, and they didn't do it.

We listened to the charts hoping not to hear 'Common People' because that would mean it would be *just* that one place higher. When number three was read out and it wasn't us it could only be one of two things, we dared to dream … for three minutes.

It was number two, the champagne remained on ice and the faces were glum. A novelty cover version had cruelly deprived us, by an extremely small margin. If we'd followed common practice and bought a dozen records in the 'chart return shops' that were used to compile the statistics, we'd have been number one. People told us how good it was really – 'Common People' charting at number two was the highest a

Britpop band had got by that point – and they were right and we'd have happily taken Top Ten before the run-down but still felt the sickening stomach drop of being called into the dentist when it was number two.

As we were beaten to number one by Robson & Jerome by something like 100,047 sales to 100,019, then perhaps the lack of zeal on re-supply cost us the number one slot. But, hey ho, it happened to us twice: we were permanent underdogs and it kind of suited us.

Our follow-up single, 'Sorted for E's & Wizz', used concert footage from our Glastonbury triumph and also narrowly missed out on the top slot. There was a huge uproar in the press about the record sleeve of 'Sorted'. It was taken to condone drug taking, which it didn't, if you listened to the lyrics. The sleeve featured a folded-up picture that I learnt later was meant to be a 'wrap', which is what powdered drugs came in. There was headline in one of the tabloids that said 'BAN THIS SICK STUNT' and a big anti-drugs billboard campaign that featured the picture of a girl called Leah Betts, who had tragically died after taking Ecstasy, which simply said, 'Sorted' above her picture.

We set off on an extensive UK tour to promote *Different Class*, supported by the outrageously camp Minty. This was the big league, with big-league press attention and big-league police attention. People outside our shows were stopped and a few arrested for drugs – but fewer than you might expect from a random stop and search outside any club on any weekend, it just wasn't that big amongst our fans. After one of the shows two young girls left a suicide note and killed themselves – there was a dark side to Britpop. I don't claim to understand it and am struggling to find the appropriate words. I'd like to think that there's something fundamentally life-affirming about Pulp's music. It trespasses into some dark areas but I hope doesn't wallow there.

Outside the Cambridge Corn Exchange a young man approached me and tried to strike up a conversation. There was something funny about him; he looked at me in this dreamy lovey-dovey way that made my flesh creep. Then he attempted to hand me a 'wrap' of drugs. I refused, and then noticed a cameraman with a long lens taking photographs. The youth then went over to this 'journalist'. So this was a set-up: think of the consequences if I'd taken that wrap, it would have been splashed all over the papers. I'd got kids and that bastard was prepared to ruin my life for a cheap made-up story. Imagine the reaction of the other parents when I went to pick my kids up from school if that one had run? And the lad was in his early teens; the journalist was using him in a quite sickening way. I'd gone on instinct, but if the lad had been a better actor I'd probably have taken the wrap, just to be polite. It's frightening how close I came to my life being ruined. He was later discovered inside a flight case trying to smuggle himself into our dressing rooms.

But the show went on as shows must and, after the Liverpool concert, we were invited to a club by the DJ playing that night, who'd helpfully written a note so we could get in. At the door I said 'I've got a note from the DJ,' to which the bouncer witheringly replied: 'And does your mother dress you?'

We wanted to go to another club we'd been invited to but our security guard Paul had reservations. The huge crescent scar on his forehead had been made when he was hit in the face with a fire extinguisher there … 'But I did not go down!' he said. He was still prepared to take us of course but somehow the club's appeal had paled. Some bands were prone to kicking off, in the full knowledge that their security would intervene if things got out of hand but Pulp weren't one of them.

Much to our surprise we ended up liking ex-hooligan Paul and I think he ended up being surprised by us. Despite appearances, our backgrounds weren't all that different. There's a kind of northern hooligan known as the 'cock' of the estate who gets their reputation by kicking someone to death in the toilets of a flat-roofed pub. At one concert, through a 'friends of friends' accident, there were known hooligans on our guest list, which cast us in a different (and misleading) light to Paul. After the show I watched him face down a hard man who wished to do him harm. They each had baseball bat-sized pieces of wood. Paul threw his down saying contemptuously, 'I don't need this for you,' and went on to verbally humiliate the guy, telling him he was a failure and washed-up in life: it somehow hit home because the guy eventually walked off, crushed. It wasn't pretty or pleasant but no one got their skull smashed. Paul had a keen understanding of psychology, which he used in preference to violence.

In Belfast a skinhead was shouting constant abuse and sticking two fingers up at us. Steve dived into the audience after him and went down. Paul ran from the side of the stage and curled himself into a ball (like someone 'bombing' at a swimming pool). Paul's jump went not only the full length of the stage but over a six-foot pit, the heads of the local security guards and about twelve feet into the audience. After the show we went back to pace out the jump, which exceeded the world long jump record by five feet. Paul had the advantage of a six-foot rise, but it looked superhuman. He bundled the guy outside. When he came back in, dusting off his hands, he said euphemistically 'Ee'll 'ave a fat lip in the mornin'.'

We had a few days off and I went to Scarborough to escape the constantly ringing phone and all things Pulp – I didn't let anyone know I was there. I was walking on the beach with the sun in my eyes and did a double take, because I was staring at a black-and-white version of myself dancing amongst the donkeys. It took a while to get my bearings and figure out that it wasn't a mirror or someone that looked like me but actually a life-sized cardboard cutout of myself. The cover for *Different Class* featured these photographs and the photo shoot for that one must have just happened there. Others in the band had similar spooky encounters with the sleeve, including bumping into people from a wedding-party photograph from the album cover at a later date. There was no getting away from Pulp.

Different Class went straight in at number one. We were the uncrowned kings of Britpop at a time when quarter of the world's music imports came from Cool Britannia. But no one much noticed because the papers were busy watching the Blur versus Oasis Punch-and-Judy show.

I kept running into a couple called Pat and Jo Skinny from Grimsby in quite an alarming way. At first it just seemed a coincidence to see them on the King's Road or at clubs but it happened further afield, even as far away as New York. We were too busy touring to make a proper video for the next single 'Disco 2000', so we got Pat and Jo to dance on lit-up squares of light inspired by the Sheffield City Hall ballroom, with ourselves played by the cardboard cutouts from the album sleeve.

The professional video maker we recruited took things to a whole new level while very much respecting the essential Pulp style. Where that style ended up was a bit too Soho-smart for my taste but it was truly original. No fewer than five bands came about from people who had been in our videos and the rumour went round that to be in a Pulp video would bring good fame – so people angled to get in them.

We were using professional models and one agency sent over pictures with vital statistics. Every model was bra-size 34, the London look of the time, with Kate Moss its most familiar face. Overconfident people who seemed to know what they wanted turned up with clipboards and it started to feel like we were a small part of a big machine.

Film crews turned up and I always seemed to be having run-ins with them because the film-makers didn't really seem to get the band and therefore earn my trust. I pretty much boycotted them all and refused to be filmed. There hasn't been a good documentary about Pulp, although there have been some attempts. There were cameras set up in the dressing room without our permission, so I unplugged them and was generally as obstructive as possible. Cameras onstage can be very intrusive and take away from the spontaneity. They get in the way of movement and I wasn't going to do a bad show to get good footage, so it was something we never really did. It's a shame in some ways, it'd be nice to have some of that seminal footage like there is of the Sex Pistols or Joy Division or Nirvana, but we did truly memorable concerts that didn't have one eye on the camera and that to me is more important than having captured them for posterity.

So it'd all gone mad in Britain and it was a relief to get out of the country and on the road in Europe where we played Le Zénith de Paris, supported by PJ Harvey, who no one was much interested in because they were waiting for the main event – so it'd gone mad there too. We were too busy to get back for 'Disco 2000' on *TOTP* and played live from the beach at Marseille. Our chums Menswear joined us for the first leg of the tour, then Cast, then Stereolab. More parties, more touring, more telly – including a memorable show in beautiful Bologna.

Outside the hotel there was a crowd of 300 screaming girls. Gosh! We didn't know we were that big anywhere, let alone Italy, so we went out onto the balcony to greet our adoring fans – only to see the real object of their excitement, Peter Andre, appear on the next balcony along. It was a funny backstage, us, Peter Andre (who was a lovely man but whose face sweated constantly) and Bruce Dickinson from Iron Maiden – who was also a lovely man and one I rather admire, though I'm no fan of the music ('Bring Your Daughter … to the Slaughter' – who would do that?). It was a live show and we stood, ready to play, as the announcer introduced us. I dampened my strings to control the rising feedback, but the introduction went on for ever and it turned out that, unbeknown to us, he was reciting the entire lyrics to 'Common People' in Italian. We kept starting the count in, then having to stop as he went on and on and on. If you are on the running blocks poised and waiting for take off in split-second concentration, three minutes feels like three hours.

You can play to a vast adoring crowd one day and be whisked off in limos. Then the next day to six bored people in a pool hall where they expect you to sweep the floor afterwards. So, after a bit, you just roll with it and don't have any expectations, just hang onto the roller coaster and see where it ends up.

When we saw all those ecstatic people at Glastonbury singing along to 'Common People', it could just as easily have been because Peter Andre had made a surprise appearance sidestage and people were cheering that.

45
Big in Japan

Arriving at Osaka airport the overwhelming impression is of having arrived on another planet sometime in the future. We wait in silent order for a silver machine to take us to an antiseptically clean lounge, where we drink a refreshing green fluid and put the cans into perfect chrome dustbins filled with perfect rubbish.

Our host arrives bowing and we bow back. Our bags disappear without our noticing, only to reappear later in our rooms. It is a cold day but huge heaters warm the outside air.

I order green tea and put sugar in it. Our host gasps and sits back in amazement.

'What's wrong?' I say, 'Is it rude to do this?'

'Oh, no!' he says, laughing, 'just unusual.'

Diplomatic incident over – respect shown – I think it's like putting milk and sugar in beer.

Awaking very early in the morning I take a walk outside and realise that I am being followed at a distance by a group of girls. After politely asking for autographs they pump me for information on our movements. There is obviously some kind of network here because, during the course of our stay, the groups become crowds. Very polite and apologetic but nonetheless there the whole time.

The eating houses have immaculate plastic replicas of the food available, which are works of art in themselves, so you can point at what you fancy. What I fancy comes back with what appear to be wood shavings gyrating madly on top. We look at each other, wondering if we are seeing the same thing. Yes, they certainly don't look alive but they still keep squirming when you pick them up – don't know what it is though – probably better not to.

Rover regards touring Japan as something akin to a well-paid prison sentence. Presumably because you can't get Watney's Red Barrel and chips here.

We go to a video games arcade, where a disgruntled teenager spends a small fortune trying to get a very realistic image of a nubile schoolgirl to shed her clothes. British shopping centres are so hard and sterile, but here they seem more soft and relaxing.

'This channel is pay TV. If you wish to continue viewing, please press the button marked "Pay",' says the hotel telly. I don't think I'll bother; the free clip involved a scantily clad schoolgirl in a bar kicking a giraffe.

On the cartoon channel all the heroes have wide eyes – perhaps we will do well here. Everything is intensely symbolic in a way that will remain forever mysterious. By accident, it may be possible to do things which key in with their symbolism and have some resonance. I don't think you should try too hard at this – it has to be something you are. The Britpop band Shampoo are huge here – apparently the colour pink they wear is associated with Lolitas and, with their gum-chewing punkiness, they look like manga cartoon heroines.

At the venue the entire street is lined with girls waving, screaming and pointing cameras into the van. I've always had a problem with the word 'fan' but here it seems apt, they really won't let us bow lower than them.

An elevator takes us to the dressing room. Westerners have been here before, so every inch of wall space is covered in graffiti – something almost entirely absent from the rest of Japan. There is, uniquely, no obscene graffiti – that will have been removed. They have however respected the western custom of no-hoper bands trying to forge a spurious immortality in this enclave.

Due to technical problems we keep the fans waiting one and a half hours in sub-zero temperatures. During the concert Jarvis apologises for this – no response. He says, 'We meant no disrespect' and there's huge applause. He receives an enormous electric shock during the concert. I've seen him throw a fit for much less than that but tonight he shows endurance.

I try on some new sunglasses, which have beams of light at the side to help me see the violin – very hi-tech – very popular.

After the concert the street is packed with kids banging on the windows, crying and being hysterical; anywhere less gentle it would be frightening. In England most teenagers own *Different Class* but we don't get this kind of thing.

Eight a.m. and, moved by the spirit to embrace all things Japanese, I have decided to eat a traditional breakfast. I do not regret this, nor do I wish to repeat it. It entailed a formal ceremony conducted in silence. I consider myself to have an adventurous palate but this utterly defeated it. The yummiest thing by quite a long chalk was raw eel. I will draw a veil over the contents of the rest of the meal – other than to say that I dare not eat anything for the rest of the day, lest the things I had consumed for breakfast gorge themselves on the new food and burst out alien-like from my stomach. Nonetheless, I feel I have passed the kind of initiation ceremony that might entitle one to join a particularly sadistic religious cult. The Japanese will eat almost anything for breakfast it seems – as long as it isn't food.

The scene at Osaka train station resembles the evacuation of Hanoi. Huge crowds bearing gifts accompany us to the bullet train, which we enter as the whistle blows. We have our own carriage but are hemmed in at either end by fans. One intrepid girl gets on at the next station to give a gift, only to be ejected without her bag. It's like the fifties here and teenagers have just been invented.

Fans have to be ejected from the lift so we can get to our rooms. Can't remember much about the concert. I *think* we gave a good show. I don't know what they make of the music; they seem to be equally enthusiastic about everything we do. What they make of the lyrics is anybody's guess. You sometimes see comical versions of the lyrics which have been translated into Japanese and then back again. After the concert we go to the hotel bar to have a drink with Rover and our host. The hotel has been cleared of fans but about ten girls have taken the precaution of booking rooms in the hotel, so they can't very well be cobbed out.

I think any fan has the right to pester a pop star to a small extent. As long as they're being pleasant, it seems part of the deal that you sign autographs, have pictures taken and answer the odd question. Cumulatively this can be very wearing but if you don't like it you can always go and work in a bank.

Some of the girls in the foyer gradually pluck up the courage to come into the bar and sit across the way, not making any nuisance of themselves at all. The women who work with us here instinctively seem to sit back from the tables and let the men get on with business. Earlier in the day, someone sees a woman asked to leave a table so men could talk business and, shock-horror, it is implied to Candida that she might be bored or offended at a meeting. She told them where to get off.

Meanwhile, the table next to us has become vacant and some of the fans come over and sit at it. They aren't taking photos, they aren't giggling, they aren't being a nuisance.

But it makes our host very uncomfortable and he shouts at the girls to go away. This is very awkward. It appears to me that if they were male, they wouldn't be treated this way. It seems rude and, well, disrespectful. However, our host is treating us very well and it's not our country. We don't want to get into a row with him or, worst of all, confront him and cause loss of face. We try to politely explain that we don't understand why this is necessary, that we don't need protecting and that ultimately it is the fans that pay all our wages. The worst thing is that the fans accept it meekly, with a slight tear in their eyes.

One of the hotel staff is now hovering around and looking anxious. It transpires that he is concerned that the girls may be underage drinkers. Those without ID are asked to leave and I must confess to being quite relieved by this (i.e. that they were being harassed because they were underage drinkers, not because they were women – fair enough). So now there are five left, all overage hotel residents.

Although it's almost midnight, our host decides that he's very hungry indeed and wants to take us out for a meal. The hotel employee also thinks it's an excellent idea and will personally escort us to a place we will like very much. We, who have not previously expressed any desire to eat a second evening meal, are encouraged to find ourselves hungry too. With many smiles and gestures we are shepherded out of the bar into the bitter cold and through a labyrinth of winding streets. Our host is much happier now.

The tawdry entrance to the eating place is billowing steam into the cold night air. It's the size of a barn, with twelve kitchen/bars with stools round them, where people eat and drink and throng through the aisles. A cross between *Blade Runner*, a pirate's den, a bookie's, a cockfighting pit and Sheffield's fish market. It's rough and ready and noisy and the prices and names of each kitchen's specialties hang from the ceiling on coloured strips of paper. Unlike everything else in Japan, it's very cheap. No one's bowing, women are laughing, being brassy and not taking tiny steps. We're the only westerners but we're here with our host, who's Japanese, and Rover, who has tattoos. So, in this wild east bar, we *kind of* fit in.

Rover has fallen in love – he just hasn't decided who with yet, but is winking and smiling at several contenders. A woman in silver hot pants swaggers over, blowing smoke in his face. Strangely, our host has no problem with this and now positively encourages us to talk to women ... and the penny drops.

Our guidebook says: 'The industrious men of seventeenth-century Japan liked to relax at the end of the day with hard liquor in the company of actresses and prostitutes.'

The Japanese guide to English etiquette no doubt says: 'The hard-working musicians of twentieth-century England love nothing better at the end of the day than to snort cocaine from the thighs of groupies.'

So *we* weren't being protected from the fans in the bar – they (nice girls from good families) were being protected from the foreign devils. They needn't have bothered, but I'm glad they did, because this place is ace. After midnight, all the deference and daintiness goes out of the window and the drunken bonhomie so familiar to us arrives on a bullet train.

People are being chummy, offering us sake and amusing themselves at our gaucheries like we'd laugh at a Japanese person putting brown sauce on his cornflakes.

Rover keeps asking for 'Tomcat soup', which turns out to be tasty things on skewers – not unlike a shish kebab. What looks like a jar of pickled onions turns out to be plums steeped in some kind of liquor, which at our insistence they serve us over ice – much to the amusement of the Japanese. We manage to get fed and reasonably merry for a total cost of £6 – which wouldn't buy a Coca-Cola in the hotel.

A woman comes over and it transpires she is offering to have sex with us all. We make our excuses and leave, having convinced her that Rover has three penises and leave him extending the hairy hand of international friendship.

The fans at the hotel in Tokyo are slightly different, enthusiastic but perhaps less fawning. Yes they think we're super-cool but think they are too – this is better.

One can forgive the older generation for feeling some trepidation at the fault lines appearing in the social consensus that has produced the jackpot for this society. I'd just like them to have a little bit more time and space to enjoy it.

'You must be feeling tired,' sympathises a fan who has been waiting up all night to see us. Well, actually, no, we always look this dog-rough but you don't want to hear *that*, do you? You want us to be plastic fantastic, you put your money in the vending machine and you get Pulp just how you want it.

Shopping! The toyshop is slightly disappointing. The real toyshop is called 'Electric Street' where you can buy a gadget for everything. I buy a Jacuzzi for sunglasses – it works, they come out clean and relaxed.

Early evening. We are taken out for a traditional Japanese meal. Shoes must be removed before sitting cross-legged at a low table. We chose a fish from a tank called a blowfish. The sexual organs of this fish are deadly poisonous. Every year forty people die from eating it along with, presumably forty chefs who must take the honourable way out. The fish is brought to the table with the organs removed and the edible strips of raw flesh arranged in a pattern at the side. The fish, however, is far from dead and leans its head upwards, looking at us.

'This fish has died for you and you must respect it,' says our host's girlfriend who is administering the food ceremony. No one is very happy about this and Rover blurts out, 'But it isn't dead and if you don't take it away and kill it I'm going to get my knife out and kill it!' We have bought cool cameras on Electric Street and snap away furiously. Bloody tourists, think the Japanese. The English are drinking sake, the Japanese drink lager.

After the meal we go for a ritual humiliation, Japanese-style. As the signs outside proclaim: 'Karaoke is Joysound.' You get a private room with your mates, who choose a song for you to sing. I get 'Trouble' by Shampoo, not something I would ordinarily be inclined to sing in company. Jarvis gets a very badly translated version of MC Hammer's 'Can't Touch This' in which 'legit' comes out as 'leggit' etc. etc. For Rover we choose 'Gimme! Gimme! Gimme! (A Man After Midnight)', which he isn't very happy about.

The first concert in Tokyo goes very well. All the concerts sold out quickly and there is anticipation amongst the stylish and supposedly reserved metropolitan crowd. I've never seen so much energy without aggression. Everything's running like clockwork.

Back in the hotel foyer, we are greeted by gift-bearing fans. In the middle of the foyer is a bar area demarcated by a complete ring of chrome about two feet high. None of the fans dare enter this magic circle. We are joined by some British models who are impossibly thin and drape themselves around the bar, nibbling nuts. They have been making more money than the modelling assignment pays by selling their used underpants, which are then sold in vending machines with an accompanying picture of the model.

Meanwhile, back in Blighty, we are being lampooned by *Spitting Image* along the lines of 'I wanna live like famous people'. There is a limited shelf life to what we do. We draw our inspiration from elevating ordinary life: therefore ordinary people relate to it, therefore we become famous, therefore we are no longer common people. We can balance on the right side of ugliness for a while, like a wedding guest in an all-white suit as the party gets more rowdy, but sooner or later it will all come crashing down on our heads.

At the second concert in Tokyo we go on to Beethoven's *9th*. There are quite a number of males in the audience, which wasn't the case at the other shows. We fight through a few minor technical problems (Jarvis has to go off to replace a contact lens) to cobble together an exciting show. Battling through adversity in a cold climate is something our cultures share. There's a certain edginess to the evening, which is a positive thing, there's a lot of darkness under all this Pulp froth.

The Japanese seem to get our style, they like a good present to be in a good box. The idea that style could possibly subtract from content would not make any sense to them.

We awake with the rising sun, like the people in the Cornflakes advert you always aspire to be. I've started rooting through my paltry belongings for presents to give back to the fans. The best I can do is sunglasses, which are much appreciated. However, the next time I'm in the foyer I see half a dozen pairs of my former sunglasses being worn by fans and it's embarrassing. Mainly because it now seems impersonal and cheap, like I'm giving them beads for land. Many of the presents we receive are very thoughtful, personal and apt. For example, someone will give you a box of matches, having noticed the brand you use, or a Japanese translation machine because they see you struggling with the language. I got given a kettle full of tomatoes and it only occurred afterwards that it was an obscure reference to an article I had written years before in our fanzine about making your own coffee out of tomatoes. I didn't get the joke, just went 'Cheers, mate'. I'm very popular here (I think they like the mod thing) and get given loads of gifts, too many to take back home, but at the concerts am pelted with soya beans relentlessly – which, it turns out, is a sign of affection. They throw five at a time to bring you luck. We give the fans so little attention – don't even bother to learn their names – and they give us so much. Why these kind, intelligent people do something, on the face of it, so uncool is beyond me, but it's appreciated.

One of the many preconceptions we had of Japan was that we would be yammered away at about other bands, much as we are in the rest of the world, only more so and in a comical Japanese accent, 'Ahhh, Elastica! You know Bobby Gillespie? You know Blur?" This is definitely not the case. It almost seems impolite to mention another band when they're so focused on you. Actually, there is one exception. They do keep giving us pictures of Menswear and assuring us that they are well, as if they are our long lost children, perhaps in the hands of kidnappers. We have seen so many cheesy pictures of Menswear grinning, red-eyed in Hawaiian shirts, that severe loss of ace-faceness has occurred.

The last show in Tokyo is less frenetic but very good; we play well and do a rare-for-us second encore.

Jarvis sustains an injury and is taken to hospital, where an already painful finger is subjected to squeezing, pricking, burning and electrocution. The tour manager only came to the doctor's office to bring the singer but they (observing he had a cold) gave him the stick and all. A man kneels on his back, attaches crocodile clips to his nose and electrocutes him so that he thrashes about like pinhead, with his neck pulsing and smoke coming out of his ears. The tour manager's cold demon is banished to the ice pits – but he says he'd rather have kept the cold than endure the cure. (God knows what they do if you're really sick, no wonder everyone looks so healthy, they're too scared to be ill.)

Our last meal in Japan, at our request, involves no live animals. We give a present to our host, who then proceeds to blub uncontrollably for the rest of the meal. Any preconceptions that these are cold people went way back. As the orders are being placed, one of the record company men pipes up 'I like beetles!' Well, almost. He stands up and starts to belt through his repertoire of the Fab Four's songs, which is quite extensive, but we're used to this kind of excellently barking-mad behaviour.

Hot sake makes you drunk and I get very lairy and tell a bloke that his tie is too wide, before crashing through a paper screen in pursuit of the toilet.

We assemble early in the hotel lobby for departure. I am avoiding the person whose tie I have insulted and whom I have been told is a yakuza, but he appears – wearing a thin tie. Jarvis has spent the night in a 'dangerous club' and staggers into the foyer, not only refusing to sign autographs but swearing at anyone who comes near him, before falling over a settee and collapsing on the floor.

Safely checked-in at the airport we ascend the escalator, waving gaily to the tearful fans. 'Please come back to Japan soon,' they plead.

'We will, we will!' we promise.

It is a promise we are to keep for it is the wrong escalator and leads to locked doors. The crowd at the bottom has not dispersed and we descend the escalator, waving to the guffawing fans.

'Welcome back to Japan!' they say.

46
Got Any Charlie?

We'd hung out with the beautiful people, but now back in London we *are* the beautiful people who everyone wants at their parties. We dress the part and take a lot of the detail from stuff we find around us. People have copied the Pulp vision of seedy glamour and we copy them back. The love hearts get put on plates in a video, the knickers end up on a record sleeve, and the feather boas go into the vibes box for aftershow parties.

Sitting in the back of a shiny black taxicab I see Alex from Blur who seems to live outside Bar Italia. He's heard of a Britart launch in an empty warehouse, with just a fluorescent bulb going on and off. Then there's something going off at Madame JoJo's, where I have a bit of a dance to 'Cigarettes and Alcohol' by Oasis. But it's all getting a bit rowdy so I go to Violets, which is run by an acid jazz outfit called the Sandals. There are party games, like pin the tail on the donkey, played to a soundtrack of music from Italian lesbian vampire films and cats with goatee beards play along on bongos.

Lazy press agents feed a lazy press with endless rent-a-quotes from Jarvis, about space hoppers and Curly Wurlies and lava lamps. I used to bring lava lamps to photo shoots to make them look Pulpy but end up hating them because they've become a cliché. Jarvis is wearing these high-end designer clothes he's been given by The Man and I begin to hate what he's becoming too. But I can't complain because The Man is giving me Levi's and Ben Shermans. Poor old Nick Banks gets given a lifetime's supply of 'Hardcore by Visage' jeans because he jokingly said he liked them in an interview.

There's an award ceremony but we won't get anything because the order of events says 'winner's dad to collect award'. So that means it's Weller again, because he's picking up everything these days, apart from best female, and nobody else would let their dad pick up an award for them. Someone tells Weller's dad that Right Said Fred are number one and he thinks it's Bernard Cribbins. My girlfriend's too sexy for her shirt and this woman who's something in the media grabs her boobs, saying: 'That's a nice dress!'

My girlfriend says: 'Thanks.'

The woman says: 'Got any Charlie?'

My girlfriend says: 'No.'

The woman says: 'It's not a nice dress then!' And blinks her eyes.

ENGLAND
2011

47
Freak Out the Squares

That was all in the blink of an eye ago for another person, and another lifetime ago for me, and now here we are headlining Hyde Park.

Tickets have sold quickly; it is a frighteningly big show and the first one in mainland Britain for me for a generation.

I lead a normal life and shop at normal shops. I don't have rock-star mates or hang out with supermodels or have a secret underground lair. And I go on holiday once a year, mainly to Scarborough. So this isn't normal. I mean, I'm getting used to it again, but put yourself in my position, it's a total mindfuck. So it's good to have people to natter with.

We're back in the trusty old camper van and pick up our friend Dorian at the Lidl car park in Sheffield. Dorian is tickled by this, as it seems to him to be very Pulp. Like meeting in Lidl car park is deliberately contrived to be whimsically down-at-heel and prosaic – but it's just a handy place to pull in.

Dorian keeps saying: 'I just want to freak out the squares.'

This gets a bit annoying, but after endless repetition becomes funny again. He also claims to be up for a challenge of any kind. In a bid to fix it for Dorian to freak out the squares I propose 'The Yoghurt Challenge'; the rules are as follows:

1. The proposer (me) puts up an agreed amount of money and places that sum with the adjudicator (Ralph).
2. The player (Dorian) puts up the same amount.

3. The player may name up to two flavours they may be allergic or particularly averse to.
4. The proposer buys twenty standard-size yoghurt pots of a brand and flavour of their choice (taking a Ski yoghurt as a standard size).
5. At an agreed time the adjudicator starts the clock and the player begins the challenge.
6. The player then has one hour to eat all twenty yoghurts and win the bet.
7. To ensure that there is no dispute about how much is spilt or left in pots – i.e. whether the challenge has really been completed fairly – if the proposer can assemble a full yoghurt pot from the leavings then the player has failed. In practise this has never been an issue.
8. The proposer has to have at least one yoghurt lined up, ready for consumption by the player, but may keep the others concealed.
9. The proposer may talk and make noises but may not touch or otherwise impede the player.
10. The player may vomit after the hour is up, but not before.
11. The player may visit the toilet but must be accompanied by the adjudicator to ensure they do not vomit.

Ralph says that Dorian is like a character from *The Mighty Boosh* but Dorian says he's never seen the programme – that's just the way he rolls. He says he is up for the yoghurt challenge too, but I suspect he may be something of a bullshitter.

I don't think Gareth had heard of Pulp before this tour and he certainly won't have heard of many of the other bands being discussed. Ralph is more of the Bowie/Roxy persuasion and was therefore a Suede fan. But Dorian is the only person I've ever met who is actually interested in 'Britpop' as a genre – which I'm not at all sure it is. He is fascinated by the minutiae of who said what to whom between Sleeper, Menswear, Powder, Salad, Elastica, Shampoo, Cast, Saint Etienne, Denim, Blur, The Auteurs, Pulp, Suede and all points in between – the more obscure the better. There's never been a more ready or well-informed pair of ears for my boring old war stories. Dorian runs a Britpop disco, though he *does* throw the records over his shoulder after playing them, so I can't be entirely sure that he isn't taking the piss and being all post-modern.

My ancient Chelsea boots are fifteen-years-old. They have been re-soled and re-heeled many times, but now the uppers have gone and if you can't buy a new pair of boots when you're headlining Hyde Park, when can you?

Women have all the fun when it comes to clothes, there is so much variety, so many ways to make an impression, create a look. There's perfume, make-up, hair, nails, fancy underwear, jewellery. None of these things are as available to men.

Yet there is a private and secret world that is one of the quintessential delights of being an Englishman: where having the good fortune to be born on these islands is to be dealt the ace in the card game of life – menswear.

For a man, and in this we have an advantage over the ladies, it is well worth buying a decent pair of hand-stitched Northampton leather shoes. They mould to fit your feet over time and build up a lovely patina, if you use a variety of different browns when polishing. They mellow with age and when the sad day comes to relegate them to gardening they glow like a chestnut fresh from its husk.

The shops on Jermyn Street are pure theatre, the service is of the 'Very good, sir, might I make so bold as to suggest,' type. Geppetto-like men with measuring tapes round their necks will whip the tapes into your crotch at the drop of a hat – which I'm not sure is strictly necessary when you're buying shoes. They offer a splendidly titled, 'Scarification Service', to scratch the soles so you don't slip.

So, proudly wearing my new Chelsea boots, I peruse the chapeaueries and regret not having the bulk of frame to carry off a wide-brimmed fedora, which would have looked good on Orson Welles but makes me look like someone playing a mushroom in a pantomime.

There were Edgar Allan Poe smoking jackets, John Gielgud nightcaps, Noël Coward dressing gowns and Aleister Crowley capes, watched over by a statue of the original dandy, Beau Brummell. The meaning of dandy has mutated over the years: the original dandies were very conservative dressers, rebelling against the overblown fripperies of the beastly continental taste and were instrumental in defining a British style typified by reserve and understatement, so they'd have liked me new boots.

I saw Stephen Fry and, confident in my new boots, invited him to the show – as he is known to be a big Pulp fan. He claimed a prior engagement but was very pleasant and courteous. He enquired as to the name of the band, as he hadn't quite caught it. Famous people, especially shy ones, aren't always nice to strangers who accost them in the street, but Stephen Fry was lovely.

Stephen Fry's view of fame is that if you are good enough you'll find a way. But Stephen Fry was talent scouted from the Cambridge Footlights revue, and the person that scouted him, when short of acts, would venture as far as the Oxford Revue in search of new talent. I don't think he ever got as far as Rotherham, where we practiced.

When I imagine an artist like Sarah Lucas or Tracy Emin hanging around Rotherham rather than Hoxton I really don't think they'd have broken through, there are lots of unmade beds in Rotherham. The idea is that if you have enough get-up-and-go then you'll get yourself to where the action is. But get-up-and-go is not the same as talent. A shy person at Oxford or Cambridge can get spotted, nurtured, coaxed and cajoled into fulfilling their potential and be allowed a few false starts along the way. Pulp would never have got anywhere if some of us hadn't moved to London, we'd have got nowhere if they'd all been like me.

Thence to Savile Row, to worship at the altar of gentlemen's outfitter Ozwald Boateng. I had attempted unsuccessfully to contact him before the tour, in the very meagre hope that I might be able to cadge a suit. I content myself with gazing at his exquisite but unaffordable wares, glowing softly in the conserving light of a hundred tiny halogen bulbs.

On Dorian's suggestion we meet at a Vietnamese restaurant on Hoxton Square and he spends the whole meal moaning about how he hates trendies. Hoxton Square is the number one place in the world to run into trendies, so methinks the lady doth protest too much. He takes us to a hipster bar and he's very down on hipsters too, which is odd, considering his appearance (Nathan Barley fallen out of a skip with some too-short Farah slacks, a school jacket and a Jelly Tots badge). He *claims* to like alienation so, theoretically, his idea of a good night out would be a Frankie & Bennys sports bar on a roundabout by an out-of-town shopping mall: but here we are in Hoxton sneering at the hipsters, who I think liven the place up. And anyway, aren't *we* hipsters? When did hip become unhip?

London is my capital city and one of the great cities of the world. In total I've spent about two years there and have been to more art galleries and clubs than the average native, as you do when you're a visitor. But there's none of that malarkey tonight, I need to get my head down, it's a big show tomorrow. Hyde Park: how on earth are you supposed to sleep with that on your plate?

48
Fashionable Camden Ennui

Show day and I desperately need distraction. I watch The Horrors, who seem uninterested – or is it just fashionable Camden ennui? Don't know, don't care. Not entertained, not taken out of myself, which is what I need just now. The Hives give it some but the audience seems quite subdued. Is this going to be a difficult night?

Nerves.

The only thing to do is to fill each waking hour with sixty minutes of faffing about. Backstage are fenced-off areas for the sole use of corporate sponsors, which flaunt their ice sculptures, largely devoid of people. We aren't allowed in, which appears counter-productive if you are flogging some kind of 'hang out with the stars' experience. Maybe the idea is that you can observe the wildlife from a distance, like a safari park? I meet a few friends but can't really hold focus because of what is ahead.

When I left Pulp, one of the sad things was that over half my social life vanished overnight. The Britpop scene relied on bumping into each other at various social occasions and all that fell off a cliff. Theoretically, it would have been possible to maintain some contact and a little of that remained for a while, but out of its natural element it withered. What are you going to do? I'm not talking about my best mates here, just 300 people that I knew well enough to have a chat with that I would never see again. One of the great surprises of this tour was how *few* of the old faces turned up backstage. It used to be full of glamorous and interesting people and I'd looked forward to running into a lot of the ones that went out of my life when I left the band. But I guess they must have grown up and got lives too.

Well, there's a welcome blast from the past! Our old security guard Paul.

Why I like Paul:

1. He had a meticulous regard for the safety of the band and audience.
2. He gave me a pair of socks.
3. He introduced me to Chris Eubank, who was a very interesting man and thought boxing was a brutal sport. Unfortunately, Jarvis put paid to that meeting of great minds at the Brits by wiggling his backside at Michael Jackson and Chris Eubank left the table in disgust.
4. He expanded my ska collection beyond 'My Boy Lollipop', 'Uptown Top Ranking' and 2 Tone.
5. He had a book signed by Mad Frankie Fraser: 'To Loony Paul'.
6. He was once overheard receiving the chilling request, delivered in broad cockney: 'Take 'im darn a B road, Po.' Which was like something out of a Guy Ritchie film.
7. When we were supported by the screamingly flamboyant Minty (Leigh Bowery's wife Nicola's band) Paul could be seen singing along at the back to 'Plastic Bag', which he pronounced 'plasteek bayeg'.
8. He had never been to prison but was a little embarrassed by this slur on his manhood, insisting 'But I should 'ave bin!'

Paul like many gamekeepers used to be a poacher, he's a very hard man – but he has prevented a lot of people being hurt and saved our lives in America.

Why I *think* he likes me are all one-off, completely out-of-character, aberrations that he happened to witness:

1. When England lost to Germany in the 1996 European Championships Paul overheard me shouting 'Fuck off, Fritz!' to the celebrating Germans singing 'Football's coming home' outside the hotel.
2. When we played a small festival in the scorching heat of the Nevada desert I wore a full suit, tie and cashmere coat: 'To show Johnny Foreigner who's boss.'
3. When I sacked a guitar tech, Paul saw me glaring with psycho eyes and gritted teeth, pointing at the tech while making a throat-slashing gesture – very East End.

4. I can eat very hot curry.
5. I have worn Union Jack socks.
6. I'm not the biggest knobhead in Pulp, there's very stiff competition for that.

Three mischievous little girls ask Ralph what he does. 'Manservant,' he says. He will rue this as they keep turning up and ordering him about.

If there are any young people out there contemplating middle age, I'd really caution against it. The angry young man turns into the curmudgeonly old git. My main gripe is my bad back. So one of Ralph's many duties is carrying my stuff.

'I'm stronger than I look,' he says, which is just as well since he looks like a contender for 'world's softest man'. I'm deeply uncomfortable about this, as it appears as if I think I'm Liberace, swanning into hotels with Ralph carrying my bags.

One's clothing options become more limited with the passing of years. I look fine for my age, but a red polo neck that looked very dashing twenty years ago with an Eye-of-Horus medallion – it gave off the general air of 'horror story writer' when I steepled my hands together – nowadays makes me look like a crozzled-up old mod. I wear a pale linen-suit and everyone else has got a decent look sorted out; we've scrubbed up surprisingly well. Still not a fan of beards though. I know they're the new black and everything but, well, they're beards, aren't they? They're for Geography teachers to get macaroni stuck in.

Gosh, I'm jumpy.

Grace Jones is on before us; she's certainly got presence, not an easy act to follow.

So the sand runs out and the time comes to head to the stage, any last requests? Yes: please let us not be some tired old bunch of fuckers who ought to have known better!

Lasers project messages onto a curtain behind which we stand. Huge neon P.U.L.P. signs go on a letter at a time, my stomach dropping further with each one. The last one glitches and crackles, the opening bars of 'Do You Remember the First Time?' start and as I hit the fuzz pedal and go into the chorus the curtain drops to a great roar and the show leaps into life.

After a few seconds onstage, all the nerves go, you relax, get in the zone and weave and dance your way through it. Calmness comes in the centre of the storm. It's a huge crowd and they know all the words, a home fixture in which we can do no wrong. As the sun sets we go into the anthemic 'Sorted for E's & Wizz', which is made for festivals. The sky streaks a violent orange, turned into a psychedelic Japanese flag by the contrails of recent jets. It's a glorious sunset and stays glowing for most of the show; poetically framing migrating birds before finally turning dark. But we are still on fire and so is the audience. It's one of the best shows we've ever played. I can't really remember it, that's just what happens. It's like the best nights out, the best holidays, the best romantic encounters; you can't remember all the details, you just know that you shared it and it was good.

After the show there is a party at a club in an underground seventies-style Soho club with mirrored walls – very Pulp. It's a good do and there are some old faces but embarrassingly I don't immediately recognise them in the dark. Nancy (who'd been in Barcelona) has turned up and after the club we all head back to my hotel in rickshaws. This turns into a hotly contested chariot race, with the drivers clipping kerbs along Piccadilly and the Strand. We pile into the hotel, to find the bar shut; but Gareth, bless him, has somehow wangled his way into parking the van in the loading bay in front of the hotel so we all go in there. It's very snug and the mystery machine bounces with dancing to bad reggae, accompanied by the hisses of beer cans. Nancy has taken to referring to the van as 'The Russ Bus'.

Rover joins us and brings the glad tidings that I am THE CREW'S FAVOURITE BAND MEMBER! Which pleases me inordinately. I'm not big on awards (after the tour I don't bother turning up at a 'lifetime achievement' one) but this is one I'm surprised and delighted to accept.

In the morning, Gareth and I walk past the bus, Nancy waves and smiles animatedly. 'Ooh, isn't she friendly, that Nancy lass?' we say and go off to breakfast. When we come back she's still waving and smiling, but when she starts banging on the windows we realise she's not waving but drowning. She'd been locked in the van all night.

On the journey back we stop at a motorway service station and Dorian puts a toy orange octopus on his head with a 'Look at me, I'm mental me, I'll do anything!' expression on his face – what a div! And to the soundtrack of bad reggae, with the repeated refrain of 'I just wanna freak out the squares' from Dorian, we wend our merry way back home.

49
My Chemical Romance

At a service station on the way to Scotland there are some big Geordie lasses – straight out of *Viz* comics, on a hen do, angel wings and white stilettos. They totter off to the loos, rorting out with laughter and fiddling with overburdened bra straps. I like Geordies, I like the accent – it's really musical and can even be sexy – but not this early in the morning.

I like the journey to Edinburgh too, through the wilds of Northumbria, past The Angel of the North, past the bridges on the Tyne, skirting the craggy east coast – with its unexpectedly turquoise bays. The world just seems to get fresher, less crowded and more open the further north you get.

Edinburgh is built on such a monumental scale that it seems to have been wrought for a race of giants. The roads are wider, the ceilings higher, the doorways taller. Edinburgh feels like a capital city in a way that the more confused architecture of London doesn't. A majestic city somewhat blighted by a shiny-faced overselling of Scottishness that dances a merry jig for the tourist dollar. No wonder the statues of David Hulme, John Knox and Adam Smith look so pissed-off.

We are staying at a stylish place described as Scotland's sexiest hotel. It has floor-to-ceiling windows that all overlook a central garden. The curtains are operated by remote control, which I keep mistaking for the telly remote: so if it's exhibitionism or voyeurism you have in mind, it's a plum spot.

The show is on the last day of T in the Park, it's pissing it down, muddy and the audience look wrecked.

My vote for 'best behaved band' goes to My Chemical Romance. They are lovely lads and a credit to their parents, I find it hard to imagine them moping around malls and painting their bedrooms black.

In our opinion we play very well indeed and put on a great show, but the audience is the deadest we encounter on the whole tour – they just look fit to drop. Objectively it was a good response but compared to the hysteria we have encountered thus far it's decidedly subdued.

On the way back we go via the island of Lindisfarne. There's something very special about the light here and Holy Island floats effulgent like a revelatory vision. We drive through the water along the causeway to get to it, but the tide is coming in and we must away before it cuts us off.

SCANDINAVIA
1996

50
Quality Knitwear

Pulp specialise in being big in places with small populations – it's part of being professional underdogs. If it's got lots of desert or tundra, we're big there. The pull of Mother North is strong and Scandinavia exerts a magnetic attraction. The prospect of fun is not part of the appeal – if pressed to explain I'd use words like 'gloomy', 'bleak' and 'depressing', which don't exactly sell it.

At the age of five my favourite TV programme was *Noggin the Nog*, a rudimentary cartoon about a Viking, which began: 'The men of the Northlands sit by their great log fires and they tell a tale …'

A screaming ball of fury, which my parents said was a 'sister', appeared and they asked me what I wanted to call it: 'Nogbad!' I said. Vikings seemed like an appealing bunch – always breaking open barrels of ale and roaring with laughter.

Then there were the Moomintrolls, creatures that hibernated in winter. They were otherworldly – but you felt they might just possibly exist. The last Moomintroll book was a disconcerting read, the other characters wait for the Moomintrolls who never show up and it's never explained why. It's sad and typically Scandinavian.

There was the notion of liberated Scandinavians with an open-minded attitude to sex. They were serious and high-minded – I could do that. Southern things seemed soft, shallow and materialistic so northern things must be harder, deeper and more real. Then there were the Abba videos, depicting bittersweet vignettes of an enviable lifestyle involving mulled wine, birch twigs, saunas, poignant break-ups and quality knitwear.

But nothing was ever rammed down your throat about Scandinavia, it just tolled sonorously like a distant bell – 'I'm here if you want me' – and we did.

We landed in Stockholm Arlanda airport where I was seized by the euphoria of still being alive after the flight, with a little added slurring from the diazepam. We were met by a very nice lady from the record company who asked us if there was anything we wanted.

'Yes, herring!' I said.

'Okay … ' she said, 'It's an unusual request but I'll see what I can do.' Unusual? *Really*? She seemed quite wary and put out.

'You're not telling me I can't get herring in Stockholm? Come on, it's famous for it!'

Well, this went on for a bit and we got dropped off at the hotel and I kept mentioning my herring and she eventually lost patience and snapped, 'Look, I can't just find heroin like that!'

She was a little sceptical, thinking I might be winding her up with our famous British quicksand sense of humour, and took some convincing that I really *did* just want to try some local food. This relieved her very much; in fact she was quite euphoric, a bit like me coming off the plane. You see, the primary purpose of the people who meet and greet bands is to please them and sort them out with what they need – and there are odder requests than herring. Anyhow, I got a variety of herring and other ingeniously pickled fish and she even tried to teach me how to salsa dance, which is bit like trying to teach a cat how to play the piano.

We played somewhere near Stockholm that involved a drive through the forest to a scout hut that held 300 people. It was packed and fans were looking in through the windows, so we were pretty much under siege, but it was a nice siege – a cross between a zombie movie and a porn film. There was a problem with the barriers in front of the stage and Rover and the crew had to spend the set propping up sweaty people who would otherwise have fallen over – mainly large-breasted girls. After the show I did the make-up of a perfect blond Swedish couple with their national flag as an eyelid design.

Driving back from the forest, there were a couple of well-known DJs in our van. It was hard to tell whether it was really late or really early because it never really goes dark. We were being followed by a police car, which kept a polite distance behind. But midsummer madness set in and the DJs went through the CDs they had been given, throwing the ones they didn't want out of the window. There was a Lenny Kravitz CD, which they took particular exception to. 'Eat the Kravitz!' said one to the other, who bit chunks out of it and spat them out of the window. The police never pulled us over; they just watched the discs spinning by. Maybe we were a red herring in some complex case involving ritual murders?

In Copenhagen we stayed in a hotel on a square that had a huge clock face, which formed the wall to one of the rooms. The whimsical cobbled square looked as if giant wooden soldiers might march in at any moment. We played the lovely Roskilde festival, where people put twenty-foot bamboo flagpoles up with individual flags on top so their friends could find them, much more civilised and decorative than the British festivals of the time. The Scandinavians seemed to really get Pulp, they did plenty of their own glamorous pop and didn't seem to think that having a bit of glitter thrown around indicated lack of depth. The journalists spoke better English than a native and didn't ask dumb questions. The language's hurdy-gurdy musicality – seemingly always raised-eyebrow astonished – was incomprehensible yet somehow familiar and I tried to pick up a few phrases. When abroad my first words would be to apologise for not speaking the language. But the Scandinavians didn't mind, and spoke English as a universal second language. Paradoxically, it protected their own languages from being subsumed by larger and louder neighbours.

Black Grape possessed the strongest herbal tobacco known to man, which they were very generous with. Blissed-out, I wandered round the venue and somehow found myself outside the fence and, with half an hour to go until we were on, unable to get back in. I ran to the stage, arriving five minutes after we were due on, to find Jarvis (who had also taken a sociable toke) squatting underneath the stage, refusing to come out. So we poked him out like you might do a trapped rabbit and pointed him towards the stage.

The tent was packed with 20,000 people in a sweaty and euphoric concert. Black Grape shambled on to 'Little Green Bag', the shambles fell into place, and they really hit the spot. Frighteningly so, because what they were was very strong. I'm not sure I always liked what they were but I admired how perfectly they communicated their thing.

We toured the same festivals as Black Grape and, as fellow northerners, cleaved together. Pulp were used to feeling for-real in comparison with other bands but Black Grape, who reeked of prisons and pubs, made us feel like a bunch of hairdressers. They were patchy and it didn't always come together, but when they caught the groove they rode it like kings. Shaun Ryder is one of the best lyricists of all time.

Shaun and Kermit crashed onstage with us at a festival, and danced and sang along to 'Common People', grabbing the mike and saying something like 'Fuck fuckin' Oasis, this is the real fuckin' thing'. So we still had the Manc seal of approval.

The Sex Pistols were playing. I went to our dressing room and psychopaths came and scared me off. Apparently the Sex Pistols' security, if you could call it that, wouldn't let anybody, including other bands, get anywhere near them. I didn't know whether it was paranoia or arrogance, but by way of thuggery they cleared the entire backstage area of anybody who wasn't them. There was no way I was going to be watching this one from the side of the stage without getting very severely injured.

So I went out front and on they came! It's an amazing sharp sound, that Sex Pistols guitar noise, and I got a flashback to what it all meant in 1977. I'm getting thrown out of the school disco for pogoing to 'Pretty Vacant'. But, at the same time, stood there with a bottle in my hand, for the first time in my life I was tempted to throw it and say: 'How dare you revisit that thing? What cheek, what arrogance.'

They got halfway through a song, a number of bottles were thrown, John Lydon sneered at the audience and they restarted the set. After three songs they were bottled off and didn't come back. Which was a shame … or was it? Not many people get bottled off these days – I've had bottles thrown at me onstage and wouldn't wish it on anybody. But John Lydon seemed like the last person entitled to complain. He threw down that kind of gauntlet so he shouldn't have been surprised that people choose to pick it up.

Norway from the air was stunning: endless lakes, fjords and mountains – there can't be a straight road in the whole country. Everyone must know some special isolated place with an ochre cabin and canoe, that they go back to year after year for generations. The people have a different look too, more Viking, more troll.

A former and very friendly Miss Norway had been employed by the record company to show us the sights – she wore leather trousers. Everyone who meets and greets in Scandinavia wears leather trousers. Oslo was very sub-zero and had a bit of the spy drama about it.

The dressing rooms were reached by boat that crossed the fjord to enter Ernst Stavro Blofeld's lair, which had a smorgasbord laid out and a commanding view of the bay, through a sloping-windowed control tower straight out of 'Modern Scandinavian interiors 1971'.

As the Norsemen of old sat round their great log fires telling stories they peered out into the forest at the fantastical shadows and heard the crashings and bellowings of monsters lurking in a world of uncertainty and superstition. When they emerged from the forest, blinking into the light, they did things in a clear, open and rational way. They never looked back to the forest and pursued modernity with zeal, certain that it was the best and only way forward. They built clean new civilisations and stripped their minds and psyches of made-up demons. Leaving them empty, open and receptive to the very real demons of their own introspection. So they drink an awful lot.

We played a concert called the Quart Festival, which was sponsored by a vodka company. There were 2,000 people and, unbelievably, 4,000 free pints of vodka. So, everyone was mind-bendingly drunk and it was just as much a blur then as it is now. Jon Bon Jovi was in town and asked if it was okay to watch us from stageside. Miss Norway was very excited about this – leather trousers, you see. But we didn't fancy the idea of trying to perform with Jon grinning and doing thumbs-up from sidestage and after that Miss Norway was a lot frostier.

In Finland there was a sign for Moominland, which I was quite tempted to go to. I didn't know whether it was actually a region where these creatures lived wild or just a theme park. I decided I'd rather not know, so the chewing-gum bubble of quantum uncertainty couldn't collapse on my face.

Helsinki was even more *Ipcress File* than Oslo. One had the sensation of being at the edge of the inhabitable world, with the harsh treeless wastes visible from the centre of the city. There was an appealing Soviet austerity about it. The Finns aren't much like the rest of the Scandinavians. The language has the same root as Hungarian and they often looked more Russian, and certainly acted it. They seemed free of the ponderous introspection of the Swedes and, at three in the morning when it was still light, they capered and leapt about in the air like young colts – off their heads on bootleg vodka.

It was all death or glory there … and the thing I'd discovered about Scandinavia was that they were very forward indeed.

In Sheffield, if a person of the opposite sex took your fancy you might attempt to catch their eye during the course of the evening. The next week you would go to the same disco and get there early. Then ask your friends if they knew any of their friends. Gradually you'd work your way to being in the same group of people. When the object of your affection happened to mention that they liked the Magazine album you'd say, 'What's your favourite track?' … and they say 'Guess.' And you say, 'Well, obviously "Shot by Both Sides" is the one most people go for me but I'll plump for "The Light Pours Out of Me"' … and, perhaps a month later, you *might* hold hands in a municipal cemetery. And, several years later, contemplate buying small yellow batteries from IKEA together.

Whereas in Scandinavia it was: catch someone's eye, if they didn't look away, you'd start shagging in the street. I'd seen people doing this – that was just their way.

The festival we were playing was in an idyllic forest by a fjord. A huge white ferry glided silently and surreally across as people paddled while watching the bands play. We watched some Lapp dancers, who didn't quite live up to expectations, before going on and doing our stuff. It was stuff they liked – how could they not? We came off enervated and tingly.

I watched Blur and, during the song 'Girls & Boys', walked out into the fjord. It was afternoon and there were already people swimming naked. A massive white ferry drifted slowly past the festival site. We had to leave that evening, which was an aching shame, I wished I was just one of the kids at the festival.

It transpired that there was nothing left to drink but tomato juice and Cinzano Rosso. This was rhythm guitarist Mark's doing. You see, other people asked for items on the rider that they actually wanted. I put Bombay Sapphire gin, Steve put Rémy Martin brandy, Nick put cooking lager, Candida put fruit juice, Jarvis put wine. People drank these things, guests and crew included, so they went. But Mark chose things that he thought were cool, or perhaps ironic, that no one, least of all him, drank. So stocks of these bloody things piled up. We'd been on the road for a bit and cabin fever was setting in. I found a large inflatable crocodile and came into the dressing room with it. 'Crocodile Dundee!'

said Nick. 'No, Crocodile Done Dee!' I said and hit him with it. We had a joke fight which knocked a bottle of tomato juice off the table and it shattered on the floor, making a glorious bloody mess. This was funny and Steve said, 'Fuckin' tomato juice,' and threw one at the wall, then stood back, a bit sheepish.

At this point, in walked Blur, who joined in the mayhem. All the tomato juice and Cinzano got smashed, in a parody of a Tarantino movie – and it was all very funny and quite a cathartic reliever of tension. Then the festival organisers walked in. They didn't shout or get angry, they explained that they were all unpaid volunteers who just did this for the love of it … and we were very, very, sorry indeed.

They were a bad influence, that Blur.

51
Nice One, Geyser

We had a flight booked to Reykjavík to play the second biggest concert the country had ever seen (after David Bowie). Although Blur weren't playing, they came along for the laugh and we had several leisurely days together away, far from the madding crowd.

The plane was a private hire, but it wasn't a Lear jet, it was an ex-Aeroflot plane, staffed by ex-Soviet air force pilots and it was brown. Our gear wouldn't go into the hold so they took the front seats out and tied the equipment up in a big net. We boarded through a little elf-door at the back. Then one of the amplifiers wouldn't go through the door, so they took the door off. Then the door wouldn't go back on, so the pilot got a big hammer and twatted it back on. Okay, I'd had enough. That was it, I was off. The tour manager headed me off at the door and soothed me into staying, saying that if I liked I could sit with the pilot, for reassurance.

Now, on dear old British Airways – gawd bless 'em – nervous passengers such as myself were sometimes introduced to the pilot, who had been doing the job for twenty years. He had the reassuring manner of a suave doctor and pointed out that I was much more likely to meet with a mishap in the taxi home than on the flight. This had a calming effect on me. That and being able to see his commanding view of the skies as the world passed steadily beneath his stately command. And, in case he pegged it, there was his equally reassuring co-pilot, Gerald. This was beneficial and instilled a measure of calm (though it did screw up the taxi ride home).

So I went to meet this so-called pilot ... who was screaming in Russian at his co-pilot and bashing big cracked Bakelite buttons with Cyrillic letters on. The window was tiny and dirty and one of the wipers was hanging off. I think I went into some kind of shock. The plane banked and bobbled alarmingly and, I kid you not, the only English words I could make out were, 'nuclear bomb', which they kept saying as a large red light flashed on and off. The tour manager got me out quick and it was explained that they were just talking about the old days in the good old USSR, but I only stopped twitching when we finally touched down in Reykjavík's Keflavik airport.

Near-death experiences are very invigorating when they are over and I was quite euphoric to be in Iceland and in a receptive state for whatever gnosis the place might offer. We were met by a bloke called Thor, who was delighted that Blur had turned up too. Iceland had the population of Rotherham but was the size of Wales and our visit was big news. A TV crew followed us round the whole time and the only programme on the only channel was 'Pulp and Blur go mad in Iceland'. After a heavy night, all we had to do was watch the telly to see what we had got up to the day before.

Straight from the plane we were all taken to the Blue Lagoon, a pool in a lava field naturally heated by the run-off from a hydrothermal power plant. Shiny silver pipes appeared through the mist evaporating from the bubbling blue pool set amongst craggy volcanic rocks. Bathers took in the health-giving vapours and coated themselves in the pale, cosmetically beneficial mud. Thor had arranged for blue-liveried bunny girls to bring blue champagne cocktails on floating trays. We looked around at each other and said, 'Well, this is the life.' If I wanted to freeze any moment and say, 'Now that's what I call glamour,' that was the one.

The pale mud was deliciously soft and squirmy underfoot and the mineral-rich water sustained buoyancy. At water-level the hanging mist obscured the view and, swimming into it, one would encounter cool areas, then hot ones where churning bubbles issued from the earth's core. Swimming away from these hot areas – hopefully to cooler ones – the parting mists revealed groups of locals smeared in the pale mud, like futuristic tribesmen. Simultaneously relaxing and invigorating – the perfect blissed-out come down from the fist-clenching flight.

Reykjavík had a frontier air and the uncompromisingly stark church steeple dominated the red ochre buildings. There was little in the way of ornament and we imagined ourselves to be time travellers visiting a puritanical utopia of the distant future. Tranquility descended; we were in the capable hands of superior beings with benign intentions, as yet unrevealed to our puny minds.

Both bands stood at the edge of a geyser, and peered down into the clear, boiling depths. It was tempting to follow the imp of the perverse and jump into the fluctuating blue lens. The geyser was heaving now, building up to a climax: the water swelled, roiled, then shot its steaming load up into the air, which danced down in veils, and drenched us in warm mist. It sighed and sucked and gurgled back down the endless bone-white shaft, and gathered its strength for the next explosion.

We explored a small pert volcano and crunched down blasted red clinker to the circular lake, from whose turquoise depths bubbled sulphurous gases. The banks were steep and unstable and the water was deep, it went down to where the earth was molten and might have decided that this was the day it blew its top.

We approached a waterfall that charged down the great continental rift and the roar became deafening. It purged dark water into an abyss within feet of our faces and blasted away with furnace ferocity, dashing down white onto the rocks below.

Raw and savage as Iceland was, it was also culturally ahead of the times. The first parliament in the world met here and this contrast between ancient and futuristic was everywhere.

It rained every twenty minutes for a couple of minutes, then the sun came out again. Thor said it wasn't worth putting on different clothes, as the weather would just change again.

We were going white-water rafting and I had a cold coming on – Thor said that jumping into cold water cured colds. We got kitted out in padded flotation suits, which protected from submersion, cold and bumps – so one felt invulnerable – and the bands each boarded a dinghy. We played a game of running round the outside of the dinghy and everyone ended up in the water. The river was a serious one and rushed down a black gorge. We raced each other along the canyon, and pushed each other off track with our oars. One of Blur fell in and I managed to pull him out and onto our boat. TV crews dashed from bridge to bridge to record this. Thor asked me how my cold was – er, what cold?

The day after there was more sightseeing and we passed through lava fields where the liquid stone had frozen into contorted black meringue, desperately populated by hardy lichens of vivid dusty hues.

Most Icelanders believe in fairies and are well within their rights to do so. When seeking to explain the intangible one necessarily resorts to metaphor, in order to translate things we can't see into things we can. I never really got the hang of advanced physics until I read the creation myth of the Norse, written in Iceland a thousand years ago. It perfectly explained multiple universes, dimensionality and everything you needed to know about the little stuff quantum physics described, the big stuff relativity described and the medium-sized stuff Newtonian physics described. It more than hinted at a synthesis of the seemingly irreconcilable conflicts between those theories and paved the way for M-theory. Those Norsemen staring into their great log fires knew what they were on about. That the metaphors they used were dwarves, giants and world trees rather than 'string' only made things clearer.

We visited an area of hydrothermal activity, where jets of steam issuing from the ground were fed into greenhouses to grow vegetables way beyond their northern limits. In the hotel the water was naturally heated, fizzed and smelt a little eggy. Pulp had interviews to do while Blur went off snowcatting on glaciers, and literally hunted wild geese.

If you've ever been out with a group of friends, with the intention of eating, you'll know how hard it is for a group to make up its mind. Somebody doesn't like Italian, somebody's vegetarian, someone doesn't like the decor. So you wander around, with everyone wanting to do something but unable to agree on what. Therefore you can imagine that a group of twenty people who haven't chosen to be friends or go on holiday together and have very different interests, aspirations, values, morals, political views, style, tastes – you name it – makes this almost impossible. Thus it's very good to have somebody like Thor who doesn't leave you any choice at all. He told us where we were going, what we were eating and what we were drinking.

There was a meal for both bands at a fantastic restaurant that had prepared a wild herb sorbet followed by very special salmon with mustard sauce and tomato sauce, accompanied by a deliciously pretty wild-flower salad, then a wild berry sorbet.

Then we hit the bars where Blur, who had escaped the distractions of Camden to record their album here knew quite a lot of people. It was an early flight back and it was not worth trying to grab a token bit of sleep; so we stayed up all night and it never went dark and the moon – for some reason best known to itself – moved remarkably quickly, seeking oblivion and avoiding the dreadful toll: 'Time to get on the plane.'

With possibly the worst hangover of all time I endured the flight without the benefit of sleeping tablets, fearful that if I went to sleep I might never wake up. All too soon we were away from this wonderful place and back into the maelstrom.

I'd splashed out on some weird Icelandic stuff for my young kids. After tales of geysers and volcanoes they took to it enthusiastically. Particularly the dental chews that had a picture of two demonic tooth goblins called Hakkur and Vrakkur on them. These were made from shark flesh that was pissed on, buried in the ground and left to ferment over winter. To my surprise, and their credit, they were rather proud of eating this stuff. So, in a small way, I'd brought a bit of Scando-macabre back home.

Nice one, geyser.

52
Zindaloo Silly Hot

Candida was still going out with our old bass player Manners and he was often around, making a nuisance of himself. The overwhelming vibe was getting very pseudy and Manners harassed, sneered at and cruelly mimiced everyone.

Manners' impersonation of me was based upon the selfless organisational toil that had earned me the (supposedly out of earshot) nickname of 'The Headmaster' and included such phrases as: 'What time do you call this, Manners?', 'You're out of tune, boy!', 'No running in the corridors!', 'I could train a monkey to play bass quicker than you!' (I did actually say that). It was delivered in a close-throated voice nothing like my own but obviously had the ring of truth because everyone found it funny.

I had my own cruel impersonation of Manners, complete with actions. One drink (with arms round shoulders): 'Hey, all right, let's have a party'. Two drinks (with tears in eyes): 'I love you, you're like a bruvver to me.' Three drinks (to lamppost): 'Yuh fuckin' bastard, yuh can stick yer job!'

Four drinks: fall over with tongue hanging out drooling.

We went for a curry with our security guard Paul and, with predictable working-class bravado, Manners wanted: 'Vindaloo. No, scratch that, Tindaloo – silly 'ot, with extra chillies, do they do a Zindaloo? Heh heh. Oh, and a pint of your finest cooking lager, bar steward.' Manners was ribbing Paul about West Ham, saying unkind things. Now, Paul's background was in football hooliganism and Manners' background was in gobbing off, so we told Manners that Paul was off-duty now and could legally kill him, which shut him up for a bit. The curry came, Manners took one bite: 'Oh, fuckin' hell!' he wafted his mouth and ran off to the toilet and wouldn't touch any more. 'You having that, Manners?' I said. Then proceeded to eat the lot. 'What's it like?' he said, 'It's all right – but it's a bit mild.' Paul liked that.

Manners pitched up at a recording and forced me to watch *Riverdance* all the way through. I got my revenge when he fell asleep drunk on the floor, and wrote 'I love Mark Webber' on his face in lipstick, which was not an accurate reflection of Manners' feelings for Pulp's rhythm guitarist.

Manners was talking to the singer of a well-known band who said to him, 'It's so refreshing to have someone talk to me in in a normal way.' 'What, are you in a band or summat, mate?' said Manners, knowing full well who he was. Manners was always sneering at any whiff of pretentiousness. Something was lost when Manners left the band, but it was not something that would ever have got us on *TOTP*. Its faint echo still lingered, it had defined Pulp as a special band and that had stayed. Amidst all of the high-cheekboned glamour, Manners was there to pull us down a peg or too and, crass as he was, I welcomed it.

Candida said I was a bad influence on Manners and I was perversely rather flattered – yes, *I* can be a bad boy too. The fact that I was, as Nick phrased it, 'so square he's weird', encouraged Manners' inner schoolboy, not that he had an outer adult. So Candida dreaded Manners going out with me, as it would often end in a scrape.

Manners and I shared a taxi to a party at Jarvis's house. Taxi drivers are widely held to be the epitome of insularity and bigotry but I'm always interested in what they have to say. Their working life is a long series of vignettes: of every triumph and disaster, routine and revelry, return, departure and depravity that a city can throw up. They see the widest range of people and go to every corner of the city, in all weathers, at all hours – insular they are not. You can learn a lot from taxi drivers. We learnt that this one supported Tottenham Hotspur.

'Jew boy! Jew Boy!' said Manners.

What? Oh, no. I held my head in my hands. The taxi driver chuckled and said 'Yeah, I'm a Yid.'

Well, they chatted and by the end of the journey shook hands as if they were best of mates. Apparently what he'd said wasn't offensive, but it was typical of the roller-coaster ride of edginess that a night with Manners entailed. At Jarvis's absurd 1970s' pimp-style pad, he had, in keeping with the decor, cooked us coq au vin. Manners ended the evening asleep with his face in the plate and Candida chided me for having led him astray yet again.

Manners was a rock of support when I was feeling anxious and would talk me down to sanity by discussing fishing at length. I would meet up with him every so often for a drink – after I'd forgotten that I'd sworn never to do it again. He always managed to totally embarrass me, insult my friends, make inappropriate passes at women, say something off colour, scare my children by removing his dental palate, or tell a joke about removing a johnny from a dog's arse – complete with lingering sound-effects – in front of Candida's parents, then fall over drunk.

When Manners turned up at the 1996 Brit Awards it was always going to end in trouble. Michael Jackson, who was surrounded by lots of very heavy and twitchy security, had dominated rehearsals to the extent that the actual Brits didn't get much of a soundcheck. After watching him rehearse 'Earth Song', Jarvis got poked off at the way in which Michael Jackson was taking over the show.

Manners and Candida's cousin Danny Doyle had been dancing onstage with us in tacky shell-suits, à la Bez, to 'Sorted for E's & Wizz'. After that they'd been drinking with Jarvis and egged him on to do a prank. So they all ran onstage and Jarvis wiggled his backside at Michael Jackson – which produced something of a commotion.

Jackson's private army came looking for Jarvis, who hid in Martin Clunes's dressing room. A policeman cross-examined Martin, who stopped giggling at the naughty intrigue as he realised it had all gotten rather serious. 'Oh, yes, and one final question, Mr Clunes,' said the policeman who was obviously a fan of *Men Behaving Badly*, 'When can we be expecting a new series, sir?'

Lawsuits were threatened and children who'd been performing with Michael Jackson came forward with concocted stories. (I knew they were concocted because I'd been in the same room as Jarvis all day.) Jarvis was taken to the cells for questioning; it was all over the front pages and looked very bad for a couple of days. But slow-motion footage revealed the truth and the fax machine at our offices spewed out endless messages of support. T-shirts saying 'Jarvis is innocent' were made and he became one of the most recognised faces in the country and something of a national hero.

We thought that we might have sold a lot of records on the back of the media frenzy but in fact there was barely a blip. To their credit, the public it seems don't really buy records because they like the person, they buy them because they like the tune. But, from that point on, the only thing interviewers wanted to talk about was Jarvis the celebrity, not Pulp the band and the Brits became a millstone around our necks.

EUROPE
2011

53
Advanced Technological Situation

All the band were supposed to be travelling on a super-duper, state-of-the art tourbus, as we had in the past. But, as the schedule got more hectic and a late show that I couldn't make was slotted in, the others pulled out, which leaves me alone on a huge tourbus. Well, not *quite* alone, as there are two drivers, Ralph and my son Ben, who load the gear onto the huge metal beast, which harrumphs on airbrakes outside my door – what will the neighbours think? The hydraulic doors open to reveal a specially adapted coach, with a lounge at the back and bunks down either side at the front. It has been kitted out with kitchenette, fridge, toilet, two televisions and a very good sound system by a colour-blind pimp with a penchant for black onyx. The bunks are of two types: 'luxury', with about three feet of headroom and the low-ceilinged type, with two feet of headroom, which come in stacks of three. I love these buses and have crossed continents on them. When we first became successful after many years of transit vans and sleeping rough, graduating to a proper tourbus finally felt like being a star.

As there are now plenty of spare bunks, we have invited a number of friends; Jack Clayton (who had been in Barcelona) and Dorian (who had been in Hyde Park). They both have Henry IV bowl haircuts; I refer to them as Henry IV Part I and Henry IV Part II. So, with eighteen-year-old Ben, there are now three 'lads' (Ralph and I don't quite count on account of seniority and general effeteness). Dorian still wants to Freak Out the Squares but has a new more-in-sadness-than-anger catchphrase: 'Lads, lads, lads!' This means: 'Stop messing about and get another can of beer opened.' And so they do and, despite my prior good intentions, I join in, as does Ralph, 'Oh, go on then, just a small one.'

And there are 'The Russian Girls' There are three of them and they call Ralph 'Meester Ralph'. I didn't know them before today but they are, as Ralph advertised, an instant party, wherever they go. I never get to learn their names and they like it this way. They send postcards, texts and emails signed, 'The Russian Girls' – I think they are some kind of art concept. Questions are answered with, 'Russian girls say …' 'Russian girls like …' Russian girls think …' 'Russian girls drink …' beer and also bootleg vodka – just to be on the safe side.

The Russian Girls take a big-sisterly attitude to Ben. They also think 'Jackclayton' is one word and always address him as such, 'Ahh, Jackclayton, please to pass the vodka'.

Dorian plays a best of Britpop set:

Saint Etienne 'Only Love Can Break Your Heart'
Saint Etienne 'Avenue'
Denim 'Middle of the Road'
Blur 'Song 2'
Blur 'Girls & Boys'
Blur 'Parklife'
Blur 'To the End'
Shampoo 'Trouble'
Menswear 'I'll Manage Somehow'
Menswear 'Daydreamer'
Elastica 'Line Up'
Suede 'The Drowners'
Suede 'Beautiful Ones'
Suede 'Animal Nitrate'
The Auteurs 'Bailed Out'
The Auteurs 'Show Girl'

At a motorway services I choose my twenty yoghurts with care.

Ben plays a best of baggy set

Happy Mondays '24 Hour Party People'
Happy Mondays 'Loose Fit'
Happy Mondays 'Kinky Afro'

Happy Mondays 'Step On'
Happy Mondays 'Hallelujah (Club Mix)'
The Stone Roses 'Fools Gold'
The Stone Roses 'I Wanna Be Adored'
The Charlatans 'The Only One I Know'
Flowered Up 'Weekender'
Blur 'There's No Other Way'
The Rolling Stones 'Sympathy for the Devil'

Ben tries out one of the small bunks and draws the curtain.

'Ha! Like vampire situation, like vampire in coffin!' say The Russian Girls.

Ralph plays sexy stuff: Roxy Music, Bowie, Gina X, Prince, Charlotte Gainsbourg, Grace Jones, Tom Tom Club and The Normal – giving the general vibe of a New York loft apartment.

The Russian Girls play Eurotrash music mixed in with post-dubstep, which they dance to then fall over laughing. It's nice to be able to retreat to the bunk with the sounds of the party going on in the back lounge as the bus wends its way towards Europe.

We're approaching the Channel Tunnel and The Russian Girls line up in size-order, looking through the front window like so many Russian dolls. The bus squeezes inside the Eurostar, which is in turn swallowed by the still larger snake of the Chunnel. The Russian girls are impressed: 'Advanced technological situation!' they shout in glee.

Customs, then the vacuum hush of the tunnel, then France.

54
Bastardo!

In pursuit of Frenchness we go via the small town near Abbeville again, and eat at the café on the square. The waiter, perhaps because there are young ladies present, is enthusiastically wielding his improbably large peppermill. He flashes his matinee-idol smile, forgetting that he's still grinding pepper onto my food. Well, I've had enough, so I hold up my hand and say 'Bastardo!' Which he seems to understand and walks off.

Jackclayton: 'Did you just call the waiter a bastard?'

Me: 'No, it just means "enough" in Italian.'

Actually, now I recall, it's '*basta!*' that means 'enough' in Italian. I got into the habit of saying 'bastardo!' because '*basta!*' sounds even more like bastard than bastardo and people turned round when I said it. For the past twenty years I've been saying 'bastardo' to waiters, houseguests and family members and this is the first time anyone's ever pulled me up on it. I'd forgotten what it meant, now it's ruined – bastardo!

With the good fortune that these kind of ventures bring, it is the town's feast day and there's an exhibition of cider making in the abbey. The venerable old presses look like torture equipment – I have press envy. My own cider press makes the nicest apple juice I've ever tasted and there are few greater delights than seeing the first golden pints come chuckling into the jug as you crank the handle and compress the pulp. It seems such a crime against nature that so many apples go to waste and the generous fecundity of the land lies rotting on the floor. But the scale of production fills my fridge and the surplus is made into a quite horrible cider.

Crab apples make an extremely sour cider – evocatively titled 'verjuice' – and a very useful jelly. The jelly starts off green but as it begins to boil and oxidise it turns brown, then a lovely, subtle, opaque calcitic pink. At which point I'd recommend reading some metaphysical poetry:

> So through the mortal fruit we boyl
> The Sugar's uncorrupting Oyl;
> And that which perisht while we pull,
> Is thus preservéd clear and full.

By some alchemical magic, it suddenly runs a brilliant clear garnet red.

I once made nice cider. A biddable teacher went along with my idea that our class's contribution to the forthcoming school Christmas Fayre should be to make cider. So, in October we raided orchards for apples and parents' pantries for sugar and sultanas. We grated the apples into plastic dustbins in the warm and suitably private library stockroom. Fermentation began and a hissing crust formed on top, filling the air with alcohol fumes – a naughty secret that ensured a willing band of volunteers, colluded in by the increasingly nervous teacher, who was also the school librarian. The crust developed an alarming furry green mould, which sent up long probing filaments. I convinced myself that it was only penicillin and everything would be all right. Straggling contributions of sugar were added to this Bitches Brew, which fed the ferocious fermentation and overran the containers as it was added. It glooped, plopped and harrumphed like a Lovecraftian nightmare – the bloody thing was developing a personality. I wouldn't have been surprised if it stalked the library at night, gobbling up books and half-moon-bespectacled librarians. The bubbling ichor was screwed down tightly in bottles for the night of the Fayre.

Peg dolls and crocheted poodles were ignored as a queue built up by the cider stall. We served it from dustbins by the beaker and, as word spread, there was a scrummage as people came back for more. The bottled stuff was very much in demand and spurted into the air, making the floor sticky and fragrant. The kids ran around madly, like pirates with an unexpected rum ration. We tried to limit it to one bottle per person but the teachers and especially the headmaster pulled rank in an unseemly way to get more than their fair share. We sold out in fifteen minutes and were surrounded by drunks chanting for more. Even in those days, the slight inadvisability of selling unlicenced alcohol to children at a school fayre dawned on the school authorities and the experiment was never repeated. But, for one glorious Breughelian moment, it was back to village life at its most rumbustious.

And it's like that here. The French revere the abundance of their land and celebrate the annual harvest with ceremony, dance and merriment.

I ring my mother, who tells me she has sold yet another of her paintings of quizzical cats: she received £50. My mother does this about once a month, which is quite a fillip for a hobby artist who only started painting in her seventies. She is not a great painter, but her pictures are winsome. I'm sure there are many people who have come out of art college and set their cap at painting with less commercial success. It sold in one of those ubiquitous shops that sell enamel containers with French words on, distressed Union Jack cushions and hearts made out of twigs.

I used to sell antique glassware to a Jewish bloke in London and took him a finely cut decanter. But he wouldn't buy it, he said it 'smelt of Dr Goebbels', which is a strange thing to say about a decanter. He said it was 'made by a man whose heart was not free'. Then he showed me a decanter he liked, with a wonky engraving of a peasant holding a cider jug, lying buck-toothed and cross-smocked, gazing up at the harvest moon. It was eighteenth-century English, with grey swirling striations, tooling marks, and other imperfections. And I learnt something there; that no matter how impressive something is, if art hasn't got heart, it's worth nothing.

But it's hard to tell the real from the bogus because The Man has learnt to fake it pretty convincingly. It's only when you get these evil totems home that they silently seep their malignant emptiness through your house. So these shops with all their bogus individuality and kookiness need the odd bit of genuinely real crap (like my mum's cat pictures) to maintain their illusion of artlessness. Of course it's not *quite* as sinister as that, there isn't some Moriarty in a top hat rubbing his hands in glee at the back of the shops.

The really annoying part is that I *like* this stuff. I almost painted my garden shed lavender and put decking on my patio – and I once contemplated making a sculpture out of driftwood. So it's particularly galling when The Man co-opts these things. Nowadays he doesn't announce himself so clearly; he's a man of wealth and taste.

But there's something miraculous about art that you can only fake for so long. The soul of the artist transmits to the medium and a message, perhaps one forgotten by the maker, shines through.

After the 100 Club show in 1986 a fan said that the song 'Separations' evoked the smell of bilberries. And I thought, crikey, that was what I was thinking when I wrote the part years ago! But I'd completely forgotten about it from that day to this and here it was preserved clear and full.

Bastardo!

55
Evil Night-time Doppelgangers

En route to the Dour festival in Belgium we sashay through France, past vineyards so regular they strobe as the bus passes. Ben is on the decks with a selection of French music for the occasion:

Brigitte Bardot 'Harley Davidson'
Brigitte Bardot 'Moi Je Joue'
Brigitte Bardot 'Ça Pourrait Changer'
Brigitte Bardot 'Ne Me Laisse Pas L'aimer'
Françoise Hardy 'Comment Te Dire Adieu?'
Françoise Hardy 'Voilà'
Françoise Hardy 'Et Même'
France Gall 'Poupée De Cire, Poupée De Son'
France Gall 'N'écoute Pas Les Idoles'
France Gall 'Les Sucettes'
France Gall 'Néfertiti'
Jacques Dutronc 'Et Moi, Et Moi, Et Moi'
Jacques Dutronc 'On Nous Cache Tout, On Nous Dit Rien'
Jacques Dutronc 'Les Cactus'
Jacques Dutronc 'L'Idole (Je N'en Peux Plus)'
Jacques Dutronc 'Paris S'éveille'
Jacques Dutronc 'L'Opportuniste'
Jacques Dutronc 'Proverbes'
Pierre Henry 'Psyché Rock'
Pierre Henry and Michel Colombier 'Jericho Jerk'

MC Solaar 'Nouveau Western'
MC Solaar 'Paradisiaque'
Air 'Sexy Boy'
Air 'La Femme D'Argent'
Serge Gainsbourg 'Initials B.B.'
Serge Gainsbourg and Jane Birkin 'Je T'aime … Moi Non Plus'
Serge Gainsbourg and Jane Birkin '69 Année Érotique'
Serge Gainsbourg and Charlotte Gainsbourg 'Lemon Incest'
Serge Gainsbourg and Brigitte Bardot 'Comic Strip'
Serge Gainsbourg and Brigitte Bardot 'Bonnie and Clyde'

There's a general consensus that Serge is God and he crops up on everyone's playlists. It seems a mystery that Serge didn't take off in the civilised world.

Next stop is Reims, the home of champagne, which delights The Russian Girls inordinately. It must be a national characteristic as there are signs in Russian outside the shops – they love their bling, those Russians. The shops sell every conceivable accoutrement associated with champagne; chocolates, patê, tea towels, ice buckets and swords. Yes, swords! Apparently it is customary at celebrations to slice the top off a champagne bottle with a sword – now that really *is* a health and safety nightmare: drunkenness, edged weapons, broken glass, severed fingers. Where's the EU directive on that one?

It is Bastille Day and there is a festival in Reims. The singer performing looks like Ralph's evil night-time doppelgänger – he wears a black double-breasted suit and trilby hat and is accompanied by three 'Black Russian Girls'. They bang out a spirited version of 'Lady Marmalade'. He really thinks he's class in that misguided way the French do, but he's more Man Jam than Lady Marmalade. Then we go on 'The World's Slowest Carousel', before hitting the road to think up more evil night-time doppelgängers as the night draws in and France flows by.

What is the evil night-time doppelgänger of the butterfly? – the moth.
What is the evil night-time doppelgänger of the bird? – the bat.
What is the evil night-time doppelgänger of the dog? – the wolf.
What is the evil night-time doppelgänger of the duck? – the goose.
What is the evil night-time doppelgänger of the mouse? – the rat.
What is the evil night-time doppelgänger of the worm? – the snake.
What is the evil night-time doppelgänger of the salmon? – the pike

What is the evil night-time doppelgänger of the rabbit? – the hare
What is the evil night-time doppelgänger of the blackbird? – the crow
What is the evil night-time doppelgänger of the crow? – the raven

Ralph stands in the middle of the bus, clinks his glass and asks for silence, then states the bleedin' obvious: 'So, we're on a tourbus, and well, we've come through the Channel Tunnel and now we're, well, you know, in France! And we're on our way to Valenciennes!'

There's a pause whilst people wait to see if that's it, then, hurrahs and clinking of glasses.

Ralph has been on the phone and has another announcement to make; shining-eyed he says: 'I've got the code to the castle!' And so he has. The hotel I'm staying in is a moated castle, like something out of 'Medal of Honor' accessed by tapping in a code. There's only one room booked and the hotel is a little jumpy about the bus from England with blacked-out windows that disgorges a stream of outlandish revellers.

I chill out in the hotel while the lads follow the fireworks, looking for further Bastille Day merriment. The festivities are just winding down but, determined not to let the day end, they follow the crowds to a local dive bar full of Les Chavs Français. Outside of the castle, Valenciennes is Le Rotherham Français. So the lads head back to the bus for a late night of vodka and music, singing 'We are the lads, we *are* the lads, we are we are the lads / We are the lads we *are* the lads, *oui! oui!* We are the lads!' to the tune of France Gall's 'Poupée De Cire, Poupée De Son'.

The bus is remarkably well insulated against sound. I open the door to be beaten back by a furnace blast of bass, and retire to my chamber in the tower.

In the morning, Meester Ralph's emollient manner has put the hotel at its ease and, after a night without mayhem and arson, has somehow charmed them into letting us have free use of a further room.

The morning is golden and hot and as I walk over the drawbridge – watching fat ghost carp lazily break the surface of the moat – the girls wave at me Rapunzel-like from an upstairs window. They are giddy with delight at being able to use a shower, when none was foretold. Girls get very miserable after a day without hygiene and every day Ralph is involved in some convoluted and often farcically clandestine shuttle to keep them cleansed, moisturised and straightened without alerting the hotel that ten people are using the facilities of one room. We breakfast on the lawn, surrounded by the castle's ivy-entwined towers; the only thing missing from this idyll is the plaintive call of a peacock.

The lads spend the morning like gunslingers, walking into dusty bars that go silent as they enter. They grudgingly file in for baths, for even lads will have a bath once a week if forced, whether they need it or not.

56
Sixties Knocking Shop

We played the Dour Festival in Belgium fifteen years ago. The day was unbearably hot and the dressing rooms airless. Guitar strings sagged like telegraph wires in the Midwest and my eyeliner melted and ran out of the end of the pencil, giving me clown-eye. We were on in the afternoon, fifty-third on the bill, and got sunbaked mudballs thrown at us – which really, really hurt. Other bands got things thrown but we seemed to attract more than our fair share and my guitar was scarred from fielding projectiles. Now we're returning to this inauspicious venue as headliners.

The backstage arrangements are amongst the most irrational ever devised and must have been dreamt up by some particularly pigheaded central commissariat. After parking behind the stage, one is shuttled across rough ground in Range Rovers, transferred to minibuses and driven several miles to a dressing room in a village school. All this has to be requested, arranged and sanctioned by the appropriate issuing of permits – both ways. So, when you get there, you'd be expecting something spectacular. But it is crap: I choose a stale bag of Quavers in preference to the fermenting sandwiches and apply to the refreshments committee for a warm beer voucher.

I go back to my lovely tourbus and have a kip. The round journey to spend five minutes in catering has taken over two hours. I am awakened by the rest of Pulp who are in some disarray as they have been held-up in catering, with show time growing ever-nearer.

'How long is it anyway?' I ask lazily.

'About ten minutes.'

'What!' I leap up and rush to get ready, this is not at all how I like to prepare for a show.

The show is raucous and life affirming. There is a large press pit in front of the stage that people from the bus are dancing in. They've been to see Ice Cube with the Klaxons who they've befriended by the subwoofers and have somehow run unchallenged into the press pit. So they dance and fall over in front of the stage, which brings the whole experience closer. A beautiful thin girl who looks vaguely familiar dances in front of me. The whole show feels like more of a party than any so far.

Dressing rooms are often unpleasant malodorous places and in my Pulp days I had taken to bringing with us a special box for 'vibing up' a dressing room. It contained, amongst other things: feather boas, rolls of silver foil, incense, lighting gels (for putting over strip lights) balloons, masks, a lava lamp, board games, plastic fruit, tea lights, string, Sellotape, a Swiss Army Knife, playing cards, catnip, scissors, silly putty, Blu Tack, fortune-telling fish and whatever other errata might make things more festive.

They've been busy back at the bus and have raided the vibes box to deck it out as (in the words of the amused drivers) 'A sixties knocking shop'. There is a Viet Cong flag illuminated by a red Soviet star; a huge cushion with mushroom prints is propped up in a corner. An oil slide-projector casts multi-coloured amoebic shadows through a web of streamers; *Fear and Loathing in Las Vegas* is on one screen and a glam rock compilation on another. 'Venus in Furs' is blasting out as people wearing feathered masks lounge, loll and spill their cocktails in a haze of incense. The squares wouldn't stand a chance.

'All the Things She Said' by t.A.T.u. comes on and The Russian Girls start snogging in solidarity.

Rover squeezes through the sapphic traffic jam to tell me that the pretty, thin girl dancing in front of me was Keira Knightley, who is supposed to be coming on the bus too. So I hide in my bunk. I don't like to meet people I admire; they can only screw it up. Keira's cool, she doesn't do too much of that showbiz stuff. When she was filming *The Duchess* near Sheffield she was really nice to the crew, and that counts for a lot in my eyes. I'll even forgive her doing adverts because they are so classy.

Speaking as a person that others have wished to meet, and having been in close contact with a major celebrity (i.e. Jarvis), I always feel we are terribly deficient at living up to people's expectations. The prize-winners who have won a 'hang out with the band' competition will, more often than not, find us lost for words and doing our ironing while watching *Casualty* and picking our noses. So it's perhaps fortunate that Keira didn't come. Her boyfriend's band The Klaxons are in party mood though.

There's a fug of reggae from Ben, which is a distinct improvement on the Gareth variety.

Althea & Donna 'Uptown Top Ranking'
Augusto Pablo 'King Tubby Meets Rockers Uptown'
Black Uhuru 'Great Train Robbery'
Dillinger 'Cocaine In My Brain'
I Roy 'Sidewalk Killer'
King Tubby 'Zion Dub'
Max Romeo 'Chase the Devil'
Tapper Zukie 'MPLA'
Willie Williams 'Armagideon Time'
Chaka Demus & Pliers 'Murder She Wrote'
Ini Kamoze 'Here Comes the Hotstepper'

The bus bobbles out over the uneven ground of the festival site, lurching dancers into each other and then onto the smooth roads with Steph the Klaxon in no hurry to leave. He thinks we're going back to Valenciennes, where the rest of The Klaxons are. What he doesn't know is that we are actually going 600 miles in the other direction and have kidnapped him.

At 4.30 in the morning, when we stumble out at a service station, the rest of Pulp's bus is there. (After much indecision they'd realised they wanted one after all). Rover is the only one awake and reports that there is some tension on the bus, with Mark Webber at the centre of it. He also complains bitterly that the boring bastards are all asleep and asks permission to board. But with Steph the Klaxon we were at bunk capacity, so there is no room at the inn. You see, even pop stars get old. At the point of my previous departure from the band I was finding the others to be a little dull and fifteen years hasn't improved this. So, staid as I may be, I'm afraid the others are worse. It's all healthy food and early nights for them. I don't normally drink before 6 p.m but, seeing as how we're doing a tour and all, I've been having the odd can at lunchtime – this makes me the wild man of Pulp. Still, if you want to talk about house extensions, what schools are good and that kind of thing, they're a blast.

57
No, Wolves Do *Not* Like Catnip

Morning in the Black Forest. The driver's first words are: 'In answer to your earlier question: no, wolves do *not* like catnip.' Fragments of the night before come back. I'd had the notion that sprinkling catnip round the bus might attract wolves. I mean, imagine waking up to find the bus surrounded by howling wolves, how cool would that be? Well, apparently they *don't* like catnip – so think on.

When Steph the Klaxon awakes in Russian Girl's pyjamas, surrounded by balloons, bottles of vodka and in transit to Leipzig – 600 miles from his colleagues – there is an amusing 'Hey dude, where's my tourbus?' moment.

We drive into East Germany listening to Kraftwerk, DAF, The Human League and Wagner. Gosh, how I miss the Iron Curtain: the intrigue, the control towers, the exotic passport stamps, the sense of *verboten*ness and da-da-doom; though I daresay some who used to live there are less nostalgic.

The first hotel Ralph found was a bit too Berlin for my taste. The rooms had pink and lime-green fluorescent lights, concrete baths, and beds that hung from chains – which isn't the perfect pre-concert Zen space. So, in the pursuit of Weimar decadence, Brutalist architecture and Ost-rock we had taken a gamble on Leipzig, which is more conveniently situated, but know little about.

Leipzig is an unexpected treat. The sinister buildings of security apparatus surveillance and incarceration stand alongside whimsical beer halls, the architecture of the past 150 years jostling together, each building evoking a different tumultuous decade. The grandeur of empire proudly proclaimed by the ornate neo-classicism of the 1880s, the bold experiments of the Secession in the 1890s, the last gasp of *fin de siècle* extravagance, the aggressive modernism of the Bauhaus, the art deco jollity of Weimar, the brutal stamp of Nazi austerity, the equally brutal Communist minimalism, the irregular polygons of sixties Soviet optimism. Each regime marching through sought to stamp its new world vision upon the city in as bold a vernacular as possible, as if in a hurry to get its message down before the next lot came along.

German art is always Grimm. From Cranach to Holbein the horrors of ghastly mortality seep sickly from every pore: each limewood crucifixion hangs from the nails in hyper-real agony, every woodcut depicts torture. At the edge of every jolly Otto Dix café a lost stranger contemplates suicide. Dürer, you say? You must be thinking of that rabbit he painted while on his holidays in Norfolk, the rest is suitably doomy and macabre. Holbein, he's quite opulent and sumptuous. Well, yeah – when he was in Merrie England! But even then his inner German couldn't resist sneaking a skull into the party.

At a café we are served steins of overflowing lager by a stout *frau* overflowing out of a well-stuffed *madschen* outfit. A distant accordion plays the humpety-tumpety strains of Brecht and oompah. It's like a scene from *Cabaret* with only a monocled lesbian needed to complete the picture. We catch sight of Steve and Mark Webber having a meal together. Sneaking up, I manage to chapeau Mark, '*Ah, Obergruppenführer Veber, was machts du hier*?' We all go to the Stasi museum for a cheap holiday in other people's misery. But our papers are not in order and we are refused admission.

The hotel is ridiculously cheap and, for the first time, everyone has a bed. The rooms are like something from the Woody Allen film *Sleeper*. There are two doors to the bathroom and a large viewing-window between the shower and the bedroom – so pulling back the shower curtain is prone to frighten the horses. There is an unfathomable coffee machine that just squirts boiling water over the side of the cup.

The lobby has a giant settee-like structure with a seat six-foot deep. It is hard to know how to disport oneself on this so we lie along it like a seal colony, ordering steins and burgers and watching a three-hour television programme in which a fine blond man in lederhosen stroked a lovely old St. Bernard in front of an alpine cabin. The hotel don't seem to mind this at all. The huge sofa thingy was probably designed with this kind of open living in mind, but I suspect we are the first clients to actually use it for its intended purpose since the 1967 photo shoot for its launch.

58
Trouble at Mill

The journey to the Melt! festival in Ferropolis (Iron City) where we are headlining goes through the noticeably less developed towns and villages of eastern Germany. Melt! must be the most unusual festival location in the world. A Soviet-era steel mill conceived on an epic scale, with rusting ten-storey-high cranes and gantries. A hospitality area atop one of the giant cranes affords a magnificent vista of the festival and adjacent tailing lagoons, where coltsfoot, bullrush and horsetail fight the heavy metals for survival.

Dorian keeps saying he'll come out and look at the festival – 'Just let me finish these couple of beers' – but he never does. It rains a lot but this seems appropriate in this concrete-and-iron *Blade Runner* world.

Backstage in a Portakabin pounded by torrential rain, Pulp rehearse rarities 'O.U.' and 'Sheffield: Sex City'. Everyone's chatting but there's a bit of an edge.

Searchlights scan the serried ranks of concertgoers and gaunt industrial leviathans looming overhead. Onstage I attempt to put myself in a trance-like state that permits free association – but there's a problem. Mark's keyboards are where I normally stand: not only am in I danger of banging into them but am unable to keep time by moving about. There is constant squalling feedback because I'm too close to the amp. I gesture to a roadie to move the keyboards, but Mark stops them – I am not best pleased with him. He grins at me maniacally, through rolling eyes like the guy in *Full Metal Jacket*. I can't figure out what is going on, there had been no hint of this earlier. I know there's been a row on the bus, maybe matters have somehow reached boiling point and he's gone mad? He certainly looks it. I'm no stranger to onstage tension but this is the first on this tour. Somehow tension isn't always deleterious to performance, it can give it an edge, and I think and hope that tonight it does.

I try to work out how to take out Mark's shins with my guitar if he lunges for me and, fearful what he or I might do, I refuse to come back on for an encore and storm off to the bus, furious.

The tour manager attempts to explain the situation because, on the face of it, the crew has screwed up. I don't think it is a crew cock-up, certainly not the onstage crew. I've seen the look on Mark's face and know there is something very weird going on.

Apparently he's been doing a lot of whingeing and that's been getting on people's nerves and he's been getting some stick. As someone who made the transition from fan to crew member to band member, Mark never quite gelled with crews. Whenever I run into a member of Pulp's crew they spend half the time recounting Mark's shortcomings. But now I'm the one moaning and am probably not all of the crew's favourite band member.

Mark rings me and while he's not exactly apologetic, he is certainly contrite and does not wish for us to be at loggerheads, which is fine by me. The reason he's not apologising is that he can't quite see what he's done wrong. He was drunk, which is very unusual for him. Now, given that Mark already has people gunning for him, there are moves afoot to get him kicked off the tour. But, despite the events in Ferropolis, I am unwilling to be the agent by which Mark is humiliated. He is fundamentally a lovely guy and I don't want to be a pawn in someone else's game. Mark may have had a reason to moan, I might have agreed with it. If I'd been on the other bus I might have been the one whingeing.

The rest of Pulp had slotted in a late show before the one in Dour and had been running against the clock, almost missing the shows and tension had inevitably resulted. It all got sorted out, but I wasn't happy that the hectic schedule the others had taken on had obtruded temporarily into my leisurely world. You see, I was still having 'a long summer holiday with a concert once a week', but they'd taken on more shows as they came up and gradually it was expanding into an extensive world tour. That I didn't do all the shows wasn't solely because of my aversion to flying. I hadn't signed up to rejoin permanently and I wanted each show to be special and unique.

59
I'll Pay You £20 *Not* to Eat It

Back at the hotel in Leipzig, the room is a swamp of people and Dorian is taking bets as to whether he dares go to the bar with a banana skin on his head. Unbeknown to Dorian, the bar can be seen from the hotel window and we all watch him *not* putting the banana skin on his head while ordering a drink. He comes back with banana skin on head and claims to have completed the bet. Oh dear, Dorian bottles it – episode seven. He's not mentioned the yoghurts once … *Dorian Bottles It* will build into a handsome leather-bound volume at this rate.

Talk turns to how much you would need to be paid to eat a slug. People are saying things like a thousand pounds, or five hundred pounds and Nancy (where'd she come from?), who hasn't been paying much attention, is asked: 'Oh, five pounds!' she says. 'Right, you're on,' says Dorian. But when someone is going to do something *really* demeaning for a *very* small amount of money, let's say pierce their scrotum for £2.50, the option exists to pay them more *not* to do it. So Ralph offers her six pounds *not* to eat a slug and the bidding goes up. In the end Nancy wins £20 for *not* eating a slug – how did that happen? (By the way, I realise how pathetic and childish this all sounds and how nauseatingly it must come across, but it's important to be honest as to the true nature of these things and portray what is undeniably a feature of this kind of life – I don't see why the reader should be spared a share of the excruciation).

We all go and see Jackclayton's band play in town. He's in a psychedelic band with possibly the best name ever: Jack and The Beanstalks. Jack wears a cape onstage, which has to be worth the admission fee alone. On a bad day they are like most rubbish bands – 'a bit like The Fall and a bit like the Velvets' (remember that one next time you see your mate's crappy band). But tonight they are on form and the place is full. They have done that rare thing and gone beyond the enthusiastic applause that naturally accrues from mates and are appealing to people who don't know them personally, so it's a triumph. But they have a row and split up. Bands are like fish, very few survive long enough to get upstream. It's got little to do with inherent worth and is more down to the vicissitudes of a hostile environment.

60
A Time of Yoghurts

En route to Sheffield. There is no room in the fridge as the yoghurts sit there passing their sell-by date. Dorian has put off eating them, with a variety of increasingly flimsy pretexts, but crunch time is approaching. He'll have to do it soon or the squares will remain forever unfreaked. Flyovers and factories pass by and, like a child avoiding bedtime, Dorian presses me for more wondrous stories of the glory days of Britpop.

'There She Goes' by The La's jangles away.

Dorian: 'Is it true that a member of Cast once got chucked out of his hotel for dismantling his Corby trouser press out of boredom?'

Me: 'Yes, he did, just like in the Alan Partridge episode.'

And still the questions come about Sleeper and Powder and Gene and Salad and Echobelly and I'm getting bored of the sound of my own voice. Then he plays the obscure Pulp song 'Tunnel'.

'Turn it off!' I say. I never know where to put myself when my own music is on, it's like being caught masturbating. 'Are you going to eat these yoghurts or what, Dorian?'

We arrive at a motel somewhere in Germany or Holland or Belgium, which is isled all around by intersections, junk food drive-ins and all-night garages. I've given up on posh hotels, the drive-in ones are so much easier.

'Would operative Dorian report to the forecourt where a customer is requiring assistance with some yoghurts?' I say.

So what's it to be then, eh? It's our last night on the road, will the yoghurt go in the bin or will Dorian eat it? I try and put him off, saying it's really not fresh and it's no fun unless really he's up for it and it's a silly thing to do. But he and everyone else knows that there's a little devil on my shoulder silently shouting: 'Chicken! Lightweight! Eat it! Eat it! Eat it!' The tension mounts …

'I'm doin' it tonight,' he says. Then goes off for a curry, oh dear me! That is just bravado and the height of folly. I clap my hands together and rub them, this promises to be a good one.

Many have taken this challenge before but none have yet succeeded. It started many years ago when I'd bought a four-pack of thick and creamy yoghurt from Marks & Spencer. My then girlfriend had eaten three, the greedy pig. She said she could eat twenty, I bet her she couldn't and the challenge was born. The relationship did not survive this test – but I won the bet, and that's what counts, surely?

You see, the beauty of it is that the feat is eminently accomplishable. Twenty yoghurts are less than four pints. Dorian drinks double that every day in beer. If people didn't mess about they'd have no problem … but they do. They all have theories and stratagems and cunning plans, which become their undoing – and I have my psy-ops.

A member of the goth band The Mission thought speed was the answer. He necked fifteen in fifteen minutes, leaving the rhubarb until the end, then just stared at it balefully for the rest of the hour, saying 'I just don't fancy rhubarb at the moment'.

Rover thought it would somehow help him to have a cold bath halfway through. So he got to about fourteen in twenty minutes. Then he got into the cold bath, his stomach contracted and he couldn't sit down: he said that he had become a tube of toothpaste full of yoghurt and if he bent in the middle it would come out of the end.

And so it begins: Dorian looks good, he's steady, doesn't rush.

Banana, raspberry, vanilla, strawberry – four down in six minutes.

He keeps up a constant stream of chipper commentary about how easy it is.

Banana, raspberry, vanilla, strawberry – eight down in twelve minutes.

This is too easy, can he have a beer and a bit more curry? Sure thing, champ.

Banana, raspberry, banana, banana – twelve down in eighteen minutes – psy-ops time.

'Very funny, but I love banana, it's my favorite flavour, got any more?' – 'Yeah, ok, enjoy the curry, did you?'

Banana – twenty minutes have passed, thirteen down.

'All right, got any other flavours?' Oh, let's see, time for music though, I think.

'I Am the Fly' by Wire. How many lagers did you have today?'

Banana. 'Kebab Trauma' by DAF. And it's down, fourteen in twenty-five minutes. He's slowing but he's still got loads of time. Cam on, Tim!

Banana, banana, banana, banana, banana, banana – all lined up in front of him.

'The Black Angel's Death Song' by the Velvets then the theme tune from *Captain Pugwash.* 'They're Coming to Take Me Away', by Napoleon XIV. Have we got any Nana Mouskouri? No? 'Cruel Summer' by Bananarama … and on the video: *Fear and Loathing in Las Vegas.*

Oh dear, he's looking a little green around the gills, needs a bit of air … and he's off. Then back, staring at the rude boys – the six remaining banana yoghurts. He starts the first and eats it very, very slowly.

Then he's off for more air, and he's gone for ten minutes, best go and look for him. But he's nowhere to be seen. Worried, we search the ditches, calling his name. I begin to feel very anxious, picture the funeral and his distraught parents and the situation feels very unfunny. But, after an endless five minutes, we find him in the hotel toilets, feeling a little bilious – that's all.

Still ten minutes left to finish the rest.

He rushes back to the bus and finishes all six, just in the nick of time to great applause – IN AN ALTERNATE UNIVERSE!

He goes to sleep it off and I place Slowpoke by the side of his pillow, the Pokémon gently cradling a banana yoghurt pot.

There's some footage of Dorian's yoghurt challenge, but it doesn't really do it justice – it's as boring as an Andy Warhol film. Perhaps we should re-film it Fitzcarraldo-style, with green make-up for when he got queasy and get him to react the way he should have? When all's said and done though, he's a cool customer and this square was *very* freaked out when he did his disappearing act. But it's not the winning that counts – it's the gloating afterwards. Dorian gave it his best shot – but his best wasn't good enough.

In the morning the plaintive and melancholy call of a peacock is heard. How strange, surely not, in the middle of all this urban snarl? But there it is, a feral, burger-fed, ditch-dwelling peacock. Magical nonetheless – a lucky omen for wish fulfillment.

I play one of The Russian Girls at chess (and when I say one of The Russian Girls, I mean all of The Russian Girls. They are all jabbering advice in Russian and I object that I'm not supposed to be playing a team. But, as it turns out, this is to my advantage as they disagree violently and curse at each other in reproach for letting down Mother Russia. The match is a draw, which isn't enough for The Russian Girls: 'Your father would be so ashamed!' says one to the other. I cheer them up with a little music box from the vibes box – it plays 'The Internationale'.

We drop Steph the Klaxon off at a Tesco on the M25 and it's quite sad. He'd been with us for a week and it had become normal to see him walking around in Russian girls' clothes: now he's gone and that's probably the last we'll see of him. That's the thing with all this rock-and-roll socialising – it only works in context, like a big holiday romance. The whole time had been more or less a constant party. Ben, as the youngest, was always the last up, keeping things going and urging others to continue. In the morning (and by morning I mean afternoon, and by afternoon I mean early evening) he was hard to rouse from his vampire situation, so others picked up the baton of merriment. But now all of this trans-Euro excess was at an end.

61
A Queer Phone Call

I was back at home in Sheffield between shows when Jarvis rang;

Jarvis: 'You'll never guess where I am?'

Me: 'The moon?'

Jarvis: 'Ceauşescu's palace!'

Before all the concerts I wasn't playing, Jarvis rang up and asked me to reconsider. He never *really* believed I wouldn't fly. People in the world of showbiz make a big flouncy deal about what they will and won't do, but drop their objections if expedient. He'd been so long in that world of casual BS that 'no' didn't really mean 'no': it was just a position, a preference, that one could be persuaded to abandon by a bit of charm – of which he has an abundance. It's nice to be asked, of course, though I must confess to a little annoyance that Ceauşescu's hitherto forbidden citadel is now so easily attainable.

IRON CURTAIN 1984

62

Now Show Me How Zey Dance in Your Country!

Having been at the Battle of Orgreave seems pretty cool and I'm happy to milk it, because, at the time, it was faintly embarrassing. I had brought leaflets into the practice room for various demos but no one else went, even though they mostly supported the causes (rendering all possible assistance, short of actually doing anything – musicians are more interested in hair than revolution). We played the odd benefit but never wrote an overtly political song until it was all ancient history.

But I was obsessed with all things communist and Eastern Europe in particular; this was the influence for the violin part for a song called 'Separations', which gave its name to a later Pulp album. Steeped in the romance of Eastern Europe I channelled the ineffable melancholy of what I imagined to be a typical mournful gypsy song, full of halts, stops, heartbreaking crescendos and a speed-up-slow-down tempo. I'd never actually heard such a thing in the flesh and headed east in the hope of encountering it. And although Pulp struggled to get bookings as far afield as Chesterfield I optimistically produced copious promotional material in Serbo-Croat in the hope that Slavic promoters would look kindly upon a fellow comrade fresh from the picket lines.

I stayed with my Yugoslav friend Z, whose family got up at the crack of dawn to milk the goats and stir the slurry pool and thought me shockingly decadent for lying in beyond sunrise. Mornings aren't my strong point, but I'm very good at staying up late and they were pussies at that. I tried giving my demo tapes to puzzled organisers of village hops, to no avail.

Z's family cooked some large blubbery squid, which I pretended to like. When poor people have shared their food there really is no other option than to wolf it all down, go 'yum yum' and ask for seconds. Then they cleared the table and danced on it, standing around clapping. 'Now, show me how zey they dance in your country!' Pogoing on a table with a stomach full of squid is no fun either, though it was the only gig I got in Yugoslavia.

Z's ancient Czechoslovakian MZ motorbike had a putter putter two-stroke engine and looked like a wasp. He had a cool black leather flying-helmet, with aviation goggles like a rider from *Orpheus*. I had a white experimental racing helmet from the 1930s, which rose a full foot above my head, like a dome-headed cartoon professor.

I'm a bit scared of bikes – well, they are dangerous, aren't they? It's not a phobia, like flying, just a rational fear. Everyone who has a bike comes off; it's just a question of how serious it is. Bikes are dirty, dangerous and can be very gruelling – but on a sunny day they are the finest and most exhilarating way to travel. I closed my eyes and let smell-vision paint a landscape of animals, forests, wood smoke and changing crops.

We rode through a high-sided gorge, with a series of blue pools cascading into each other, sprouting long vegetative strands, which were petrified by the limestone-rich water to form travertine marble. Such places almost always contain the remains of ancient man, it's where we came from – a paradise lost.

On the road to Mostar we entered Bosnia, passing artichoke-scented sunflowers which turned to face the sun. The skirts of the women in the fields got longer and eventually became culottes, then an unfamiliar crop that had the presence all powerful crops have – tobacco. What a sight a tobacco field is, like something from Culpeper, so self-possessed.

Thence to Sarajevo. We journeyed through sleepy villages, with each cottage a different shade of blue. The road dipped down grassy at either side to the cottages, where storks nested atop chimney pots. Chickens and geese squawked and ran out of the way, the whole of nature conspiring to present a fairy-tale idyll. Swallows swooped from the rooftops and escorted the bike, dipping and swagging. One cheeky swallow swooped between the wheels of the bike for the sheer joy of it. Freedom, the open road, a new place each day.

I was so used to having to be the grown up in Pulp, I set up the concerts, printed the leaflets, spoke to the promoters, hired the vans and herded the cats. But it was good to let go and be the passenger for once.

I was sick of being in a small band, playing Sheffield and the odd dismal awaydays we could afford. I had ambition; I wanted to play exotic places like this and was frustrated that no one else seemed to share my urgency. I gave out leaflets and demo tapes but didn't get any concerts. But one has no idea how these things will turn out. For all I knew we could have become the biggest band in Yugoslavia and I could be writing about what a master stroke it was. It would have been a very good idea if it weren't such a bad idea.

63
Stock-cube Mule

Oh, don't go to Romania, it is a sad country,' pleaded my friend Z's baleful uncle, unaware that to my ears this just sold it. We planned the route, but there was one road his uncle objected to: 'Too many snakes!' Z was a reckless character, he threw his motorbike round blind bends and ate out-of-date sausages, but he was wary of snakes. I was intrigued by what a place with so many snakes that they represent a hazard to transport might be like: do they form in piles and block the road? Do they link head-to-tail and garrote you between posts? Do they leap from trees at your throat? Do they puncture the tyres with their ickle teeth?

So we took a long detour and ended up in an off-the-beaten-track part of the country beyond Bela Crkva, where horses and carts were the norm and heads turned to see a strange vehicle in town.

A woman walked towards us, she was heavy-set, had cracked heels and a couple of bruises on her arm. She was far removed from the anorexic beauties I normally went for but was womanly and stomped heavily and lazily towards us, swaying like a galleon. She was wearing a stretchy nylon top and had the most impertinent pair of breasts, too big to jiggle, they joggled braless and pointed this way and that – to the extent that I involuntarily looked at what they might be pointing at, like someone following a tennis match. She passed us with a look of haughty contempt and proceeded across the road. Rural Yugoslavia is not a great place for flirtation. We had been staying with hoary old uncles and had not seen a woman put out a sexual agenda of any kind, knowingly or otherwise, towards ourselves or humankind for a fortnight. So this display attracted our attention. She looked like a nasty piece of work and to stroll around quite so brazenly in a small village implied some backstory. A mustachioed brute with a fleet of clapped-out old carts guarded by snarling dogs backed up this assertiveness. This was the back of beyond, the last village before Romania, it didn't sell postcards.

The border approached, a no-man's-land separated by coils of barbed wire and a chain of observation posts, an Iron Curtain. A barrier and signs with exclamation marks interrupted the road. There was no sign of life from the bunkers around it – maybe it was unmanned? Maybe we could just drive through? Or *maybe* there were guns trained on us, hoping we would do just that and add our shredded tyres to the others lining the road? As Z went round the barrier an officer hurried out, putting his cap on. A young soldier with a rifle slung over the shoulder of his ill-fitting uniform followed.

The older man spoke to Z and the conversation was long, they went inside.

I grinned and leaned casually against the bike, affecting relaxation. The younger soldier smiled and lolled himself, but his rifle slipped down and he hitched it up alarmingly towards me.

They needed to search us. I'd got twenty half-kilo packets of Vegeta (vegetable stock) in my rucksack, would that be a problem?

I should explain that Romanian cuisine (such as it is) features soup quite heavily and some dictator or other (naming no names, Mr Ceauşescu) had forgotten to put stock cubes in the five-year plan. So we were told Vegeta was like currency over there. In the more relaxed atmosphere of Yugoslavia it had seemed like a good idea. Z's worrywart of an uncle had said there'd be no problem, but he wasn't here acting as a vegetable-stock mule.

I opened my rucksack.

'Vegeta?' said the officer, suspiciously.

'Vegeta!' I said, smiling as if he'd unexpectedly got the correct answer to a difficult question. I tore one open, he sniffed it, narrowed his eyes, 'Hmm, Vegeta' I proffered it to him as a gift. '*Ne!*' he said, angrily.

I silent-comedy-mimed that now it was open I couldn't put it back in my case without spilling it, making sad face with tear. He reluctantly accepted, as if doing me a favour. The young soldier hut-hummed, so I opened another packet for further inspection. He sniffed and nodded assent: it was Vegeta all right, and he might as well have it now, hadn't he? He looked across at the older man, who gave a nod and rolled his eyes.

Then I pulled out the cassette tape with which I hoped to get concerts for Pulp. They looked at it in puzzlement, then started to pull the tape out in a loop. Was it secret microfilm? '*Ne, ne, ne!*' I said, '*musika, musika!*' Oh, *musika*, delivered by some strange means of conveyance unknown in Romania.

'Giuseppe Verdi?' said the older man, hopefully.

'*Ne, ne, ne e Giuseppe Verdi, e Pulp!*'

'*Pulp? Ne for Romania!*' He confiscated it. How was I going to get any concerts without my demo tape? Still, on the plus side, we were banned in Romania. Is that cool? Seems pretty cool. I'd not had much success as a booking agent; if circles beyond the village hop existed, I hadn't found them. And neither had I come across any authentic gypsy music. But Romania, as the natural home of gypsies had promise.

Then he shook my tub of aspirins, but couldn't open the childproof lock. I opened it (by sorcery it appeared) revealing the suspicious white tablets (I was beginning to see the world through their eyes and most things are suspicious to a Romanian customs official).

'*Drogheria?*' he said as if he'd caught me out.

'*Ne, ne, ne, medicina, medicina!*' But when I saw the dubious look on his face I handed them over. I was beginning to wonder where this would end. It was starting to feel like a slow-motion robbery. Would we end up driving off naked, with a sack of Vegeta?

Then he took out my address book and puzzled over it. This was a neat little item about the size of a credit card. On one side was a picture of a red post box and on the other, a picture showing the outside of a door, with a pair of eyes peering through a letterbox. He consulted with the other guy, this was a find, there was definitely something fishy about it.

Z told me that he wanted to know what it means. What did it mean? Oh, well, I guess if you didn't realise what a red post box was and hadn't figured out that the eyes were looking through a letter box it would seem like something suspicious – something a spy might own. He tapped it, shook it, listened to it. It didn't tick, fortunately. Oh, how to mime this one? How do you mime letterbox? And even if you do, it's not a letterbox, is it?

Might as well get this over with. You see, this address book was actually two plastic halves that were held together by magnets. These concealed a concertina of A to Z leaves of lined card for writing addresses on. It was really neat, you had to write really tiny to fit the addresses on. I opened it, stretching both arms wide for effect and the concertina of addresses sprang open and sagged down. The man stepped back and gasped, the young one looked around nervously and held onto his rifle. They seemed to think they'd got us bang to rights here. The officer beckoned me to hand it over and took it gingerly, as if it might have another trick up its sleeve and emit poison gas. He put his specs on, this was serious.

Suddenly it wasn't a joke any more. It kept going through my head that the whimsical Holly Hobbie style of the graphics made it impossible to get concerned, but they were taking it very seriously. Z had more explaining to do and was worried now. They went inside and made a phone call. I imagined the person on the other end of the phone being consulted; two strangers (and they didn't get many round here) had this gadget that sprang open to reveal hundreds of tiny names, addresses and phone numbers. They were going to hold us, this was going higher up and they had what looked like a cell. Oh, shit! Would this be a good time to mention that I was a flag-burning republican communist?

The officer came and spoke in a raised voice – I didn't know what they were saying but Z was pleading. I pointed to Z and pointed to the 'Z' in the address book/network of subversives and mimed that the numbers were a telephone – this didn't help. Then more numbers, 'Droog' I said, which means comrade in *Clockwork Orange*, which is the nearest I get to Romanian. 'Engleski droog!' And the next number? Sherlokski was onto something here. 'Devotchka' ('girl' in *Clockwork Orange*), which they understood. And the next, 'devotchka' also, then another 'devotchka', the young soldier smiled and raised an eyebrow at the older one. Lotta devotchkas here – you know what these spies are like! I pretended that the next names were devotchkas and they were impressed. Then I said 'mama', sentimentally, like something from an Italian comic opera.

'He wants to know where your mother is,' said Z.

'*Engleski mama*,' I said.

The colonel pointed at me, '*Engleski?*' he said, not believing a word of this nonsense.

'*Da, da, da, Engleski! Me Engleski!*'

'*Pass-o-port!*' he said.

I reached into my inside pocket, the soldier pointed his rifle at me. '*Pass-o-port*' I said, as I slowly took it out. The soldier lowered his gun. And there it was, the glorious large black passport, with inset lozenge. And there was my photograph, set amongst the elaborate and calm calligraphy, each page of which looked more plausible as currency than anything this tin-pot dictatorship could produce. If you'd never seen one in the flesh before – and they hadn't – it looked like something someone of an elevated status would have, a high-up party official or a diplomat. They might have seen one in a film when they were doing national service (which they did somehow) – maybe *On Her Majesty's Secret Service*?

And there was her majesty demanding that Johnny Foreigner allow – 'without let or hindrance', mind! – her most esteemed subject to be set free on pain of incurring her majesty's displeasure. And you don't want that, do you? Yeah, we'll see now, what's it to be then, oh my friends and brothers? The officer instinctively began a salute, and the young soldier stood up straight. I nodded curtly, as if inspecting troops, and raised a patrician hand for him to stand down and desist from entering into any spontaneous applause, which he might otherwise feel compelled to do. Oh yeah, English: read it and weep. They might not have heard of Pulp – but they'd heard of her majesty. Flag-burning republican communists – don't see many of them round here, do you?

We were all friends now: 'Zed, Zed, Zed' said the now avuncular officer, smiling indulgently. Z had a Yugoslav passport in slimy-country red, it was dog-eared from much travel and an examination of the stamps resplendent with elephants, temples and palm trees – revealed that the last three countries he'd been to were Malaysia, Cambodia and Laos; or the Golden Triangle, as I believe it's known in heroin-smuggling circles. Oh, here we go again.

Z was searched and out came a stack of long, tapering Camden Carrots – giant fucking spliffs. These he had bought quite openly in the gift shop at Laos airport as a souvenir. They were not dope, as possession of dope carried the death penalty in Laos and they wouldn't sell them at the airport shop, would they? But try explaining that when you don't speak Romanian! They looked just like spliffs or, more accurately, like a film prop from a Cheech and Chong film. Honestly, ossifer, there's a perfectly innocent explanation – you see, it's all quite amusing actually. Z managed to talk his way out of it by saying: 'Do you *really* think I'd be stupid enough to carry something that looks so obviously like drugs?

Then they shook hands, smiled and let us go. We'd been there over an hour – it had been touch and go and I'm not sure anyone but Z could have talked their way out of it. The combination of Z and I's nationalities meant that they were more wary of detaining us than letting us go, but it probably didn't help that Z was called 'Z': I mean, it's a pretty good name for a spy, isn't it?

64
The Extremely Sad Toy

Romanian petrol disagreed slightly with the MZ. But it was made in Czechoslovakia and not used to the finer things in life, it would run on lard if need be.

We slowed as we approached a sentry box and the MZ protested with a series of staccato backfires like gunshots, which brought a dozing soldier out, clutching his gun.

'*Americhki* cigarettes?' he said. We offered him Yugoslav Drinas. Nope, worse than useless. He pressed the corners to demonstrate: soft packets, you see. The important thing was hard packets.

'John Player Special?' he asked, forlornly. John Player Specials' shiny black packets were the preferred smoke for a Western dream involving onyx tables, a poster of a red Ferrari and a Philip Castle print of Farrah Fawcett-Majors with breasts metamorphising into torpedos.

No. Sorry, mate, only this shit: what can you do?

He smiled sympathetically, have a nice day anyway, fellow paupers.

We had guns pointed at us about twenty times in Romania, which you'll agree is quite a lot for a one-week 'holiday'.

There was a lot of budget circa-1968 modernism in Romania. The kind of 'architecture of pleasure' you occasionally get at seaside resorts. The construction materials always looked sub-standard and possibly hazardous. Mostly it was poorly finished, if zealously enthusiastic, and gave no quarter to function or comeliness.

In some forgettable town on the way to Cluj, a supermarket had eight aisles – each one filled with a different pickle such as gherkins, sauerkraut and beetroot. And the toy department, 'Ages 5–18', was an aisle full of wooden ducks pulled by string that opened their beaks as they walked. This was one of the saddest things I'd ever seen. Imagine you are seventeen and that is your Christmas present and your little brothers' and all your mates'. There's a lot to be said for the primitive life. I envy tribesmen who live in yurts, follow the herd and live on blubber. But to be somewhere that has left behind all that was attractive about the past, to live in a bureaucratic, repressed, polluted world pursuing industrialisation for its benefits … and that is the best it can give a teenager. I know it seems vaguely comic and not the worst thing in the world, but walk a mile in those shoes.

By the roadside, we found a bull's skull and strapped this to the front of the bike so that light streamed though the eye sockets and then rented a woodland cabin in a desolate spot and listened to the wind in the trees, feeling slightly uneasy. It was the kind of place you wouldn't split up and wander off from if you've seen enough horror films.

The crunch of gravel from a car shone headlights into the cabin, music blared from the stereo. Two policemen got out clutching a bottle of booze. Then two girls in gymslips: fellow campers, how delightful. We tried making conversation but they were laughing to themselves and whooping it up. It was an assignation of some kind. The girls, who were neither sufficiently abstemious nor svelte to trouble Nadia Comăneci, drank vodka and laughed unconvincingly loudly at the policemen's comments. The policemen went into the cabin to wait for the girls, who lingered, chatting to us. Neither Z nor I were so good looking that we got offered a lot of modelling work but, lolling on the MZ with the cow's-skull light, we were sufficiently young and exotic to provide more interest to these racy young women than their current paramours, who were double our age and weight. But these girls knew which side their bread was buttered in Romania 1984, and made a blithe show of being less interested in us than I think they were. The blokes were waiting in the cabin and their tone was getting increasingly irritable. With a resigned blown kiss and a raised eyebrow the cheeky girls made their way to the cabin to do the deed, fortifying themselves with plenty of vodka and shared brassiness.

The signs outside a black factory complex proclaimed 'Heroism! Socialism! Romania! Ceauşescu!' A steam whistle blared and hordes of workers streamed out, it looked like a scene from a constructivist propaganda poster – but the figures didn't strike such heroic poses, they looked beaten and broken. No jutting jaws and fierce eyes fixed firmly on the future, just hung heads and Lowry stoops. The pervasive hand of surveillance and suspicion filled the air, neighbour feared neighbour.

Man-of-the people Ceauşescu lived in the largest and most opulent palace ever conceived, from which a fifty-foot image of his reassuring face smiled down, surmounted by huge red letters. Perhaps he's smiling because of the irony, the letters bear the legend: '1984'.

Any remaining notion I might have had about Romania being some kind of worker's paradise had long gone. Clearly this was evil and oppressive, something that common decency dictated one should oppose without thinking. I'm surprised how quickly I adjusted to the truth. Reading George Orwell helps: Romania under Ceauşescu seemed to have used *1984* as a template for how to construct a society.

When one has woken from a dream it's hard to remember just how real it felt at the time. Now that the Iron Curtain has been drawn, it's difficult to picture the dictators as anything other than paper tigers, slightly laughable anachronisms who were destined to fall. So it's impossible to imagine the permanence and solidity it seemed to possess back then. But stability is an illusion, a sandcastle built by a child unaware of the incoming tide.

Ceauşescu's Romania cured me of communism but Pulp retained a fascination for oppressive regimes – it was something that we referenced amongst ourselves. Steve, who became a significant driver in the band, would note with approval when something looked 'Brutalist', 'Soviet', or 'eastern bloc'.

I had run Pulp People, the band's fan club, and initially contributed most of the content for the fanzine *Disco-very*. Mark took over the running of both but I still contributed articles including a 'Hardline' crossword and a recipe for 'Mussolini Tomatoes' that played to this theme.

Aficionados will recognise several songs from Pulp's earlier periods with an overtly Eastern European flavour, but one anecdote from our heyday perhaps typifies this theme's persistence.

We fed the press a made-up story that we were getting the worlds' biggest stylophone – the size of a grand piano – made. The stylophone was actually invented by someone called Jarvis, of all things, but we pretended that the inventor was Otto Prutsinger, who was constructing the instrument in Düsseldorf. The idea of it being made in Düsseldorf particularly tickled us; it was appropriately brutal and industrial.

But there's another pull exerted by the east – something older and more impenetrable, deep-set and intense. It's European, and therefore familiar, but it's so different that it's something else all together. The flavour and fascination of Eastern Europe did have an influence on our music and presentation. You'd probably find it hard to ferret this out from the overall tapestry, but it's definitely one of the colours in the palette.

There have been a number of references to 'Eastern European disco' in reviews so some people picked up on the influence. But when I try and put my finger on exactly what that is, it slips away elusively.

PORTUGAL
2011

65
Cave Centipede

Now, where were we? . . . I dimly recall this all started out as a story about Pulp's farewell tour in 2011 and we've spent the last goodness knows how long wandering around Eastern Europe in the 1980s rather than just going straight to Portugal, where the next show is.

This is essentially a family holiday punctuated by a concert. It's a once-in-a-lifetime chance for my now adult kids to travel this way and – despite his fears of it being a bit weird having him along as 'a hairy manchild', as he puts it – Ralph fits in fine.

There is a mix-up with the hotel booking and we have to find somewhere on the fly. This is a great stroke of fortune, as we end up in Porto (or Oporto in old money). Porto has been preserved in picturesque decay, with warrens of winding streets and barques on the river bearing the casks of port that gave the city its name. With its crumbling tiled buildings, it's down at heel, in an old colonial way and it doesn't take much imagination to picture oneself in the world of doubloons and pieces of eight.

The drive to the concert is through scorched badlands full of burnt trees. Fire is a part of the ecosystem here and renders it largely uninhabitable. The heat is intense; to walk outside the bus is to walk into an oven. There is a whiff of the spaghetti western, which is no surprise as many were filmed here.

It seems unlikely that there should be a festival in such a backwater and we haven't seen any adverts. But there it is and it's a lovely set-up: people camp by the river, cook on campfires and live the outdoor dream that Glastonbury used to offer. It's a small (ten to twenty thousand) audience compared to the others on the tour.

The atmosphere backstage seems to have calmed down a bit.

At the last minute Jarvis springs on Ralph the fact that we need his assistance playing keyboards on 'Common People'. He introduces him wryly as, 'The master of the keyboards, Mr Ralph Razor', which delights everyone, apart from an embarrassed Ralph, who feels the heat because he plays some bum notes. This is Pulp, Ralph, you're *supposed* to play bum notes.

Rover shuffles over, reluctant to get too close. He is dressed all in black with a hooded cowl and looks like a thirteenth-century peasant on the scrounge for a turnip. His face is ashen, he's got crew-flu, poor love, and is voiding at both ends. He won't shake my hand as he doesn't want to infect me. On a tourbus, when one person falls ill with something infectious, it's near certain that it will work its way round the vehicle, given the close proximity and low resistance that this kind of life entails. Coming offstage in a shirt drenched in sweat into chillier air pretty much guarantees that you'll pick up whatever is going round. Crews rightly dread this lurgy, but accept it as an occupational hazard. Two roadies will split a course of antibiotics when there's something going round if two aren't available. This is a dangerous game because if you don't kill the bug you'll have made it stronger. But such was the mighty dread of crew-flu that they were prepared to self-medicate in this dangerous way.

On one tour I travelled overnight on my bunk, unable to lie down, coughing all night on all fours, straining a new muscle with every cough. Another time I had a mouth infection, which turned my mouth green, but was unable to get any Corsodyl – you try finding it in Luxemburg on a Sunday. I was shown a bottle of fluid that was used to clean the microphone heads. That was all they had, I declined and suffered.

This time round I'm taking no such chances and have brought heap big medicine chest ... and feel as fit as a fiddle.

On the way back we stop at Bilbao, the capital of the Basque country where, unfortunately, the women aren't in national costume. But – glory be! – we *do* find tapas worthy of the name and wander round the bars, trying the various specialties. It's a feast day again and the wacky sound of a brass band playing a Pogues song heralds the arrival of a milk float with a huge *Scooby-Doo* dog's head, which lurches dangerously back and forth like a bull along the narrow cobbled streets with the band following. It drives into bars, knocking over tables as the band gets drunk, stumbling and chaotic. It's got a berserk pagan mayday feel and doesn't seem like the rest of Spain. You can see how this part of the world was the interglacial refuge of the tribes that later settled Britain. They are more raucous here, that's for sure.

We stay at the ancient Occitan fastness, Carcassonne, which is as fairy-tale a medieval walled city as it's possible to find. I'll resist the temptation to get all Sunday supplement on your ass about Carcassonne – it's very beautiful and all the things it should be. I rather fancy buying an absinthe fountain, but the ones in the shop all have tacky plastic chrome-effect fittings – ugh. You see, pop stars have troubles too!

The kids find a frightening creature in the bath that looks like two eyelashes joined together. Apparently it's a poisonous cave centipede and, this being Carcassonne, the centipede must have come from a cave stuffed full of Cathar gold. Now all we have to do is crack the code, kill the albino, go through the secret passage and find the grail.

What is it with all these new creatures anyway? When I was a boy it was just lions and tigers and donkeys and a few creepy crawlies like earwigs and slugs. You never saw anything that wasn't in the *Observer Book of Insects*. Now all you have to do is imagine some twenty-foot-long piece of wobbly chewing gum with prehensile ears and, hey presto, some chipper Yank from Wisconsin is patiently explaining how you catch one on the Internet. There's definitely something fishy going on. We didn't have cave centipedes when I was a lad; we got by without 'em and were none the worse for it.

66
Say What You Like About Reading

Gareth parks the van on unprepossessing spare land at the side of the hotel we are staying in for the Reading festival. For all I know, there may be some great bits to Reading, but I shan't be going there for my holidays – Carcassonne it ain't.

Ralph gives one of his morale-boosting speeches: 'Well, so, well, we're in Reading and erm, say what you like about Reading but ... [long pause as we lean in waiting for the revelation] well, what can you say? [yes, what *can* you say] Well, so, here we all are ... in Reading!' Hurrah, cheers, clink of glasses, magnificent speech! We have established that we are indeed in the place we know ourselves to be. Ralph has excelled himself with this one. When one considers the great eve-of-battle addresses – Churchill's 'Never was so much owed by so many to so few'

and Henry V's on the eve of Agincourt – surely 'We're in Reading' will rank amongst the most inspiring?

It is quite a high-pressure concert because it is the only one being filmed. Looks okay on the telly to me, someone lit a red flare. The reviews that are thrust under my nose are pretty universally glowing but someone makes mention of me looking 'bucolic' – which I did – so I get some pale foundation after that.

So that was Reading, we came we played, we got muddy wellies, we left: end of. There are a few people we know at the show but I am glad we don't run into them and inflict our less than inspiring wet-weekend-in-Wales upon them and damage the reputation of the bus. Not one for the scrapbook.

I've got very little to say about the show and I know that must feel like a cheat to the people who shared it. I don't like the word 'fan', it implies inferiority, but can't think of a better one. None of my friends are Pulp 'fans' – or at least if they are they don't go on about it. But I'm really proud of our fans. They inspired us, they found their way into the lyrics, they influenced our style and without them there would have been no band. I've met thousands upon thousands of them and, with the odd exception, they are a lovely bunch of people. I recognise their names on the credits of television shows. If I watch a late-night arts programme I'll often see a face from the Pulp moshpit. There can be few bands whose audiences contained as many creatives as Pulp's. But that isn't because they liked Pulp – it's because they were like that anyway. For the first few years I read and replied to all the fanmail and that was a pleasure. So I've got nothing to say about Reading, apart from the fact that a show like that means I can bow out of this thing with no regrets: and for that I owe a huge debt of thanks to those that were cheering us on.

People ask me what I miss about being in Pulp and, you know, there's very little. What I do miss is playing a concert then hanging out with a bunch of cool kids who show me their hometown. So, thank you, Reading and goodnight.

I recently cleared my loft including some fan mail and was slightly tempted to reply to several letters I hadn't managed to respond to at the time:

> Dear Miss X,
>
> Forgive my tardiness in replying to your letter of the 17th inst. October 1995 in which you made a very generous offer. I wondered if now that you are the age I was when I received this letter (to wit 34), whether the offer still stood or whether the passage of time has rendered it null and void?'
>
> Sternest regards
>
> R. Senior esq. (Bsc. Hons, Mercury Music Award, Ivor Novello Award. Best behaved band in Europe etc. etc. etc.)

1996
GERMANY

67
Something Changed

There had been a tour of UK arenas and it must have been vindicating to play to over 10,000 people in our home city and several nights at Wembley Arena, but I have no recollection of the concerts. Some will have been exultant life-affirming experiences, but an arena concert is not always a special moment; it's an entertainment consumption option and I'd much rather play a scout hut in a forest.

We did a song called 'Something Changed', the last of four singles from *Different Class*. I wasn't proud of my part, it seemed like a bog-standard recapitulation of things I'd done before and the track itself seemed like we had come full circle – back to the kind of songs Jarvis wrote on his own. It got to number ten in the charts.

With the heightened security that came with our greater fame and the threats made after the Brits, we were increasingly sealed inside a bubble where we only met accredited and particularly pushy people. One never met the casual fan and I really missed that. The social life got worse and the only thing I remember is hanging around bored in corridors. So it was with much relief that we got back to down and dirty touring in Germany.

In Berlin, several people seem to want to take us out for a meal, but no one is obviously in charge. As it turns out, it is just a random collection of people who happen to be there. Some are fans, one is a hotel employee, another a former East German skating champion, several who think it must something to do with the wedding they are attending, and a Down's syndrome lad who has lost his carer.

We head over the bridge into east Berlin like the pied piper. At the restaurant Rover, who was practicing his German and trying to flirt with the waitress, calls her 'a little snail face', which is taken amiss. The tour manager, who's not slept for three days, shouts at Rover, 'You don't behave like this, this is Pulp!' But it's really hard to figure out what's going on. The Down's syndrome lad is getting excited and keeps clapping his hands, which lends lends a riotous air to proceedings.

The tour manager storms off.

When the bill comes it transpires that we're paying for everyone's meal and they don't take credit cards. Cash is scraped together, including a big pile of pfennigs and no tip, which the restaurant isn't very happy about.

We skulk back to the hotel, return the Down's syndrome lad to his relieved carer and see the tour manager with his head down on the bar. A bloke chucks a peanut at him and Kraken wakes: 'If you throw another effing peanut at me I'm gonna put you through that wall' says the man who collected the 'Best Behaved Band in Europe' award. We've not played a concert yet and things are getting very sketchy, in a way that normally only happens after a month on the road.

In the morning the tour manager can't be woken. No one's got any money and we await further instructions, which don't come. So, in need of food, we go down to the venue to see what's on offer.

The Longpigs, who also hail from Sheffield, are supporting us. They are a volatile bunch and prone to smashing their instruments and each other up. They have a female keyboard player who, as a worker with primary school children, takes it all in her stride: 'boys will be boys'.

The venue holds 2,500 and is sold out, our biggest headline show outside the UK.

The concert is hot and enthusiastic. Like audiences the world over, people throw an arm or two up at frenetic points in the set and even the gentlest of German indie anoraks does an involuntary one-armed salute, before catching themselves and putting their arms down embarrassed.

In the dressing room there's a large wedge of watermelon and I bang this against my forehead until it is all over my face and clothes.

The show feels a bit disconnected, like it sometimes does in England now. That people like us on a superficial pop level and just want to hear the hits. This is fine, but I'd like there to be something more and I'm sure there is, but it's not at the forefront. One doesn't get a spiritual feeling from a show like that. It feels like a job, which you take pride in doing well, but a job nonetheless. There's no reason to complain and we get treated very well – especially by an American lady who turns up backstage offering us a massage. The suspicion is that it's some kind of seedy ploy. But, as it turns out, she's the finest masseuse in Berlin and just kind of collects all the bands.

We set off for Hannover, sleeping overnight on the bus. I'm woken by vigorous shaking and the words 'You wake up now!' by a leather-clad dominatrix, who drags me by the arm, bleary-eyed, to some kind of railway siding. She then marches me into an underground chamber to be interrogated with a light shining in my eyes.

'So, why did you come back to Germany, when you were only here six months ago?'

The members of Pulp who have also been dragged here look at each other, puzzled at this hostile line of questioning: 'Well, we were asked to do concerts.'

'What are your influences?'

Time is called on the interview by the leather-clad lady, who turns out to be the rep from the record company. I do prefer the German way of doing things – they have their allocated slot, then they bugger off and leave you to it. It's all very efficient and it does run on time. But, like many things on tour, if you're not in the mood for it, it can wind you up immensely.

After the show she-who-must-be-obeyed collars the very tired and drunk Steve in the lift, insisting that he fill out some kind of questionnaire. He is indignant, bemused (and, I suspect, slightly aroused) by this.

The day after I'm practising my violin, swishing the bow back and forth to make helicopter noises, and the rep takes umbridge: 'Just because I wear leather does not mean that I am into S&M and domination and I think people's sexual preferences are their own business!' She storms off.

Whoever said that travel broadens the mind should get out more. In our experience it only confirms the stereotypes. When people write to us from Germany, it is usually on graph paper.

After the concert we come offstage, having lost several litres of body fluid in sweat, which is replaced by refreshing mint juleps.

So, hangover occurs … but we get over it and, before the next show, watch the England versus Holland match and England win 4-1. There's a lot of squaddies over here and a lot of Union Jacks, which I'm a bit ambivalent about at a concert (even though I wear Union Jack socks). We go onstage and let the crowd know the scoreline, which is very popular. It is lively and more laddish that we're used to – more like an Oasis audience.

We're doing very well in Germany but it's getting a bit boring. One arrives at a place and forms an impression, but what you see is very artificial. You're judging it by transportation, hotels, dressing rooms and the people you meet – who are a very self-selecting minority. So we're not really seeing Germany, we're doing a hermetically sealed concert tour of Germany, which is a very different thing.

It's nice to think when you're setting out on a tour that you're embarking on an *Apocalypse Now*-like journey to the heart of darkness and that you're going see strange things and have unusual experiences. This one started off quite promisingly but after a week it's just petered out and I'm looking through the drizzle at a gravel car park feeling like I'm doing a very mundane and workmanlike thing. You can't force fun to happen, you can't stop it happening either. If you try and pursue normality, strangeness will find you.

Sleep overnight to Czechoslovakia.

Awake to find that we're not at the festival site but in a Chinese shantytown, surrounded by hundreds of masturbating garden gnomes: just one of those porcupine in a bucket things that happen a lot when you are on tour.

The Chinese people keep shouting at us to go but we've got to wait for the truck driver. Then we've a mad dash to the festival and the best directions we've got are: 'a camp site near Prague'. It's five hours until we're due onstage and it takes six hours to get to Prague, so the show has to be cancelled. We had all the right papers too … so much for Bohemia. Incidents like this do nothing to calm the incipient xenophobia that sets in after a week away from home.

We head along the Rhine to the next concert, passing at least ten castles, several of them gay, and end up in a drizzly car park awaiting the equipment bus driver, who's been detained by Czech customs for the past thirty-six hours.

'What you been up to, mate?'

'Been held up at the German–Czech border.'

'Did they torture you?'

'Yes, but I didn't tell them anything.'

'Did your lovable scouse humour win them over?'

'I did get a bit feisty.'

We play a small festival to a stadium rock audience, which is a nightmare. We are supporting Iggy Pop, who is wearing transparent trousers, not a pretty sight. Our set is filmed for posterity and doesn't look half as bad as it was in terms of going through the motions.

My guitar is stolen and Richard Hawley of The Longpigs is so furious that he smashes up *our* dressing room. I'm not that bothered; it's just a guitar, a tool to do a job. I haven't called it 'Lucille', or polished it lovingly with finest Manuka beeswax. So that's the kind of guy Richard is, a complete drama queen, but fiercely loyal to his many friends and passionate about guitars. Whenever I've bought a guitar I've always taken Richard with me. I stumble through 'Smoke On the Water' on the bottom string, then Richard plays 'All Along the Watchtower' with his knob, better than Hendrix, and the shop gets out all their nice guitars. Richard gets out his micrometer and takes measurements and tells them that it's the 1963 import, when they switched to using mahogany instead of rosewood, and the price comes down. Then I buy an amp because I think it's pretty. Richard approves of my purchase because it's got a 'very full bass response', whatever that is, then tears his hair out because I turn the bass down to zero to get the tinniest sound possible.

In Munich we record two songs at a television show and, much to our surprise, it's a concert with 1,500 people. The audience has paid half price, so they aren't expecting much, but we put on a full show and it's great.

We arrive at the Biscuithalle in, what's the town called? Don't know, let's look on the itinerary, where the blinkin' heck are we? We're in Bonn! We go to the venue at eleven in the morning and there's nothing to do except wait around all day. I have a shower and put my suit on and, all bright and breezy, go onto The Longpigs' bus to wind them up because I know they'll be in a right tangle.

'Come on, chaps, shake a leg, let's not miss this splendid morning! *Schnell! Schnell! Raus! Raus!*'

Richard Hawley is in vampire situation and I ask him how their television interview went.

'It was very strange because it was like we were having an autopsy done on us.'

'Are you speaking metaphorically here?'

We sit outside playing chess as Richard slowly sobers up, good-naturedly nursing his hangover in front of bemused fans.

Taught The Longpigs how to play poker – that was a mistake, think they might have played before.

Play the concert in the Biscuithalle, that's good, then drive to Münster, where we are now.

It's England versus Germany in the semi-final and we're going to have to figure out somewhere to watch the match where we aren't outnumbered – so we can cheer on England and still stay alive. I love Germany's friendliness, its high-mindedness, much of its music and its cack-handed attempts at humour. Things can easily get out of hand though because English and German people are always trying to get on and overcompensate for that little bit of misunderstanding we had a few years back.

England lose on penalties. We start applauding and the Germans start applauding so it was quite nice actually.

It has struck me that, when it comes to talking about concerts, I've got very little to say about them. And I find it very difficult to remember any details. I know a feeling from it whether it felt good, or bad, or in between but that's about it. And yet there's nothing to say about it from an insiders' point of view. Time slows down just before you go on, then it really speeds up, you're no sooner on than you're off. Like a dream you remember it for about fifteen minutes then it fades.

I'm not overly keen on the analogy some people make between being onstage and sex. It's stimulating in many ways, but only in the same way that eating is like sex. It's a sensual experience but a different one. But the amnesiac quality, especially when it's good, is part of it. Bad concerts where you don't really connect drag on for ever. Good ones flash by: you know it was good but you can't quite remember who did what to whom; when and how and where; and how it all was; but you know it was good … so, in that respect, I have begun to understand the analogy.

ENGLAND
2011

68
Unicorn in Asda

Autumn's approaching and it's getting quite nippy now. Leeds is the closest we are playing to Sheffield, so it is something of an awayday for friends and family. Hometown shows can be a right bunfight. There's always somebody left off the guest list who needs to be attended to when you should be concentrating on the show. I hate this stuff – it's really tedious – and do my absolute best to ensure that anyone I have invited gets in. But there are always cock-ups and someone who shouldn't be left outside is. Conversely, there will be someone inside bending your ear who you'd really rather wasn't. It's like five gypsy weddings all at once. I still cringe at the thought of my undemonstrative father being unable to get in to see his son's triumphant homecoming or Steve's mum not being able to get backstage when someone (and I suspect my own guests) pretended to be her. I've been on the other side of this many times too and, don't hold it against those who should have made sure I got in – well depends actually. Once I couldn't get into an award ceremony where we were receiving an award. Stuff like this is very depressing but I have developed an answer: 'Well, if my name's not down then I'm not coming in!' and storm off, but it's tough if you've travelled. It's also an occasion where the Machiavellian politicking that surrounds Pulp, and I guess most bands (and, I guess, most organisations) has full rein to rear its ugly head. It's survival of the pushiest. Stuff like this made me want out, but today it's not too bad, largely because I've put off almost everyone I know from coming.

It is very cold and the band huddles round the gas fire backstage. My mum forces me to wear a fake fur coat she has brought. Mum, I'm not nineteen and I'm not in the Manic Street Preachers!

It is a huge crowd, they love us and we love them. Shame it isn't filmed.

Backstage is lively because of all the families and other guests. My mum befriends our old drummer Magnus, who sits grinning benignly with his dreadlocks and Hindi face tattoos.

In 1987, when signing on, I saw Magnus in full monk's regalia, complete with tonsured head. He rode off on a bicycle and went all the way to India. No one heard from him for several years and we thought we'd never see him again. Then he just turned up, his face covered in Hindu tattoos. He'd joined a cult, then tried to leave but had been forcibly kept prisoner.

'Do you want something to eat?' I said.

'Oh, no, I don't eat,' he said, which somehow seemed quite plausible with him.

'But you must eat *something*?'

'Just jelly balls and nuts.'

And now here he is, live in Leeds, bold as you please – like a unicorn turning up in Asda.

So the line-up from the album *Freaks* is almost complete and … but there's someone missing from this line-up of twisted toyshop escapees. Manners is now working with young offenders. He's perfect for the job, as he has home-made tattoos of insects running up his legs and those little dots on the knuckles. They'll certainly relate to him and he'd be the last person to patronise them. Though whether he'll teach them to stop stealing, or how to do it more effectively I couldn't say.

69
The Old Abandoned Aftershow

The Brixton Academy is one of those double-galleried old theatres that manages to be big while still remaining intimate. We played in the nineties and there's some footage of it, though thankfully not the bit where I stepped backwards onto my diminutive guitar tech, who was scuttling across the stage and ended up carrying me along in what must have appeared to be a carefully choreographed routine – a kind of dwarf sleigh-ride bonanza.

There's a great view of London from the hotel and I watch it moving for half an hour like a slow-motion firework display. London is a great city and has far surpassed its rivals of twenty years ago, there's really only New York that compares to it. I never thought of London as a beautiful city until I saw it from the river at night, with all those iconic buildings and fine bridges reflected in the water.

We head to the venue and London traffic going nowhere rattles even the normally placid Gareth. In Brixton he crashes into a lamppost – and comes out to inspect (honestly, we play reggae *all* the time, it's not just cultural slumming).

The soundcheck takes ages with all the new songs we will play, to make sure each set is very different for the few who have bought tickets for both nights at Brixton.

In an otherwise sparky show Jarvis rambles on a bit too much between songs. The rest of us look around, hoping he will wind it up. Mark starts noodling his guitar to let him know to get on with it and Jarvis snaps at him: 'It's just fucking rude!'

The audience goes 'Oooh' in a 'Hark at him getting all stroppy!' way.

Jarvis says: 'This next song is dedicated to Mark, if you're not part of the solution you're part of the problem.' It's prissy and unpleasant and kills the mood.

Steve, to his credit, takes issue with this kind of thing and I'm not mad on it either. Although after Mark's antics in East Germany I'm not really minded to stick up for him, I end up doing so anyway because it's just not fair. The point is that it's not right to slag someone off if they don't have a microphone to respond with, you leave that to the dressing room. So it's all getting a little bit niggly and, yet again, I'm glad I'm not on the same bus, amid all the fester.

The next day I go to soundcheck and practice the fresh songs we'll be playing. I lazily knocked out the guitar part for 'Something Changed' shortly before I left the band in the nineties, so I've not played it that much – so little in fact that I never really felt ownership of it. But now I find it deliciously mellifluous and beguiling in a way I didn't at the time.

Again it was a good show and thankfully tantrum-free this time. Peace has descended. There's only one more show to go, then we can all go our separate ways.

So many people have elbowed their way backstage that the dressing room is a hard place to get dressed in. When you think about it, what a dressing room is actually for, it's a bit weird that so many people insist on forcing their way into your changing room – but there you have it. Imagine if someone came to your place of work and insisted on hanging around the changing rooms? There are so many very important people in London it would seem. But I don't know who the fuckers are, so I go to the aftershow, which is more sparsely populated than the dressing room. So it's a London aftershow that the London end of the band don't turn up to, which is a pretty poor show if you ask me.

Outside the infected road crew load out past fans who have been waiting ages for autographs in the chilly night air and I feel a like Prince Prospero callously eating a lamb shank while darkness and despair and the Red Death hold indomitable dominion over all, then get another glass of champagne.

I see a few old faces, including Luke Haines of The Auteurs. Some of Menswear are supposed to be here, but I don't see them or maybe we just don't recognise each other after multiple pile-ups with time's winged chariots.

Back at the hotel, according to Ralph, I have an argument with someone I don't even know and storm off but I've no recollection of this – so maybe I was bored and just wandered off, maybe I've just got a miserable resting face, maybe I didn't have the energy for my own aftershow. I *do* remember there was a really nice chair in the room though.

I'm glad there's only one more show to go, I've had all these conversations before. It's all such a bore; I can't tell one person from another and I want my life back. The only things I feel like saying now are bitter. I could try and settle some scores and put the world to rights but that would be unedifying, so instead I'll tell you a story of another journey in another land far, far away.

USA
1996

70
Pigbum Dollar Twenty-five

Land in San Francisco. Jet lag is good for two reasons. Firstly, it makes you feel like a time traveller from another dimension and secondly, it means you aren't on jets.

Huge letters saying 'ROOMS' announce our motel. Despite the Californian acceptance, nay encouragement, of euthanasia, smoking is strictly prohibited and my room has, for my 'comfort and convenience', been designated a zone of zero tolerance. Of course, we rebellious rock stars aren't bothered by such trifles – except when trigger-happy water sprinklers are pointing towards them.

My showbiz chums and I eat at a diner where our waitress wears a badge that states 'I saved a special smile just for you.' By the time our drinks are served we have discovered:

A. Her name
B. Her star sign
C. Her boyfriend's name
D. Her therapist's name
E. That she gets a little grouchy when she's 'on her cycle'. Well, don't we all!

When I awake in the morning, my hand is trembling. No, actually it's the bed. No, actually it's the motel. No, actually it's 4.8 on the Richter scale. Jarvis is filming the swaying 'ROOMS' sign with his Super 8 camera when an 'O' detaches itself and falls onto the bespectacled singer, encircling him. It's a lucky escape but he's grazed his arm and a rather seedy Denholm Elliott-style doctor takes cash up-front to diagnose that he is suffering from cold turkey on account of what he mistakenly takes to be track marks on Jarvis' arm.

There's time to kill and Nick Banks and I hire a tandem and head for the beach. This is full of inconsiderately bronzed and beautiful people anointing at the temples of their own bodies. We expose our doughy English flesh to pitying glances. The sign outside the diner proclaims 'PIGBUM $1.25', which is the last thing I fancy after riding behind Nick. At a bogus Native American carving emporium, Nick is tempted by a huge sculpture of a rampant bear rolling its eyes in onanistic ecstasy. I buy a gun, which fires suckered darts.

We have an 'instore' to do. This entails going to a record shop and signing autographs. I'm sunburned and puffy-faced and only have my casual clothes. I take one of the sucker darts from the sucker-dart gun, pull the sucker off and put it onto the unsuckered end of the other sucker dart, place it sideways in my mouth and suck it. The suction sucks my cheeks in and the shaft of the sucker dart makes me lisp like Andy Warhol. I crudely daub the rudest words I can think of on my face with shoe polish – 'tits', 'fanny', 'arse', 'tosser', 'pigbum' – and controversial slogans on my arm like 'feed Satan', 'eat beetles' and (my personal favourite) 'destroy conformity' but I do it in the mirror and it looks like Russian.

There is an old Pulp custom called the 'CD sweetener', which we inform the record shop of just before the signing, then show surprise that they haven't heard of it. What happens is they give us a CD for every 100 autographs. This is a just reward for the vicarious kudos you bestow on their humble shop.

A black London-style taxi takes us to the instore – it could hardly be more conspicuous and in the light of the Michael Jackson business something of a security risk because at least 10 per cent of Americans …

A. Like Michael Jackson. That's twenty-five million.
B. 10 per cent carry guns. That's 2.5 million.
C. 10 per cent are mad, so that's only a quarter of a million potential assassins then?

Around 1,000 of these potential killers are cunningly disguised as Pulp fans; colour-clash babes, suited-up scooter boys, misshapes, mistakes, misfits. The compère, who has obviously been doing marathon dances, tries to get them to whoop and holler but they're not having it. We sign a lot of bras and underpants – nice work if you can get it.

The last time we did a signing in America we'd flown overnight, hadn't slept and, boy, were we grouchy – but we didn't get a sweetener because fewer than 100 turned up. Do you want to know how many fewer than 100 people turned up? One hundred fewer than a 100. Yes, it's true, I know it happened in *Spinal Tap* but I'm not making it up, everything that happens in *Spinal Tap* happens in real life. So we sat there for two hours, all tarted up, with silver marker pens and no one came. The manager got his staff to pretend to be fans but we saw them on the way out, ducking behind the counters.

We awake in LA after sleeping overnight on the bus. The front lounge where the band hangs out is fairly civilised; books are read, chess is played. The rear lounge, or 'ambient tequila lounge', is where the road crew listens to loud music, gets drunk and watches trashy videos. It's a bad idea to have a bunk near the ambient tequila lounge and I've bagged mine near the front. Newcomer to the band Mark has drawn the short straw. The noise, other people's socks, and the occasional 'special friend' of other members of the touring party have to be turfed out before he can get in. Eventually, after weeks of living on top of the sounds, smells and habits of would-be complete strangers you begin to hate the colour of their socks worse than fascism.

The show is sold out, it's the place to be for the hip crowd and the burgeoning mod scene. After the show we go to a social/business function called a 'meet and greet' – an American custom whereby the record company, journalists, DJs and anyone else who can blag their way in gets to meet the band.

If you entered this holy of holies, what might you see? Would you see bacchanalian acts of unspeakable depravity? Would you see a white light leading down a long tunnel with no need to be afraid? Or would you see a portly drummer reading *What Car?* magazine while bursting a crisp bag and someone (perhaps Thom Yorke?) sitting in a corner, holding his head in his hands and rocking slowly back and forth in melancholy madness?

After shows, bands will either be gloomy or ecstatic but almost always intensely facetious. You may be a big cheese, but this doesn't mean that an overtired, undersexed musician isn't going to tell you your tie is vile, make a cack-handed pass at you, pretend that you're a waiter, or vomit on your Guccis, because if you sell records they like you and if you don't, then ... well, nothing. Maybe the way down is a little softer but who the hell cares about that?

Anyone who does anything remotely glamorous has, or affects, an air of bored nonchalance and goes on about what a drag it all is. This is supposed to signify 'Hey, I'm not industry', or 'Hey, I'm industry, but I'm cool.' Everything is either cool or it sucks.

A perky little man with a neatly trimmed beard says: 'Hey, I'm your publisher, if you're ever in Seattle drop into the offices and ... [observing my face] we'll bore you.'

The rest of the band are flying so I'm travelling with the crew, who accept me very much as wolves do feral children. They teach me the skills vital to survival within the pack, like how to play Metallica basslines and roll massive joints. I did have a toke on one of these but can assure the public that I did *not* exhale.

The land is raw and unfinished, the desert endlessly the same and endlessly varied. We drive uphill but the river runs uphill too. The driver stops and we roll uphill past a warning sign and skid marks where other travellers have been bewitched by the same illusion. The land from horizon to horizon is striated with alternating bands of red-and-yellow sandstone, which are tilted and give a false impression of where true level is.

A sign advertises a café 200 miles away, which is like advertising a Scottish café in Sheffield, but the miles and the signs tick by and we're there.

Following the simple maxim, 'Never eat anything bigger than your head,' I decide, for the first time, to order something American that I can actually finish – it's called a 'biscuit'. This turns out to be two large savoury scones with bacon and cheese, and I eat them all – huzzah! The waitress brings an extra one and asks what I'd like for the first course.

Driving through the desert at night.

On a lonely stretch of desert road a man with a petrol can flags us down. I've seen the films and don't want to stop but the driver does, saying 'He's one of all of us.' We sail on as night turns to day and back to night again and the radio plays all the songs it should: Crystal Gayle, The Band, Creedence Clearwater Revival, Gram Parsons and Ry Cooder. Our driver looks a bit like David Duchovny and is big on philosophy, alien abductions and storm chasing – which I become obsessed with too. We scour the immense skies for storm clouds.

At night we are eating a so-called 'short stack' of twelve pancakes at a lonely truck stop, when the place goes quiet. A man with long black hair, Charles Manson eyes and a huge swastika tattooed on his bare chest goes round the tables, asking in a polite gentle voice if anyone can give him a lift. He comes over to our table and cutlery is grasped in tense readiness. I'm glad we're with Paul our security guard.

All the band, apart from Jarvis who is still in LA, too sick to travel, arrive in Denver but the concert is cancelled. This is painful, the whole reason we're here, for coming all this way, has vanished and the people looking forward to it will be let down. I'm not in the mood for raving so retire to bed with tacos, a jar of salsa and a cigarette.

A red light begins flashing
So from the covers I am thrashing
To stub out the embers
Into the salsa jar

Too late, the siren's wailing
And the hotel is a shaking
As evacuating residents
Pour down the corridor

I'm thinking of escaping
And my underwear am chasing
When footsteps come a pacing
Towards my chamber door.

Then comes a tap tap tapping
Followed by a crash crash crashing
And a voice demands I open up
Forthwith my chamber door.

Gingerly I open
To see who has thus spoken
Why – 'tis a friendly fireman
With an officer of the law.

Oh humbly I beseech thee
I've extinguished it completely
And from this day henceforth
Shall spark up – nevermore

The fireman (who'd been sleeping) waved his axe towards the ceiling
And with eyes that have the seeming of a demon that is dreaming
He stamped upon the floor …
Quoth the fireman – 'Nevermore!' *(Apologies to Poe)*

The driver, crew and myself gravitate towards an Anglo-friendly club which promises 'goth-mod-spanking' and turns out to be a kind of heavy-metal bondage club. On a wooden 'X' a volunteer from the audience is getting a bit more than he bargained for in the form of a red candle – everything's bigger in America.

We enter the Midwest. There's a valley with thousands of wind turbines that speed up and slow down as fast eddies churn though them, illuminating the texture of the orange air. At the start of *Easy Rider*, the heroes threw their watches away before embarking on an odyssey across America. I did this too so don't know whether it's sunset or sunrise the wrong side of another day.

Candida's on the bus and we play poker crossing the desert with a margarita in the ambient tequila lounge. Margaritas don't give you hangovers on account of the hydration from the ice, and the overdose of vitamin C you get from the limes. The ever-present risk of scurvy is banished too. (Touring bands have actually got scurvy from the diet of junk food.)

'Gambling's for fools,' said Lemmy in 'The Ace of Spades' – but the average person will come out the same as they went in, which makes poker a cheap form of entertainment. I know there's a downside but, within reason, enjoy that too.

I have a special pack of poker cards that are extra wide (for men's hands!) that came free with a bottle of bourbon. Candida, who has the hands of a consumptive Victorian child, keeps dropping them. The British Poker Association's 1933 rules are printed in our itineraries, to avoid any arguments. Poker only makes sense if you are playing for hours with the same people: then you can establish a personality and gain the benefit of being a reckless bluffer when a good hand finally turns up. Some say poker is all about luck, but luck evens out in the long run.

Everyone is dealt decent cards, so there is quite bit of money in the pot before anyone drops out. But now there are three people left and hundreds of pounds on the table, this is getting gnarly. Pretty much all the money in the bus is there. Rover has to write an IOU to double my stake – he loses. The crew have lost that week's wages on a hand of cards, but they would have only wasted it on tasers, strip clubs and food. Rover wants to 'get his money back'. His money, excuse me? So we play 'double or quits' and now he owes me £1 million pounds – which he promises to repay 'when his band gets a major deal'. So, never then.

The barometer is dropping and 'Only Happy When It Rains' by Garbage comes on as a cloud bursts; it's one of those perfect moments.

We play a Midwest gig with Radiohead in the baking heat. The crowd is a real rocker mob: long shorts, tattoos, broken teeth, death metal T-shirts. I put on extra make-up, Union Jack socks, polish my shoes, tighten my tie and button up my cashmere coat. We come on to catcalls and abuse, play our rockiest numbers and, not for the first time, our defiant posturing when our backs are against the wall wins us friends. The show builds to an enthusiastic, if slightly ironic, chant for an encore. 'These limeys are a bunch of fags but they're kinda cool.'

The audience is silent throughout Radiohead's set except for calls for 'Creep', which is a big hit in the USA. They play it for the encore and everyone goes mad. Radiohead are more morose than usual, they are on an endless soul-sapping tour of America and 'Creep' has been a millstone of raised rock expectations.

I play Radiohead at scrabble; they know a lot of big words.

I've been trying to work out how they got the amazing double-stutter guitar noise before the chorus on 'Creep' and have put something like it into our song 'Joyriders'. As it turns out, it was just a tape glitch that they decided to keep. They are self-deprecating about this serendipitous accident, but it takes genius to be in that place at that time and be open enough to let the accident stand. Creativity is often a thin thing and disparaged by those who possess it; it comes so easily that they don't feel ownership. It's just a knack, but not everyone has it.

At night the tunes going round my head keep me awake, like Hieronymus Bosch demons. They start off original then go through variations and end up turning into something recognisable, like 'Smoke on the Water' or 'Puff the Magic Dragon'. I figure that it is better to start off with an existing tune, then keep varying it until it is unrecognisable from the source. In the morning I try to sing these tunes but my vocal abilities don't allow it, which is terribly frustrating. I sometimes have this great tune locked in my head but it won't come out of my mouth. So I'll play it on the guitar and get it wrong and find something else appealing on the way.

These tunes often feel troublingly familiar and usually turn out to already exist. The most frustrating ones are those that no one can put their finger on at first but then a couple of weeks later someone would will say 'Ooh, that's the bassline from "Babylon's Burning",' and you'd sigh.

Then there are *really, really* frustrating tunes that seem familiar but no one can place. These are original tunes, but they don't *feel* original, they feel like fossils trapped in the rock for millions of years that you have just happened to expose. You don't feel ownership because you've just been lucky enough to find one and dash off with it before someone else can. It's just persistence and a bit of luck, so there's no reason to get big-headed.

I've heard it said that pop music is an easy kind of music to make. This is absolute rubbish. In rehearsals Pulp were able to knock out very passable genre music: reggae, blues, heavy metal, funk and soul. They are easier because there is a formula. But there is no formula to a three-minute pop song. A hook can be anything from a melody, to the noise of a crazy horse. It can be a line as simple as 'Lucky, lucky, lucky', 'Yeah, yeah, yeah' or 'Lager, lager, lager'. Actually, maybe that *is* the formula, just say something three times?

The rest of the band have tired of flying and have come to shatter the idyllic calm and space of the bus. There are fourteen bunks, fourteen seats and fourteen people and there's crap everywhere. Overflowing ashtrays, drinks, dirty clothes and the mortal enemy of bus travellers: pistachio nuts. Getting out of a bunk with bare feet onto an empty pistachio nut shell is not a good start to the day, but not as bad as the slightly open ones, which give a nasty nip.

Someone has used up all the batteries on the mobile talking to their dog in England, so we can't find out the address of the next venue. Multimedia ordeals are happening all over the bus and music of many different stripes blares out from different sound systems. Some people are more considerate, some are more tolerant, but everyone in their own way is a total pain. It all depends on what you want to be happening but I'm not sure anyone has an ideal. A bus is as smelly as the smelliest and as noisy as the noisiest. You're on top of each other and it's only going to get worse. Little civilising influences, like playing chess, take the edge off, as does the de-civilising mayhem in the crew room – whatever gets you through the night.

We hit a truck stop for booze and fags and nibbles, and I buy an onctable (I don't know what this is, but that's what it says in the diary – perhaps a monocle for an octopus?).

Yoko Ono has a similar effect on Pulp as she did on The Beatles. You see, Mark likes her (or possibly enjoys winding people up by pretending he does?) and puts this awful caterwauling on, to much protest. By this point the band are in the front lounge and the crew have claimed the back lounge. So Mark goes into the back lounge, turns off the Garbage album and puts on La Monte Young's *The Second Dream of the High-Tension Line Stepdown Transformer From the Four Dreams of China*, which ain't heavy metal, followed by Yoko Ono's challenging blackboard scrapings and sits there in silence.

There's been a storm a-brewin' between the crew and Mark over various niggly things. He's new and only a short while back was working as a crew person. Like new teachers, he tries to lay down his authority by bossing them about, as if they're servants rather than equals who work for you, and they don't like it. When he customised his Marshall amp logo to say 'Warhol', they customised it to say 'Arshol' – but this is just about the final straw. So they lock the door and won't let him back in. Which means that he's playing some dreadful arty nonsense down the front now. I escape to the sanctuary of the ambient tequila lounge, where they're watching Japanese disaster movies and headbanging to the theme from *Banana Splits* as a 'Fuck you, I won't do what you tell me' protest.

Riverport Amphitheatre, St. Louis, Missouri. I catch Garbage's last few numbers: the crowd is lacklustre but the singer is a rare orchid and genuinely loses herself onstage. She might feel as if she's going through the motions – we all do sometimes – but has obviously lost herself so many times that she just doesn't know how to do it any other way.

The lowly Pulp are due to play on a pub-size stage with other pub-standard groups. Fortunately, our equipment driver has run out of gas and isn't here and it looks like we might get out of playing. Then he shows up saying 'I'm an asshole,' there is general concurrence, but not for the reason he thinks.

It's a basic show, five songs and no gin and tonic – but it's fun to be back playing a little concert like this and we play for all we're worth and at the end some girls are screaming.

An anvil cloud of biblical proportions looms over the festival.

We lose our way and find a diner with rusting fifties petrol pumps, where they take a long time to appear. A woman with horn-rimmed specs says that since they built the interstate folks don't pass through this way much. When she finds out we're a gen-u-wine English pop band she calls her husband and, although they've never heard of us, they're mighty thrilled that we've come. We give them T-shirts and they give us an alarm clock which ain't much but it's got the name of the diner on so we can remember them – because it's a real honour to have a pop band come all the way from Merrie England to their diner. It's like every conversation in America is something from a film and you look round in case there's a hidden camera, but they really do want you to have real nice day. The fire hydrant going off isn't a prop, it's just like that all the time and, after coming here with my sniffy knee-jerk anti-Americanism, I've realised that they really are the friendliest people in the world ... although the place is utterly spiritually dead because nothing is old, nothing is rotted and there's no patina. They put plaques up on things saying 'Built in 1938', because there's no ancient history and no accretion of meaning.

The radio station plays sentimental country music that, in its natural habitat, feels apt and poignant. A revivalist preacher vibrates with wrath: 'And His vengeance on that day-uh will be right mighty and He shall smite-uh the unworthy from the earth and a great calamity shall befall the sinners-uh and the fornic—' Oh, crikey, does he mean us?

That tornado alley overlaps with the Bible Belt seems no coincidence. The vast earth over which we scurry like inconsequential insects is loomed over by a judgmental God, ready to send down a finger of destruction out of caprice or retribution. The tension on the bus is dissipated by the overwhelming sense of menace coming from the wall cloud that dwarfs our earthly preoccupations. Set against the majesty of nature, the choice of listening seems inconsequential – as long as it isn't Yoko.

Carole King weaves a tapestry as a violent electrical storm dances through the wall cloud.

Our driver is in CB radio contact with another trucker forty miles of bad road ahead and knows all the lingo, maintaining a folksy Chuck Yeager hominess between two souls crossing the empty plains. The rain is getting heavier, scowling clouds make the immensity of the plains feel low and claustrophobic. The wall cloud crosses the road in front of us and, as we enter, the sky takes on a greenish tinge and the hail begins.

The local radio announcer screams: 'Tornado on the ground, take cover, get in the basement, get in the basement!' We look back at the cloud, knowing that somewhere within it a tornado is wreaking destruction. During the daylight I was keen to get as close as possible to a tornado, but at night it seems as appealing as jumping into a dark lake with a crocodile. There is some debate as to whether to turn back and try to see the tornado but in the end it is only Candida (who is a huge fan of *The Wizard of Oz*) who wants to go.

After the storm, the air is bursting with juicy uplifting ozone. Mark had the camera going the whole time but is a big Warhol fan, so there are twenty minutes of him mumbling while painting his nails.

The crew plots a jape to play on Mark. He will awake to find the bus being rocked from side to side, while they clomp about on the roof making a racket with the sound of a twister turned up to full volume on the stereo. The lighting guy will rig flashes and green light and, as Mark looks out of his bunk window, he will see ice cubes and the contents of the litterbin being thrown off the roof and blown back by the wind machine. The twister itself will be conjured by setting fire to a rubber tyre. He will then be instructed to get outside and into a ditch, preferably a slimy one, where the jape will be revealed – sadly this never happens.

It's a tradition (so they tell us) for crews to play japes on bands, especially on the last night of a tour. Japes, they say, are always proportional and appropriate to the vanities, peccadillos and self-obsessions of the person or persons being japed, as is the level of viciousness.

One of Pulp's requirements on coming offstage was a lit fag. At the end of one tour we returned to the dressing room to find it entirely cleared apart from one chair with one cigarette and one non-functioning lighter. At another, the set lists, which normally started with the song 'Do You Remember the First Time?' just had the words 'Do You Remember the Set List?' on.

On one tour a singer, who was a vegan, had been making themselves disagreeable by insisting that everyone else was vegan too. So roadies, as well as having to subsist on a diet not of their choosing, were forced to discard their customary leather boots and jackets and wear some kind of biodegradable eco-clobber. The band's drummer had also been giving them stick about not having enough cups of water. There was a general consensus that this was out of order and at the end of the tour payback came in the form of the crew dropping goldfish onto the stage, where the singer ran around trying to save them by putting them into the 200 cups of water that had been superglued to the drummer's riser.

Had Mark's amp cases been searched at customs he would have had quite a bit of explaining to do: they had become the storage place of choice for any illegal or embarrassing items – such as dildos full of cocaine – that the crews wished to take across borders.

One expends a lot of adrenaline onstage, of which one only has a finite supply. You can borrow a bit, artificially, but boy, is the interest rate high. After touring for a while your body knows to completely shut down before a show and go into suspended animation to recharge the batteries. Time slows and comes to a halt and your blood solidifies to lead. Two hours before going onstage it seems utterly impossible to summon the energy required to do anything but stare into space and moan in dismay. And you know no fear because you just don't give a toss, and realising this scares you, and the fear kicks in about half an hour before and you start going through the rituals, which transform you before crossing the boundary to the stage where time speeds up and you feel no pain.

We're in Detroit. Ian Astbury from The Cult has played the night before and has scrawled a messianic message in the toilet to us and Garbage, who are playing here tomorrow. There are phrases like 'Pulp and Garbage through the eye of a storm united in pain and death.' It seems profound, troubling and prescient.

We park the bus in front of the venue in daylight on what seems a fairly ordinary street. When we come out later it is dark and the street is mean. On the short walk to the hotel to retrieve our bags we pass two pools of blood. A guy walks along with us and says, 'I killed those two police last night,' and laughs. Paul natters away at him in incomprehensible cockney as we get on the bus. An ugly crowd forms across the street and hard-looking crews bounce down the street in souped-up gang cars, blocking it off. The man who said he'd killed the coppers is waving a gun and urging the crowd to take us on. Paul stands his ground, arms blocking the doorway of the bus. I pass him the baseball bat but he says, 'I can't bat bullets away,' and tells us to go and lie down in the middle of the floor.

The cavalry arrives in the form of four massive coppers, who stand with guns drawn. Rover drops a microphone and four guns are trained on him. Somehow, Paul persuades one of the cars blocking us in to move and we get out fast and onto the interstate, where the crew celebrate their escape from death by attempting to kill themselves bus surfing. Rover gets out of the rear-lounge skylight, crawls along the roof of the moving bus and comes in through the front-lounge skylight.

There's this character called Dave Two-Yeah on account of how he always says 'two-yeah' at soundchecks. He's a big feller, over six foot and he just about manages to squeeze through too.

But Dave Two-Yeah's got this mate from Blur's crew who looks just like him and is also called Dave. But this other Dave is massive, maybe six foot ten. He's like Chewbacca or Dave Two-Yeah's dad, so he's called Double Dave. And this Double Dave manages to squeeze out of the rear skylight and he's a long time on the roof before his legs come through the front and he's stuck and there's a bridge coming up. So they push him back up and he pounds along the roof. I run to the front and tell the driver, who slows but can't brake in time because that would throw Double Dave off the bus. He drops down the rear skylight as we go under the bridge and there's a reassessment of the health and safety aspects of bus surfing.

On arrival at a hotel with a road crew an oft-heard phrase is 'Where's the swamp?' The swamp is the room of someone who doesn't mind loads of people coming back to their room for a party. The room gets messy, hence the name, and its resident will be up late. But it may be fun and will doubtless involve at least one of the holy road crew trinity of sex, drugs and rock and roll. If the booze runs out, the ever-resourceful roadie can get the hinges off the mini-bar fridge without needing to trouble the lock. They are able to take the power down to deactivate the smoke alarm, and also rig up a Maglite to run off the telephone power line for a bit of mood lighting. If any pay per view material is watched, the morning after will go like this.

Rover: 'What are these additional items for films watched?'
Receptionist (sotto voce): 'They are for, ahem, pay-per-view films sir.'
Rover (not sotto voce): *Massive Melons*, I didn't watch that, I've seen it before, it's really good, have you seen it?'
Receptionist (noticing other roadies clipping toenails in foyer): 'No, sir' Rover: 'You should, it's really good, you'd like it, it's got hundred of big—'
Receptionist (stage whisper): 'Yes, sir, but there's also another film!'
Rover: '*Anal Assault on Precinct Thirteen*! Not my bag, have you seen it?'
Receptionist: 'Let's just strike these items from the bill, shall we?'
Rover: 'But I watched *Sapphic Traffic*, it's got these—'
Receptionist: 'On the house, sir, sorry for any inconvenience.'

I don't think we'll be picking up 'Best Behaved Band in the USA'.

In New York, a middle-aged lady called Cynthia Plaster Caster, who looks as if she ought to be running a hand-painted ceramics workshop in Greenwich Village, arrives with a bag of plaster and two pneumatic young assistants who act as 'fluffers'. Cynthia achieved fame in the sixties by taking plaster casts of famous rock stars' genitalia and you know you have arrived in New York when she turns up. I wish I could tell you that we fought the good fight and that she ran out of plaster, but sadly only one member of the band is up for it.

71
The End

Lush's drummer Chris Acland was the life and soul of the Britpop party. He was the epitome of the 'scene that celebrates itself' and made everyone's face light up when he entered a room. One felt like he was an old mate after meeting him a couple of times. He seemed such an easy-going chap, but was bitterly disparaging of his own abilities to an extent that went beyond the natural self-deprecation of such a likeable and unassuming man. He said he was playing 'the bog standard indie shuffle', for which he had scant regard.

If, for me, Britpop started one night in Paris with Chris as its brightest ornament, it ended when he committed suicide. I was probably about three-hundredth on his list of best mates but he was in my top twenty, he was in hundreds of people's top twenty. The funeral was in his home village in Cumbria and hundreds of what I had taken to be rather a shallow bunch of people made the trip up. The vicar said 'When Chris's batteries were running low he used to come back to the Lakes to recharge them, but this time he was running on empty.' It was a poignant service and afterwards a rainbow appeared.

Jarvis was the second most recognised person in Britain at the time – below Princess Di, but above Tony Blair and the queen. A young relative of Chris's asked for Jarvis's autograph at the funeral (if by any chance that young relative gets wind of this, please don't feel bad about it, it's natural). This was about as far as it could all go. The essential spirit of Britpop had mutated from something that might have come from a beach, meadow or garret to something more of the pub and football terrace. There was a lot more to go record-sales wise for music that would be called Britpop, but for me it was over.

I played my final show at Barcelona and, early in 1997, left the band.

Being in Pulp wasn't always fun but we still talk to each other occasionally without the aid of lawyers, which isn't the case with all bands. So the Pulp story is a happy one; we stayed true to our roots and managed to capture the mood of the nation for a few heady months.

I've been asked a hundred times why I left at the height of our success and I've given a hundred different answers because there are many reasons. I could write a book about all the negative things about being in Pulp but this isn't it. A better question would be to ask why I stayed for so long. The answer to that is simple: we made great music. But I knew there was no more juice and the well had run dry, we'd never make a great album again. When we were recording *Different Class* I felt an urgency to get what we had preserved – clear and full – because I knew we were losing it. The only reasons for me to stay were money, fame and fear of the unknown and they weren't big enough reasons.

When pushed to explain why Britpop came to an end my answer would be: why shouldn't it have? It had run its course, ennui had set in and people had nothing left to say. My own path was symptomatic; I've always been an early adopter and an early departer. Chris Thomas once said to me at a party, 'It's 2 a.m., in ten minutes' time it'll be six in the morning, it's time to go home.' So I did.

IRELAND
2011

72
Hotels Don't Have Morgues

On the way to Ireland for the last show. Ralph's girlfriend Alicia and her mate, a cocktail waitress called Charlie, have arrived at the hotel and she's got him running around looking for a false eyelash (oh, where's the cave centipede when you need it?).

Next morning, with many a flirt and flutter, we leave on a big bus for Ireland, holding up traffic in Piccadilly (where, fortunately, people are renowned for their patience) and within an hour are free of stop-start London traffic: hurrah, it's cocktail time! Charlie is definitively the worst cocktail waitress in the world; her technique consists of pouring random spirits into a glass with no ice, no mint, no cherry and no umbrella. Mixtures of things that are a lot worse together than apart. On the plus side, she's a right laugh and wanders around in camiknickers – a Catholic girl gone bad St Trinian's-style.

At a service station a friendly fellow with a Hulk Hogan moustache from another tourbus befriends us – the camaraderie of the road. There is a sign in his bus window that reads, 'Band on tour, overnight relationships welcomed.' Very dry, very droll, very counter-productive.

We pass straight through Wales like a dodgy burger.

Ralph has told everyone that the ferry will be the height of sophistication, with casinos and dancing girls. Ben is dressed like a nineteenth-century Irish peasant emigrating to America, complete with flat cap and cravat. And everyone else is dressed in tropical casj (short for casual) as if it was a 1920s cruise from the golden age of steam, rather than a wet weekend in Wales. Spanish Anna is wearing a Carmen Miranda outfit. I've been on this ferry before and it's a lot more Wallander than Wooster. We have brought a cocktail mixed by Charlie named 'Tropical Casj'.

I'm worried we're going to get smacked for looking so absurd but, as it turns out, we aren't the most absurdly dressed people on the ferry as there are quite a lot of people from places where mullets and pink shell-suits are all the rage.

Ireland seems to have taken a turn for the worse since I was last there. The Celtic Tiger has bitten great chunks out of the countryside, leaving toytown bungalows in its wake, such a shame. Oh, mystic isle of Erin, haunt of banshee, scholar and poet: where art thou?

The hotel is in a suburban area of a new-build dormer town with paviors, offices and all that jizz.

Alicia is tired and emotional, extremely high-maintenance and has disappeared. A search party is dispatched. I come across her in the foyer and she asks me if I can help her find her room. She is upset and says that she keeps getting lost and got trapped in the morgue. I point out that most hotels don't actually have morgues, but she isn't convinced – she says she can 'smell flowers and death'! So we go wandering through this weird Escher-style hotel, which has levels between levels, and eventually end up in a room with signs in Polish, those big heavy-duty opaque plastic strips hanging down, red floors, fluorescent lights, stainless steel slabs and a bunch of fragrant white lilies. Okay, maybe *this* hotel does have a morgue.

No wonder I'm getting irritable, I'm coming down with crew-flu; headache, runny nose, sore throat, aching limbs. Ugh. So I spend the night waiting for the four hours since I took the last lot of paracetamol to pass, so I can take another dose and control my temperature. There is something particularly horrible about being ill while away from home that is compounded by being on the move and unable to get creature comforts. Feeling like that and having to go and leap about onstage and remember your part and act all lively when you really should be in bed is uniquely horrible. There are much harder things, like being in a trench in the First World War, but don't expect me to be in a good mood about it. I spend most of the night feeling sorry for myself and composing my speech to Alicia for the next time she gets on my tits: 'Listen, love, if anyone's gonna be high maintenance, if anyone's gonna make unreasonable demands, if anyone's gonna throw their toys out of the fuckin' pram and act like a prima donna it's gonna be me, cos it's my bus and I'm the one going onstage! All right?'

The day after, Alicia is being perfectly lovely and my speech is wasted. So I get irritated at the crappy excuse for a fountain that springs from six inches of muddy and litter-filled water outside my window, which drunken idiots were splashing about in during the night.

It seems there has been some naughtiness overnight. The other girls and possibly some of the boys took Alicia up on her offer to lend them her prized Vivienne Westwood dresses. In the early hours, they decided to go for an adventure in the pouring rain. As they were already soaking wet, and perhaps a little drunk, they decided it would do no harm to jump in the 'swimming pool', which turned out to be the muddy fountain.

So Alicia's prized dresses are muddy, fag-end strewn and missing sequins. Alicia, surprisingly, is very good about this and doesn't make a fuss – but then I don't think she's got her contact lenses in. Anyway, isn't Vivienne Westwood supposed to be punk? Just get some safety pins.

This cheers me up a bit.

We go off looking for the 'real' Ireland, hoping to encounter peat bogs but the bus is far too big for the country roads. Travelling light has a lot to recommend it; the bigger you get the harder it is to get places.

We attempt to go to New Grange, which is a reconstructed Celtic burial mound, but the last tour has already gone. The museum won't even let us book tickets for the next day. You have to come and queue up. The spurious rationale for this is that it's 'fair'. This is nonsense, we've come a seventy-mile round trip to see this thing and they are saying that we should do the same again on the off-chance that we might be able to come in. What are we? Thirties dockworkers signing on the dole? We're bloody tourists, we want to see the monument! The monument that by some shady act of appropriation the authorities have seen fit to deny to the freeborn Britons whose birthright it is to gaze upon such wonders bequeathed to them by their ancestors.

Julian Cope, in his excellent book *The Modern Antiquarian*, is rather sniffy about New Grange. But then Julian Cope thinks Stonehenge is johnny-come-lately bling. Julian, you were right, New Grange is the monument The Man wants you to see: neutered, sanitised, over gift-shopped, sugar coated with guilt-inducing greenwash for a miserable, false-jollity, face-painting, family fuckin' fun day. He didn't put it like that, but I bet that's what he was *really* thinking. Did I mention I had a bit of a cold?

On the way back, an excited lady with two children pulls up in front of us and is terribly disappointed to find it is a lowly Pulp person rather than the hoped-for One Direction, whoever they might be.

Backstage, there's a present from Bono: it is bottle of champagne and a bottle of Guinness, which makes yet another horrible cocktail. The note reads, 'This town ain't big enough for both of us – so we got out.' Too right, pal, I wish I could.

Onstage I wear a hat and coat. I don't care what I look like – I'm shivering and it's freezing. Between songs I warm my shaking hands on hot drinks, praying for it to be over so I can go and collapse somewhere warm. Despite the cold, many people have their shirts off and go absolutely crazy. This might be the best reception we've ever had, so hats off to them.

What an odd way to play your last ever show: feeling crap, amazing reception, can't wait to get home. In fact it was so underwhelming that I didn't even notice it being particularly underwhelming at the time. I'm just struggling to say anything at all about it. So there you go, done, finito, the end, thank you and goodnight.

I hole up on the bus in my bunk while the party gets into full swing. Jackclayton and Ben begin a 'psyche-off', which entails them taking it in turns to play the most 'Far out, daddy-o!' tracks they can lay their hands on, squares should prepare to be freaked out.

The Electric Prunes 'I Had Too Much to Dream (Last night)'
The Magic Mushrooms 'It's-A-Happening'
The Knickerbockers 'Lies'
The Open Mind 'Magic Potion'

The dancing starts.

The Jury 'Who Dat?'
Shocking Blue 'Send me a Postcard'

It's gone off-*Nuggets*, it's all kicking off!

The Leaves 'Hey Joe'

Charlie says that she had to leave Paris when she ran out of money because she had spent it all on expensive cheese. I have a bizarre vision of mustachioed French chefs rolling great cartwheels of cheese into her room while she throws her head back and laughs maniacally, oblivious to the expense.

Fun 'n' groovy with 'Psyché Rock' by Pierre Henry

It turns out that it was 'shoes' (with a posh accent) not 'cheese' that Charlie had spent all her money on. Shame, cheese would have been better.

Pierre Henry and Michel Colombier 'Jericho Jerk'

The bus lurches, throwing the dancers over.

The Castaways 'Liar, Liar'

The bus comes to a stop outside the hotel.

The Sonics 'The Witch'

At the start I knew what was going on but now I just peek my head out of the curtain and see everyone doing their own thing. It seems as if the trip has become an entity in itself; a complete thing with a variety of flavours as other people were added to the mix and the permutations increased. I like the whole dynamic of this rolling group of people. I suppose in a way I am the host, but certainly not the most engaging guest.

The Sonics 'Strychnine'

The power on the bus goes off, I go to bed in the hotel to be ill and suffer.

I can hear 'Dive Into Yesterday' by Kaleidoscope through the walls.

It's gone tripped-out hippy. The bus party are continuing the psyche-off in Ralph and Alicia's room with 'Incense and Peppermint' by Strawberry Alarm Clock.

Going onstage drains all adrenaline, I've got a cup of tea and I take sugar and I can see the sugar bag there – but can't muster the energy to get it.

Jefferson Airplane 'Somebody to Love'

They're jumping on the bed making a right racket to 'Wild Thing' by The Troggs.

Suddenly there came a rapping as of someone loudly tapping on the chamber door … The music is turned off and there is clattering as everyone but Ralph goes to hide in cupboards. Shush!

Ralph, affecting sleepiness, opens the door. It is a member of staff complaining about the noise … The man goes and the music restarts.

Status Quo 'Pictures of Matchstick Men'

Hey, mate, goddany Quo?

Ralph plays Serge and apparently Ralph's dancing – can cats dance?

There's another complaint and they are ejected from the hotel and move back to the bus to carry on the party. They splash about in the fountain in their underwear, then get chased down the road by shouting security guards, then sneak, shushing loudly, back to the bus.

There's nothing as noisy as someone trying to be quiet.

The day after is carnage. Everyone is much the worse for wear, having 'had a bad banana', as they say in Ireland. Onto the ferry with a sky like lead and a storm forecast they go on the top deck, reluctant for the party to end and in a way it never ever does.

THE END

Acknowledgements

Thanks especially to Vicky who has given tireless support and critique.

To Rupert, Robin, Josh and Jennifer who have made numerous suggestions for improvement, and my publishers Aurum Press for taking a gamble.

To the people in the book, many of whom have made contributions. To concert goers, record buyers and letter writers.

To Colin, Steve, Richard, John, Eddie, Mark, Scotty, Sian, Mike, Solj, Andy, Roger, Justin, Neil, Mick, Liam, Jack, Rachel, Ben and Dave, whose words I have borrowed and twisted – annoying, huh?

The roadie is paid to do a job and the job description doesn't involve being discussed or analysed. They aren't paid to be your mate, even though some of them are. So 'Rover' is a generic title used for the many people who acted as road crew, who can confirm or deny anecdotes according to whom they are trying to impress or placate. Road crews are the last true wanderers in western culture, a race of men as noble in deed as they are in bearing: oh, gentle roadies, I salute you!

Apologies …

… to those parodied and paraphrased including: Andrew Marvell, Mark E. Smith, Kilmister, Oakey, Hawkwind, Shampoo, Patrick Leigh Fermor, Serge Gainsbourg, Beowulf, Jane Austen, Steve Coogan, Bill

Clinton, Damon Runyon, Edgar Allan Poe, Barry Hines, Nick Clegg(!) and Enid Blyton.

Dates are approximate and events are elided to make a more coherent narrative.

There are characters that don't really exist. Those that do often didn't do what I say they did. Many of the cleverest things they said are attributed to me.

This story is best regarded as historical fiction based upon real events. I had a blast and hope you did too.

Russell Senior, Sheffield, 2015

Index